RESEARCHING CLASSROOM DISCOURSE

This practical guide to doing classroom discourse research provides a comprehensive overview of the research process. Bringing together both discourse analysis and classroom discourse research, this book helps readers develop the analytic and rhetorical skills needed to conduct, and write about, the discourse of teaching and learning.

Offering step-by-step guidance, each chapter is written so that readers can put the theoretical and methodological issues of classroom discourse analysis into practice while writing an academic paper. Chapters are organized around three stages of research: planning, analyzing, and understanding and reporting. Reflective questions and discourse examples are used throughout the book to assist readers.

This book is essential reading for modules on classroom discourse or thesis writing and a key supplementary resource on research methods, discourse analysis, and language teaching and learning.

Christopher J. Jenks is a scholar of language, communication, and discourse. He has worked as a professor in a number of countries, including the United States, England, Hong Kong, and South Korea. Christopher specializes in the study of language in society and is particularly interested in the political and cultural implications of the global spread of English.

RESEARCHING CLASSROOM DISCOURSE

A Student Guide

Christopher J. Jenks

LONDON AND NEW YORK

First published 2021
by Routledge
2 Park Square, Milton Park, Abingdon, Oxon OX14 4RN

and by Routledge
52 Vanderbilt Avenue, New York, NY 10017

Routledge is an imprint of the Taylor & Francis Group, an informa business

© 2021 Christopher J. Jenks

The right of Christopher J. Jenks to be identified as author of this work has been asserted by him in accordance with sections 77 and 78 of the Copyright, Designs and Patents Act 1988.

All rights reserved. No part of this book may be reprinted or reproduced or utilised in any form or by any electronic, mechanical, or other means, now known or hereafter invented, including photocopying and recording, or in any information storage or retrieval system, without permission in writing from the publishers.

Trademark notice: Product or corporate names may be trademarks or registered trademarks, and are used only for identification and explanation without intent to infringe.

British Library Cataloguing-in-Publication Data
A catalogue record for this book is available from the British Library

Library of Congress Cataloging-in-Publication Data
Names: Jenks, Christopher Joseph, author.
Title: Researching classroom discourse: a student guide / Christopher J. Jenks.
Description: Abingdon, Oxon; New York, NY: Routledge, 2020. |
Includes bibliographical references and index.
Identifiers: LCCN 2020010145 | ISBN 9780367208707 (hardback) |
ISBN 9780367209018 (paperback) | ISBN 9780429264023 (ebook)
Subjects: LCSH: Interaction analysis in education–Research–Methodology. |
Discourse analysis–Research–Methodology. |
Classroom environment–Research–Methodology.
Classification: LCC LB1034 .J46 2020 | DDC 371.102/2–dc23
LC record available at https://lccn.loc.gov/2020010145

ISBN: 978-0-367-20870-7 (hbk)
ISBN: 978-0-367-20901-8 (pbk)
ISBN: 978-0-429-26402-3 (ebk)

Typeset in Bembo
by Newgen Publishing UK

CONTENTS

Preface ix

PART I
Planning 1

1 What is classroom discourse analysis? 3
   1.1 What is classroom discourse? 4
       1.1.1 Classrooms 5
       1.1.2 Discourse 9
   1.2 What is discourse analysis? 13
   1.3 Why do classroom discourse research? 16
   1.4 Creating a plan for classroom discourse research 19

2 The logistics of classroom discourse research 20
   2.1 Practical considerations 21
       2.1.1 Access 21
       2.1.2 Time 23
       2.1.3 Technology 23
       2.1.4 Ethics 24
       2.1.5 Empirical issues 26
   2.2 Collecting data 26
       2.2.1 Recording data 27
       2.2.2 Managing data sets 33
       2.2.3 Making sense of your data 33

2.3 Transcribing your data 34
    2.3.1 Open and closed transcripts 34
    2.3.2 Representation and transformation 36
    2.3.3 Transcription practices 39

PART II
Analyzing   43

3   Conversation analysis   45
    3.1 What can I investigate? 47
        3.1.1 Turn-taking 47
        3.1.2 Turn shape and placement 52
        3.1.3 Repair 55
        3.1.4 Interactional competence 57
    3.2 What are the methodological considerations? 59
    3.3 Key terms, constructs, and people 63

4   Discourse analysis   65
    4.1 What can I investigate? 67
        4.1.1 Triadic dialogue: IRF/IRE sequence 67
        4.1.2 Floor management 71
        4.1.3 Teacher questions 75
        4.1.4 Discourse markers 79
    4.2 What are the methodological considerations? 83
    4.3 Key terms, constructs, and people 86

5   Critical discourse analysis   88
    5.1 What can I investigate? 89
        5.1.1 Power 90
        5.1.2 Language ideologies 94
        5.1.3 Neoliberalism 97
        5.1.4 Racism 101
    5.2 What are the methodological considerations? 105
    5.3 Key terms, constructs, and people 108

6   Narrative analysis   110
    6.1 What can I investigate? 112
        6.1.1 Identities 112
        6.1.2 Teacher cognition 115
        6.1.3 Reflective practices 119
        6.1.4 Learner diaries 123

    6.2 What are the methodological considerations? 127
    6.3 Key terms, constructs, and people 131

PART III
Understanding and reporting   133

7   Classroom ethnography   135
    7.1 Purpose and principles 137
    7.2 The importance of context 138
         7.2.1 Doing fieldwork 140
         7.2.2 Field notes 142
         7.2.3 Thick descriptions 144
    7.3 Understanding your context 146
         7.3.1 Ethnography of communication 146
         7.3.2 Autoethnography 149
    7.4 Key terms, constructs, and people 151

8   Reporting and writing   153
    8.1 Purpose and principles 154
    8.2 Describing your research 157
         8.2.1 Identifying your objectives 158
         8.2.2 Reviewing the literature 158
         8.2.3 Explaining your study 161
    8.3 Presenting your data excerpts 162
    8.4 Key sections of a research report 165

References   *167*
Index   *180*

PREFACE

Classroom discourse is an interdisciplinary research project that receives contributions from scholars working in a number of disciplines, including education, psychology, sociolinguistics, and applied linguistics. Modules on, and even tangentially related to, classroom discourse are thus common in many university programs. While many university students in the humanities and social sciences are introduced to classroom discourse, few books provide accessible overviews of how to conduct such research. The contents of this book address this pedagogical need by providing university students, novice researchers, and curious readers with a practical overview of using discourse analysis to conduct classroom research.

Although this book does not require any specialized or advanced understanding of discourse analysis, some basic knowledge of research may be helpful. Readers enrolled in university programs that deliver modules in applied linguistics, teaching of English to speakers of other languages (TESOL), English-language teaching (ELT), or intercultural communication will find this book particularly helpful. Furthermore, readers preparing to be teachers or teacher trainers may use this book for their professional and academic projects.

The aim of the book is to provide an easy-to-understand overview of the research process as it pertains to classroom discourse analysis. When read sequentially, chapters provide step-by-step guidance for students carrying out research on classroom discourse. The key theme of this book, and the characteristic that differentiates it from existing titles, is the focus on practice: Each chapter is written so that readers can put the theoretical and methodological issues of classroom discourse analysis into practice while writing an academic essay or research paper.

The book is the result of my many years of teaching and supervising university students interested in both discourse analysis and classroom discourse. Recommending books that bring together both topics is difficult, as authors have traditionally focused on one topic while neglecting the other. For instance, although there are several existing and seminal titles on "classroom discourse," most books report on research findings while overlooking the writing and research needs of university students. Furthermore, while many existing "discourse analysis" books are catered to the needs of university students conducting research, such titles pay little to no attention to classroom discourse. This gap in the literature forces me to recommend multiple books, which often creates unnecessary financial and logistical challenges for university students.

After reading this book, readers will establish a broad foundation of knowledge from which to conduct, and write, a study on classroom discourse. The book does this, in part, by developing both the analytic and rhetorical skills needed to write a research paper. In other words, students using this book, either independently through self-study or in a teacher-directed context, will have a broad foundation from which to conduct research on some aspect of classroom discourse. Chapters accomplish this objective by using many examples of classroom data, asking readers to reflect on important empirical issues, providing example research questions, identifying seminal and helpful references for further reading, and offering practical advice on researching and research writing.

The book has eight chapters; these chapters are organized into three stages of research: (Part I) planning, (Part II) analyzing, and (Part III) understanding and reporting. Each part includes a range of theoretical, thematic, and analytic issues. Thus, the book can be used as a main title for a module on classroom discourse. Alternatively, the book would provide an excellent supplementary resource for a module on research methods, discourse analysis, or language teaching and learning.

PART I
Planning

1

WHAT IS CLASSROOM DISCOURSE ANALYSIS?

Classroom discourse research spans many disciplines, is informed by a range of theoretical frameworks, and has been carried out with a number of different methodologies. Defining classroom discourse research requires deconstructing the very terms that represent this area of study. That is, how do researchers understand and approach classrooms, discourse, and analysis?

The answers to these questions establish what has been done in classroom discourse research, and how discourse analysis informs such work. Although addressing these terminological issues is a necessary first step in explaining how classroom discourse can be studied, such a discussion is inherently selective and somewhat superficial because of the interdisciplinary nature of this research. For example, discourse analysis is a collection of approaches that covers many methodologies and methods, and therefore some analytic issues will be naturally excluded from this book. To complicate matters, the meaning of classroom discourse varies according to theoretical frameworks, methodological tools, and empirical interests. For instance, a scholar with an interest in turn-taking practices will have a different theoretical understanding of classroom discourse than a critical researcher examining how race and ethnicity shape teaching and learning. This chapter, which attempts to make sense of these diverging views, should thus be read as one interpretation of classroom discourse out of many.

Many questions must be asked when defining classroom discourse research. For example, what does it mean to be in a classroom and what types of teaching and learning take place in these pedagogical spaces? In the same vein, what does it mean to examine discourse, and what discursive features shape, and are shaped by, classroom activities? The idea that classrooms represent a set of discursive phenomena that can be investigated is based on a host of methodological issues. In other words, a discussion of classroom discourse also requires you to understand what is meant

4 Planning

by analysis, or more specifically, discourse analysis. That is, what methodological issues shape all discourse analytic approaches?

The first two sections of this chapter answer these questions by reviewing the main theoretical and empirical issues associated with classroom discourse and discourse analysis. The aim of the chapter is to provide an introductory account of classroom discourse analysis, which means avoiding lengthy and convoluted theoretical explanations. Instead, this chapter points readers to supplementary references that offer detailed accounts of classroom discourse analysis if more advanced reading is necessary. Furthermore, the chapter aims to walk readers through the research process as it pertains to classroom discourse analysis: tables and figures are used throughout to illustrate the basic principles of the research process. The chapter ends with a research outline that can be used to not only plan an empirical investigation, but also make sense of the basic contents of this book.

1.1 What is classroom discourse?

If you are considering using this book for your research, then you should already have some understanding of what classroom discourse is and how it can help you achieve your academic or professional objectives. You may not, however, have a clear understanding of the different empirical issues that can be, and have been, investigated in the classroom discourse literature. That is, you may have a general understanding of what a classroom is and what constitutes discourse, but it may not be clear how such terms can be approached in a research paper. After reading this section, you will be able to start conceptualizing your research paper and selecting the appropriate methodological tools to carry out such work. Before defining classroom discourse, it is helpful to reflect on what your understanding is of classroom and discourse.

1. What are some defining characteristics of a classroom?
2. Are classrooms only located in schools and universities?
3. What types of discourse do teachers produce?
4. What types of discourse do students produce?
5. How do classrooms influence the types of discourse used by teachers and students?

Classroom discourse is difficult to define because scholars have different empirical interests that are, unfortunately, sometimes viewed as competing ideas. These divides are largely unhelpful and discouraging, as all researchers interested in classroom discourse work towards a common goal: to improve teaching and learning. With this common goal in mind, rather than explain the myriad theoretical and methodological reasons for debate within the literature – indeed much has already been reported on such issues (for competing viewpoints on discourse, see Jaworski & Coupland, 2006) – this section addresses the different ways the aforementioned questions can be answered.

Classroom discourse is defined in this book as the language (e.g., words), communication (e.g., teacher-led talk), practices (e.g., correcting a mistake), texts (e.g., coursebooks), and social structures (e.g., societal expectations of teachers) that make up, as well as influence, teaching and learning. Classroom discourse can thus be seen as what teachers and students do and say (e.g., Walsh, 2006a), and all of the social conditions and factors that shape how this "doing" and "saying" are conducted. While this definition may offer some basis on which the study of classroom discourse operates, it does not help you select a research topic and begin devising an initial outline for your project. Therefore, the discussion will now focus on some of the more common ways of investigating classroom and discourse. In the interest of simplicity, each term will be addressed in a separate section.

1.1.1 Classrooms

Attempting to devise an outline for your research paper first requires identifying an empirical agenda – that is, what general direction will you take in your research? This is a highly variable task, as classroom discourse research includes a range of empirical topics investigated by scholars working in many different fields of study. Although some scholars believe establishing an empirical agenda requires first immersing yourself in the research literature, which is good advice, a more practical way of devising an initial outline is to begin with the notion that the classroom is a site of investigation. Beginning the research process with the understanding that the classroom is a site of investigation can save valuable time by narrowing down the number of keywords that you use when searching the literature. This notion of saving time when searching the literature will become clearer later in this section.

Establishing a site of investigation without knowing much about the precise nature of your research requires momentarily suspending any consideration of classroom context, such as providing explicit correction, teaching oral communication skills, learning in groups, and giving students evaluative comments. Your research outline will need to be eventually narrowed down to this level of context, but for now it is more helpful to think of your research setting. The key difference between *context* and *setting* in relation to classroom discourse are as follows:

1. *Setting:* The classroom as a place (e.g., chat room, school, library).
2. *Context:* The discourse that occurs within this place (e.g., instructing).

The difference between setting and context is a useful starting point for planning a research project. Again, rather than begin with identifying a contextual issue or phenomenon to investigate, which requires combing through thousands of potentially interesting ideas, it can be more efficient to think of your research setting. For example, is your research going to be based on a physical classroom surrounded by four walls within a school? (Figure 1.1)

If you answered yes, then your research is likely going to involve conventional teaching and learning roles and classroom relationships. In this setting, teachers

6 Planning

FIGURE 1.1 Starting point question

often possess some degree of institutional power, which allows them to deliver instructional materials, provide feedback, and evaluate learning according to performance markers, to name a few. Scholarship demonstrates that this institutional power manifests in classroom discourse in many implicit and explicit ways, providing researchers with a range of contextual issues to investigate.

This classroom setting will likely be organized according to a number of other predetermined factors, such as lesson start and end times, learning goals, behavioral expectations, participatory roles, and class size. As with institutional power, predetermined learning variables manifest in discourse in various ways, creating a range of contextual issues that can be investigated. For example, the notion that a predetermined learning outcome can shape student participation is investigated by Seedhouse (2004), who shows that the organization of classroom discourse is intimately connected to the type of learning a teacher is trying to promote, such as fluency or accuracy.

Table 1.1 offers some exemplary studies conducted in traditional classrooms, and identifies several keywords that may help you establish a direction for your initial outline and research. You can use these keywords to search relevant scholarly databases, including Google Scholar and Linguistics and Language Behavior Abstracts (LLBA). You may also locate studies relevant to your interests by using these keywords to search within specific academic journals, such as *Classroom Discourse* and *Language Teaching*.

You can begin your research outline by identifying several keywords that represent some of your research interests. The studies listed in Table 1.1 should give you some indication of what methodologies have been used to investigate particular keywords. In some cases, your keywords may converge into one clear methodology. For example, turn-taking, sequence organization, and teacher talk are three keywords that naturally point to conversation analysis. If this situation applies to you, then you could, but need not, jump straight to the analysis chapters that introduce empirical topics in more detail (cf. Chapters 3–6). In many cases during these early stages of devising a research outline, you may not be able to come up with keywords that point to a clear methodology. This is a common situation: Identifying a list of keywords that represent your research interests may require extensive reading beyond the contents of this book.

TABLE 1.1 Traditional classroom research

Keywords	Example study
knowledge display, learner initiative, learning opportunity	Waring, H.Z. (2011). Learner initiative and learning opportunities in the language classrooms. *Classroom Discourse, 2*, 201–218.
teacher belief, classroom interaction, teaching practice	Li, L., & Walsh, S. (2011). "Seeing is believing": Looking at EFL teachers – beliefs through classroom interaction. *Classroom Discourse, 2*, 39–57.
identity, ideology, critical pedagogy, neoliberalism	Chun, C.W. (2009). Contesting neoliberal discourses in EAP: Critical praxis in an IEP classroom. *Journal of English for Academic Purposes, 8*, 111–120.
discourse markers, concordance, corpus, lexical features	Hellermann, J., & Vergun, A. (2007). Language which is not taught: The discourse marker use of beginning adult learners of English. *Journal of Pragmatics, 39*, 157–179.
code-switching, pedagogical focus, language choice	Üstünel, E., & Seedhouse, P. (2005). Why that, in that language, right now? Code-switching and pedagogical focus. *International Journal of Applied Linguistics, 15*, 302–325.
content and language integrated learning (CLIL), English as medium of instruction (EMI), immersion, medium of instruction	Wannagat, U. (2007). Learning through L2: Content and language integrated learning (CLIL) and English as medium of instruction (EMI). *International Journal of Bilingual Education and Bilingualism, 10*, 663–682.

If you answered no to the question posed in Figure 1.1, then the empirical issues that you may investigate extend beyond the traditional classroom topics discussed previously. Your research may, for example, in addition to including topics related to traditional contextual issues (e.g., instructing and learning), address empirical topics that challenge established notions of teaching and learning. For example, teaching that occurs outside of traditional schools and classrooms may not follow conventional turn-taking patterns, such as a teacher asks a question and then a student responds (see Sinclair & Coulthard, 1975). Indeed, a teacher may not be present in the learning process, such as in settings where students help each other in the absence of predefined institutional roles and goals (e.g., student-led chat rooms or tutorial sessions).

Furthermore, the discourse that students produce in nontraditional classroom settings may challenge what it means to be a teacher. For instance, the person doing the teaching may be a fellow student. While teaching roles can also be negotiated in traditional classrooms, there is often less opportunities and pedagogical space to exploit this possibility. When searching through the literature on nontraditional classrooms, it is not uncommon to come across terms and categories, such as expert, novice, and learning in the wild. Researchers use these terms and categories to highlight the fluidity and hybridity of teaching and learning that are common in nontraditional classrooms.

8 Planning

TABLE 1.2 Nontraditional classroom research

Keywords	Example study
repair, corrective feedback, learning in the wild	Theodórsdóttir, G. (2018). L2 teaching in the wild: A closer look at correction and explanation practices in everyday L2 interaction. *Modern Language Journal, 102*, 30–45.
conversational floor, computer-mediated communication (CMC), online community	Simpson, J. (2005). Conversational floors in synchronous text-based CMC discourse. *Discourse Studies, 7*, 337–361.
immigrant adults, power, church-based learning	Chao, X., & Kuntz, A. (2013). Church-based ESL program as a figured world: Immigrant adults learners, language, identity, power. *Linguistics and Education, 24*, 466–478.
professional discourse, English for specific purposes (ESP), corpus tools, language corpora	Hafner, C.A., & Candlin, C.N. (2007). Corpus tools as an affordance to learning in professional legal education. *Journal of English for Academic Purposes, 6*, 303–318.
moment analysis, translanguaging, discourse identity	Wei, L. (2011). Moment analysis and translanguaging space: Discourse construction of identities by multilingual Chinese youth in Britain. *Journal of Pragmatics, 43*, 1222–1235.
lingua franca, English as a lingua franca (ELF), membership categories, chat rooms	Jenks, C.J. (2013b). "Your pronunciation and your accent is very excellent": Orientations of identity during compliment sequences in English as a lingua franca encounters. *Language and Intercultural Communication, 13*, 165–181.

Table 1.2 provides some example issues that can be investigated in learning spaces outside of traditional classrooms. As with Table 1.1, the keywords identified do not represent a comprehensive list of empirical issues associated with nontraditional learning spaces. The studies and keywords identified, however, will provide you with a foundation of ideas from which to begin your research should you decide on examining such classrooms.

Tables 1.1 and 1.2 demonstrate that studies of classroom discourse can be categorized into keywords. Keywords are important in these early stages of planning your research, as they highlight several aspects of an investigation that can be used to locate other similar and helpful studies. Specifically, keywords may be related to the following aspects of a classroom discourse investigation:

1. The classroom setting.
2. The contextual issue under investigation.
3. The methodology used to conduct the investigation.
4. The theoretical framework or paradigm followed.
5. The terminology or constructs that define the investigation.

When devising an outline, it is important to therefore identify your own list of keywords that represent the different aspects of your research.

This brief overview of "the classroom" establishes several important points related to identifying an empirical focus and thus beginning the research process. First, notions of what it means to be in a classroom vary from one theory, methodology, and scholar to another. The polysemous (and somewhat ambiguous) nature of the term means that the literature on classroom discourse is varied, expansive, and interdisciplinary. Second, and related to the first point, it is your responsibility as a researcher to comb through this expansive literature to identify a specific empirical topic to investigate. An efficient way of doing so is to begin, not with a set of possible contextual issues, but rather the setting that you would like to investigate. Another efficient way of establishing an empirical focus is to use the keywords adopted in previous studies to search academic databases, which also helps you understand how your research builds on existing scholarship. Third, what makes a classroom a site for teaching and learning is not based on predefined definitions, but rather the discourse that occurs in such spaces. The discourse that represents teaching and learning is addressed in the next section.

1.1.2 *Discourse*

Classrooms are often viewed as spaces with four walls, one teacher, many students, and predefined learning objectives. In recent years, scholars have expanded their investigatory lens to include not just traditional classrooms, but also settings outside of such spaces. Although important contextual and pedagogical differences exist between traditional and nontraditional classrooms, as discussed in the previous section, there is one similarity that connects both spaces together. That is, both spaces are occupied by participants that actively work together, in their discourse actions and orientations to discourse structures, to engage in practices related to teaching and learning. What these discourse actions and orientations to discourse structures look like is the topic of the current section.

In simple terms, discourse is about what people say and do, how this communication is managed, and why such behavior is performed the way it is. Thus, classroom discourse is what people say and do while teaching and learning, how teachers and learners engage in this communication, and why these roles are performed in such a way.

The list of discourse actions and orientations to discourse structures that can be studied in a classroom setting is expansive (e.g., O'Halloran, 2004). Introductory books on discourse analysis provide excellent resources for you to learn what can be investigated in classrooms and how (e.g., Coulthard, 2014; Markee, 2015). These books collectively represent hundreds of features and aspects of discourse, and indeed much time is needed to acquaint yourself with just some of this literature. Therefore, in the interest of simplicity, and for your immediate goal of planning your research, this section breaks classroom discourse into two distinct, yet sometimes overlapping, areas of investigation: discourse actions and orientations to discourse structures.

Although this distinction is admittedly somewhat crude, it should provide you with an easy way forward during these early planning stages. In other words, the distinction presented in Figure 1.2 ignores the subtle differences within and between these two foci, but discourse actions and orientations to discourse structures nonetheless provide a useful way of narrowing down your research into a manageable set of topics or keywords.

Discourse actions refer to the all of the language and interaction that occurs within classrooms both in written and spoken form. It is the discourse that is constructed in real time, including all of the language that can be heard, seen, and read while teaching and learning. Discourse actions include, but are of course not limited to, turn-taking, student essays, written responses to texts, spoken utterances, telling a story, correcting a mistake, pointing to an object on a wall, discussing homework, beginning a lesson, providing instructions, dealing with silences or nonparticipation, teacher-fronted instruction, and repair strategies.

The empirical issues discussed in Chapters 3–6 are all related, to varying degrees of focus, to discourse actions (as well as discourse structures). Much of the classroom discourse literature is based on discourse actions because scholars have historically been more interested in examining the discursive features of teaching and learning than in uncovering the larger discourse structures that shape, but are not always visible in, classrooms.

Discourse actions and orientations to discourse structures can be investigated at the same time within a single investigation (e.g., Brooks, 2016), as both areas of focus speak to each other in interesting and productive ways. With that said, however, there are several reasons why discourse actions have been the focus of many classroom discourse studies. Namely, discourse actions bridge the conceptual gap between what classroom discourse researchers are interested in empirically and what can be gained pedagogically from such investigations. In other words, the discourse of teaching and learning offers concrete ways of evaluating the success of a lesson, as discourse actions represent both the object of empirical investigation and the things that teachers and students do and say in classrooms. For example,

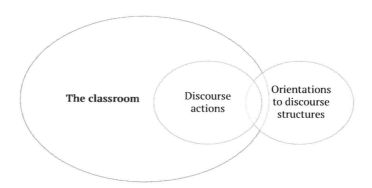

FIGURE 1.2 Types of classroom discourse

a researcher interested in student participation may examine how teachers ask questions and the time allowed for students to respond. This focus on questions and response time represents the object of investigation, but also the discourse actions of teachers and students. Thus, discourse actions provide a familiar way for teachers and students to understand, and adopt should they wish to do so, the findings of an empirical investigation. Although discourse actions represent the bulk of classroom discourse research, orientations to discourse structures are no less important, as will be highlighted later in this section.

Table 1.3 offers several example studies that represent prototypical ways of examining discourse actions in classrooms. Additional discourse actions references are provided in Chapters 3, 4, and 6 (Chapter 5 is based on orientations to discourse structures). As with the studies identified in the previous section on different classroom types, the references in Table 1.3 are merely examples of discourse actions and should not be interpreted as an exhaustive list of empirical topics.

While the discourse actions identified in Table 1.3 occur inside a classroom, they are often shaped by external variables, which often include the unnoticed social, cultural, institutional, and historical variables that shape teaching and learning. Put differently, a discourse action, such as turn-taking, may unfold in real time as teachers and students engage in teaching and learning. Such turn-taking practices may appear to unfold as if they were detached from other social factors (e.g., power dynamics between teacher and students), thus leading researchers to conclude that classroom turn-taking possesses an organization unto itself. However, it is problematic to believe that discourse actions are detached from the larger social milieu. As we know from our personal encounters both in and outside of classrooms, and at work and during personal time, what we say and do while communicating with

TABLE 1.3 Discourse actions research

Discourse action	Example study
IRF (initiation–response–feedback) sequence	Nassaji, H., & Wells, G. (2000). What's the use of "triadic dialogue"? An investigation of teacher–student interaction. *Applied Linguistics, 2*, 376–406.
Turn-taking	Garton, S. (2012). Speaking out of turn? Taking the initiative in teacher-fronted classroom interaction. *Classroom Discourse, 3*, 29–45.
Repair strategies	McHoul, A.W. (1990). The organization of repair in classroom talk. *Language in Society, 19*, 349–377.
Using the first language (L1)	Raschka, C., Sercombe, P., & Chi-Ling, H. (2009). Conflicts and tensions in codeswitching in a Taiwanese EFL classroom. *International Journal of Bilingual Education and Bilingualism, 12*, 157–171.
Floor management	Jenks, C.J. (2007). Floor management in task-based interaction: The interactional role of participatory structures. *System, 35*, 609–622.

others may be shaped by a number of cognitive, psychology, social, and critical issues and phenomena that are not always immediately visible in discourse actions. Anxiety, self-efficacy, covert racism, emotional states, prior learning experiences, and political forces are several of the many issues and phenomena that often lay hidden under discourse actions. Such issues and phenomena are referred to in this book as orientations to discourse structures.

A "structure" is an important principle in classroom discourse research, as it suggests that discourse actions are bound to a system of pre-established social norms and expectations. A discourse structure encourages teachers and students to talk or behave in a certain way. What this expectation to talk or behave sounds or looks like is often determined long before a lesson has started. For example, the power that teachers possess (to allocate turns to, and evaluate responses from, students) is a historical artifact developed over many generations of teaching and learning. The term "orientation" (in orientations to discourse structures) thus suggests that teachers and students will, to varying degrees, attend to this power dynamic. That is to say, structures are not always a factor in how discourse actions unfold in classrooms. Research on orientations to discourse structures contributes to the literature in significant ways by uncovering how discourse actions are intimately connected to the world outside of classrooms. Table 1.4 identifies several noteworthy discourse structures.

The extent to which you examine discourse structures is based on what methodology you wish to use in your research. In other words, your methodology will typically determine whether you should examine discourse actions or discourse

TABLE 1.4 Discourse structures research

Discourse structure	Example study
Power	Martin-Jones, M., & Saxena, M. (1996). Turn-taking, power asymmetries, and the positioning of bilingual participants in classroom discourse. *Linguistics and Education, 8,* 105–123.
Language ideologies	Lee, J.W., & Jenks, C.J. (2016). Doing translingual dispositions. *College Composition and Communication, 68,* 317–344.
Neoliberalism	Gray, J. (2010). The branding of English and the culture of the new capitalism: Representations of the world of work in English language textbooks. *Applied Linguistics, 31,* 714–733.
Gender	Hilliard, L.J., & Liben, L.S. (2010). Differing levels of gender salience in preschool classrooms: Effects on children's gender attitudes and intergroup bias. *Child Development, 81,* 1787–1798.
Linguicism	Auerbach, E.R. (1993). Reexamining English only in the ESL classroom. *TESOL Quarterly, 27,* 9–32.

structures. For instance, conversation analytic principles have a very rigid interpretation of how to analyze discourse structures: The methodology is not in the business of examining historical and economic issues, such as neoliberalism. Therefore, although it is possible to examine discourse structures using conversation analytic tools, it may be difficult finding existing work to begin your research. The point in using this conversation analytic example is to highlight the importance of understanding the theoretical expectations of researching classroom discourse. In addition to understanding the varied ways in which you can study classrooms and discourse, establishing an empirical focus during these early stages of research requires some knowledge of methodological issues. In other words, what discourse analytic tools will you use in your research?

1.2 What is discourse analysis?

Discourse actions and orientations to discourse structures are objects of investigation. Their definitions in the previous section establish *what* classroom discourse researchers investigate. It is now necessary to address *how* classroom researchers approach the study of discourse actions and orientation to discourse structures. That is to say, what is meant by analysis in classroom discourse analysis?

The diverse literature on discourse analysis means that it is necessary to be selective in discussing how researchers analyze discourse actions and orientations to discourse structures (for an excellent overview of discourse analysis, see Jaworski & Coupland, 2006). To this end, rather than list all of the analytic approaches that can be used to study classrooms, this section identifies some of the more common methodological issues that shape how you will conduct your study. That is to say, this section reviews methodological issues rather than methodologies. Methodologies, and their relevant methodological principles, such as the principle of next-turn proof procedure in conversation analysis, are discussed later in this book (see Chapters 3–6).

Focusing on general methodological issues (at the beginning stages of research planning) will give you a deeper understanding of why methodologies differ, thus allowing you to more confidently narrow down your empirical interests and foci. Relatedly, and perhaps more importantly, establishing a general understanding of the methodological issues that shape all discourse analysis will help you argue why a particular methodology is more suitable for your specific empirical needs.

So, what is discourse analysis? McCarthy (1991, p. 5), in his seminal book publication on the subject, defines discourse analysis as "the study of the relationship between language and the contexts in which it is used." What McCarthy refers to as "language" is what this book means by "discourse." The latter term is more suitable for investigating classrooms, as discourse represents a wider range of empirical possibilities (cf. discourse actions and orientations to discourse structures). For our research purposes, the idea that there is a relationship between "language and context" suggests that what teachers and students do and say is a reflection of their classrooms and how these classrooms are organized is based on what is done and said.

Therefore, classroom discourse analysis can be defined as the study of the interplay between discourse and classroom. Classroom discourse analysts want to know how discourse actions are used in teaching and learning and what discourse structures are made relevant in such accomplishments.

Many approaches to discourse analysis have been used to investigate classrooms, including speech act theory, ethnography of communication, narrative analysis, interactional sociolinguistics, discursive psychology, critical discourse analysis, and conversation analysis. While space does not allow a review all of these approaches, nor is it the aim of this book to address the theoretical and methodological nuances that exist in discourse analysis, it is helpful to highlight some of the methodological issues that will influence how you approach the study of classroom discourse.

Approaches to classroom discourse are underpinned by unique methodological assumptions (e.g., the role of context in communication as understood by conversation analysts versus critical discourse analysts); to this end, Table 1.5 identifies five general methodological issues that distinguish one approach to classroom discourse from another.

Table 1.5 does not represent a comprehensive list of methodological issues that shape how to conduct classroom discourse analysis research; it should, however, provide an adequate understanding of what discourse analysis requires of you when carrying out your research. References identified in the third column, as well as in subsequent chapters, should be read to gain a fuller understanding of how classroom discourse analysis is put into practice. The four approaches to classroom discourse introduced in this book are discussed in relation to these five methodological issues at the end of their respective chapters.

Some overlap exists across the five methodological issues identified in Table 1.5, so it is important to remember that the perceived boundaries that demarcate approaches to classroom discourse analysis, such as the differences between conversation analysis and narrative analysis, are somewhat imagined. For instance, an analysis of micro-level features does not mean that you cannot, nor should not, examine macro issues. Furthermore, how you approach a particular methodological issue may be based on other methodological decisions. For example, your level of analysis will typically influence data presentation (e.g., how much linguistic information you include in a transcript).

The issue of data collection is addressed in Chapter 2 at a general level, and the discussion is based largely on spoken communication. Data collection requirements are specific to methodological approaches, and thus the chapters later in this book should be read for further information. At a general level, data collection can be divided into two types of classroom discourse: *participation* and *reflection*. Rather than select a methodology and form your research according to its methodological principles, you may find it easier to identify a topic or question by determining whether you would like to investigate what teachers and students do in the act of teaching and learning (i.e., participation data). Alternatively, do you find it more interesting to examine the ways in which teachers or students think about their teaching or learning (i.e., reflection data)?

TABLE 1.5 General methodological issues

Methodological issue	Description	Further reading
Data collection	Discourse analysis requires collecting data (e.g., embodied movements or student essays). The type of data that you collect, and how you engage in this important part of the research process, are shaped by your selected methodology.	Meyerhoff, M., Schleef, E., & MacKenzie, L. (2015). *Doing sociolinguistics: A practical guide to data collection and analysis.* London, UK: Routledge.
Data presentation	Presenting your data is an important part of doing classroom discourse analysis research. Like data collection, how you present your data is shaped by the methodology that you adopt, as well as your intended audience.	Jenks, C.J. (2011). *Transcribing talk and interaction: Issues in the representations of data.* Amsterdam: John Benjamins.
Type of analysis	Three general types of data analysis exist: describing, interpreting, and explaining. Most approaches to classroom discourse analysis include describing and interpreting; some methodologies attempt to explain as well.	Gee, J.P. (2014). *How to do discourse analysis: A toolkit.* London, UK: Routledge.
Level of analysis	Three general levels of data analysis exist: micro (e.g., turn-taking, prosodic features, lexical collocations); macro (e.g., government policy, laws, historical events, power); or meso (i.e., links between the macro and micro).	Ellis, D.G. (1999). Research on social interaction and the micro-macro issue. *Research on Language and Social Interaction, 32,* 31–40.
Role of context	Classroom discourse analysis requires you to look beyond the description of surface linguistic and communicative forms and features. You must also show how such forms and features are situated within a context (e.g., interactional context, social context, historical context, political context). Much variation exists in what context means, and how it is incorporated into an analysis.	Duranti, A., & Goodwin, C. (1992). *Rethinking context: Language as an interactive phenomenon.* Cambridge, UK: Cambridge University Press.

Data presentation is how you organize your data for dissemination (i.e., sharing or reporting your findings). All classroom discourse data, whether spoken or written, must be organized and presented in a way that is readable to your audience. Like the sentences within a research report, the data from which your analytic observations are based must be constructed and presented in a systematic and rule-governed way. Data presentation conventions are based on not only a particular set of methodological principles, but also what your empirical objectives are. Furthermore, there is an added presentation challenge in researching spoken communication in that such data require attending to a number of transcription rules (see Chapter 2).

Types and levels of data analysis relate to your objects of investigation. That is, what are you investigating and how are you going about this analytic task? Type of analysis refers to the extent to which your observations are descriptive. A researcher's interpretation of context will often influence what type of analysis is conducted. Level of analysis is also based on interpretations of context, and refers to the extent to which observations are limited to the discourse of what is immediately said or done within a communicative exchange. Chapters 3–6 are dedicated to unpacking how types and levels of analysis are shaped by the methodological principles that are established by a particular approach to classroom discourse.

The fifth methodological issue, the role of context, is based on a principle that underpins all discourse analysis research. That is, discourse analysis is more than just describing the surface linguistic features of language; it is about demonstrating how such features are shaped by, but also shape, contextual variables, such as a lesson, proficiency of students, pedagogical objectives, and institutional goals, to name a few. Chapter 7 discusses the importance of context from the perspective of classroom ethnography.

Before ending this section, it is important to note that discourse analysis research is highly subjective, as it involves a great deal of researcher manipulation (e.g., pointing a camera in one direction, transcribing only some aspects of talk, potentially disrupting a class by recording a lesson). One way of addressing, but by no means eradicating, the issue of researcher manipulation is to reflect on the ways in which your involvement in the research process shapes what is ultimately reported and disseminated. This reflective process is often referred to as reflexivity. Researcher reflexivity is a topic of several important publications (e.g., Rymes, 2015), and can offer an important resource for how you write up your research paper.

1.3 Why do classroom discourse research?

Research is a vague term in that its meaning varies according to context and purpose. Accordingly, before answering the question established in this section's heading, it is necessary to briefly address what is meant by research. The term is used in this book in reference to primary research, which means conducting an investigation using data collected in a classroom. That is, the discussions contained within this book regarding classroom discourse research are based on you collecting, transcribing, and analyzing data (typically in the form of video recordings or written records of teaching and learning). Primary (classroom discourse) research presents a host of logistical challenges that often get overlooked in introductory books on discourse analysis (see Chapter 2).

Secondary research on classroom discourse involves using data from existing sources (e.g., using existing transcripts in a published empirical paper). Although this type of research does not entail collecting and transcribing your own data, such investigations require you to think about how to manage and present your secondary sources (again, refer to Chapter 2 for more details). Using secondary sources is a common way of investigating classroom discourse, and many excellent studies have been conducted with this type of research – for example, some of the studies identified in the tables presented in this chapter are secondary research. Secondary research will likely be the preferred option for readers that are writing an essay for a module assignment – this is because modules often set out rigid deadlines for when to complete and submit a research paper. In other words, if you are completing an assignment for a module, then it is not recommended to collect your own data because time will be a scarce resource. Conversely, readers conducting advanced graduate-level (e.g., doctoral thesis) research should, and most likely be required to, collect primary data. Exceptions always exist, so readers should defer to their unique working circumstances and specific empirical objectives.

In concrete terms, classroom discourse research, whether primary or secondary, requires thinking about what type of data to collect, how much of it to analyze, why readers will benefit from your investigation, the degree to which context is incorporated into your analysis, and the ways in which issues of transcription representation and readability shape your analytic observations, to name a few.

Now that a basic understanding of research has been established, it is possible to move onto why it is important to investigate classroom discourse.

Discourse analysis continues to have a significant impact on all aspects of life and society. In academia, discourse analytic studies contribute to high-impact disciplines, such as health communication, psychology, law, and of course, education. Such disciplines benefit and grow from the ability of analysts to bring out nuance and detail in the study of discourse as situated, context-dependent activities (e.g., Tannen, Hamilton, & Schiffrin, 2015). For example, health communication has benefited from the conversation analytic work done on how medical professionals deal with complex issues during patient encounters (e.g., Antaki, 2007), and pedagogical theories and practices have evolved over the years as a result of classroom researchers uncovering the interactional structures that facilitate good language teaching and learning (cf. Walsh, 2011). Therefore, you should do classroom discourse analysis research because you can make an important contribution to your respective academic discipline or area of study.

In professional practice, discourse analysis is used as a tool to bring about immediate change in the workplace. Such work is referred to as action research, and tends to sacrifice analytic rigor and detail in the interest of communicating findings and observations to nonspecialist co-workers (e.g., Sagor, 1992). For instance, transcripts created by a teacher using action research in order to increase student participation levels will omit communication data, such as prosodic features, that is typically found in some empirical studies published in scholarly journals. In other words, you should do classroom discourse analysis research because it equips you with the tools to make an impact on how work is conducted at your school.

It is easy to identify the larger contributions that have been made as a result of discourse analysis. For example, in both scholarly and professional research, discourse analysis is helpful for its ability to uncover the many ways in which spoken and written communication shape, and are shaped by, social practices. However, identifying the specific reasons why you should engage in classroom discourse analysis is a difficult task, as reasons for learning and carrying out any type of research are based on highly personalized justifications. Your personal circumstances will dictate what aspect of a classroom you look at, and how you conduct your analysis of discourse. With that said, however, there are several motivations and justifications for doing classroom discourse research that should resonate with most readers, including creating solutions to learning problems, developing new materials, critically reflecting on your professional development, understanding classroom behaviors, uncovering how teaching and learning is situated in discourse, training pre- and in-service teachers, and establishing new institutional guidelines for good pedagogical practice.

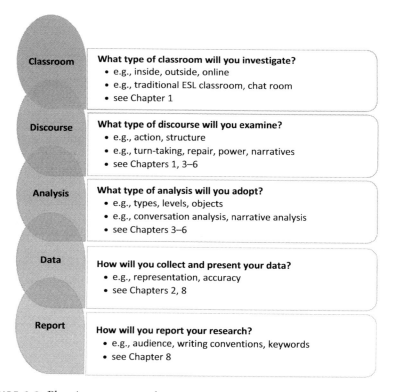

FIGURE 1.3 Planning your research

Although the specific reasons for engaging in scholarship will vary from one individual to another, and indeed the motivations for conducting work in classrooms may be unclear to you at this point in the process, it is important to remember that all good classroom discourse research is based on a genuine empirical interest or practical concern. As you read through subsequent chapters, try to think about your specific motivations for doing classroom discourse research and how a specific methodology may help you best achieve your objectives.

1.4 Creating a plan for classroom discourse research

This chapter has established a foundation from which you can plan your research on classroom discourse. A number of empirical and methodological considerations have been introduced, including different notions of classrooms, discourse, and analysis. Figure 1.3 provides a visual representation of some of the issues that you should consider during these early planning stages of conducting classroom discourse research.

Figure 1.3 presents your outline as five overlapping aspects of classroom discourse research. It is helpful to conceptualize the investigatory process in such a way, as what you decide to do in one aspect of research will influence others. For example, how you transcribe your data recordings will be influenced by what type of discourse you are interested in and the level of analysis adopted. It will become clear, as you read through the chapters of this book, how these different aspects of research influence each other. Readers that are in the early stages of research with no predefined empirical focus can use Figure 1.3 as a planning tool to identify the key aspects of their study.

2

THE LOGISTICS OF CLASSROOM DISCOURSE RESEARCH

Now that you have a better understanding of what classroom discourse is, and the ways in which discourse analysis lends itself to examining teaching and learning, it is important to start thinking about how to move forward with your initial research plan. Implementing your research plan is like planning a vacation. You have to think about how much time you have (e.g., what is your deadline for submission?), where to go (e.g., what classroom will you visit?), and what resources are available (e.g., what recorders will you use?), to name a few. Much like a dream vacation that is poorly planned, a theoretically sound plan that reflects an excellent understanding of the academic literature is useless if you do not have the resources to carry out such research. For example, a longitudinal study on language learning may not be feasible if the final research paper must be submitted at the end of an academic semester. Therefore, in addition to thinking about your empirical interests and reflecting on what has been done in past studies, your research plan must consider the realities of doing classroom discourse research.

One critical reality that gets overlooked in a research plan is the need to record and transcribe classroom data. Recording and transcribing possess unique practical and logistical challenges, and the decisions that you make regarding your data will have an impact on how you complete your research project. For example, how you report your findings, and what you ultimately write in your research paper are based on data recording and transcription issues. Therefore, your initial plan should consider the relationship between what you may want to research (see Chapter 1) and how you will go about doing such work. This chapter will help you make this important connection.

Because the planning decisions that you made in the previous chapter are intimately connected to how you attend to the logistical issues discussed in this chapter, you may find yourself revisiting some of the issues discussed in Chapter 1. It is important to be open to making changes to your outline as you read through the sections in this chapter. It is also equally important to remember that researching classroom discourse requires balancing logistical issues with theoretical frameworks and methodological principles, as you will see in subsequent chapters.

2.1 Practical considerations

The practical decisions that are made during these early planning stages reflect a consideration that underpins all aspects of your research. That is, where does your data come from and how will it be used? The answer(s) to this two-part question will have an impact on your ability to carry out any plan or objective established in the previous chapter, such as the setting that you wish to investigate (refer again to Figure 1.3). Again, be prepared to make changes to your plan while you reflect on these five logistical considerations: access, time, ethics, technology and empirical issues (see Figure 2.1).

2.1.1 Access

Your ability to answer a research question, to achieve a particular empirical objective, or to otherwise do what you plan on investigating is dependent on a number of variables, but the issue of access is perhaps the most influential. Access refers to whether you are allowed to use a classroom – either yours or someone you know – as a site of investigation. Simply put, you will be unable to begin your study if you do not have access to a classroom (or classroom data).

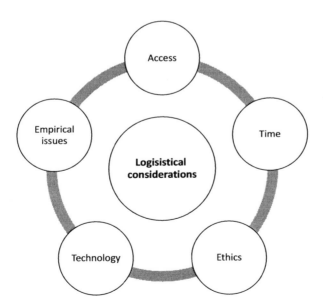

FIGURE 2.1 Logistical considerations

Obtaining access to a classroom may not appear to be a significant issue, especially if you are currently teaching in one. However, access is not only about accessing a physical space, such as a classroom. Access is also closely related to permission (an issue that partly forms the basis of discussion on ethics in Section 2.1.4). Obtaining permission to collect data in a (physical or online) classroom requires knowing who is responsible for such decisions. This person, often referred to as a *gatekeeper*, may be a school principal, a parent of a student, an administrator at a college, a work colleague, an online site administrator, or an institution. If you are currently teaching in a classroom, then chances are you must seek permission from a gatekeeper before using your own students as data. Seeking permission to collect data is an integral part of doing research, and should be approached with care. Waiting for a gatekeeper to grant you access may take a long time, and in the end, the outcome may not be what you want to hear. Access can thus be thought of as two interdependent questions:

1. What classroom will I be able to use as a site of investigation?
2. Who is responsible for granting me permission to collect data in this space?

Furthermore, the issue of access will determine what type of research you conduct. For example, if you only have access to a classroom for one day, then it will be very difficult to research how students develop interactional practices over time. Similarly, if you only have access to a second-language writing classroom, then you may not need to worry about the logistical challenges of transcribing spoken discourse. Therefore, before spending many hours reviewing the academic literature on your particular empirical focus, you should first address the issue of access.

Data sources are also relevant to this discussion. While access is commonly thought of as entering into a physical space to conduct some type of research, it is important to remember that the ultimate goal in finding a classroom is to collect data. With this in mind, access can also be thought of as the source of data used to conduct your research. Your data source can be primary or secondary. A *primary data source* is a classroom recording, transcript, or artifact collected by the person responsible for conducting a particular study (i.e., you). A *secondary data source* is a classroom recording, transcript, or artifact collected by someone else responsible for an existing (often published) research project. Primary data entails collecting your own data or using data collected by you from a past study. Secondary data entails accessing an online corpus, extracting transcripts from published research articles, sharing data with classmates, or using data from old postgraduate theses and dissertations, to name a few.

Using secondary data, as with using your own classroom as a site of investigation, requires obtaining permission from the author/owner/publisher of the data source. This may entail paying a subscription fee for an online corpus or emailing the author for permission to use an existing published transcript. Sections 2.2 and 2.3 address data collection and transcription practices.

2.1.2 Time

Like all things in life, logistical considerations in classroom discourse research is constrained by time. The amount of time that you can spend on your research is finite, and will therefore be a factor in how you manage your data and write up your findings. As with the issue of access, you should plan your research and modify your outline according to time constraints. For example, if you only have two months to complete your research – a common situation for MA students – then it will be difficult to collect, transcribe, and analyze your own data. In other words, you may find it easier to conduct your research using secondary data sources if you only have two or three months to complete your project. If you are in a privileged position where you can pay for, or have access to, a research assistant (e.g., paying for transcription services or getting help from a colleague or friend), then the time to collect and transcribe data will of course be less of a constraint. The issue of time is also less of a concern – whether or not you have access to a research assistant – if you decide to transcribe and analyze a single stretch of communication.

Much variation exists in how you manage your data: How much data you collect, where it comes from, whether you will combine primary and secondary sources, the level of detail offered in your transcription, and the possibility of getting help from a colleague or classmate are just some of the issues that are influenced by time constraints. Such temporal issues must also be addressed by factoring in your readership and disciplinary expectations (e.g., what does your supervisor expect of you or how much data is considered enough for conducting a corpus-based study on classrooms). To complicate matters, your decision to use a single transcript or a set of transcripts, or focus on a type of utterance or a list of different lexical constructs – again, decisions shaped by how much time you have – must to some extent reflect disciplinary and methodological expectations; such expectations are topics of discussion in subsequent chapters.

2.1.3 Technology

Students discussing technology in the context of classroom discourse research often ask the following question: Is there a software program that will transcribe my data for me?

The temptation to rely on technology to bypass some of the steps required to do classroom discourse analysis is great, as recording and transcribing data is an exceptionally laborious task that many researchers struggle to do given existing time constraints. While technological advancements in recording and transcribing software and hardware have made it easier to carry out classroom discourse research, at the time of writing, there are no reliable methods for automating the very time-consuming process of data management, including and especially transcribing recordings of spoken communication. For instance, there are several applications and online services that purportedly have the capabilities to automate the transcription process: A user uploads a data recording, and after several minutes, a transcript that "accurately" captures what has been said is produced. Such promises must be approached with caution, as classroom discourse is highly nuanced and multifaceted, often comprising multiple participants interacting in and with a language that is itself marked with complexity in terms of prosodic features and syntactic composition (Cook, 1990). More importantly, transcribing data recordings is an important part of the analysis process, as producing transcripts brings the researcher closer to her data, revealing crucial information about the participants and the interaction that may have been overlooked had some "automated" service been used (Jenks, 2013a).

With this in mind, an important logistical consideration in planning your research is the availability of technology. Do you have access to a recording device? If so, what type (e.g., a mobile phone or GoPro device), how many, and where will they be placed in the classroom? As noted in the previous paragraph, classroom discourse is multifaceted, and thus having access to only one recording device means you will be limited in what you can actually investigate. For example, one recording device placed in the back of a traditional classroom space, pointing at an instructor in front of the class, will not pick up student facial expressions, nor will it reliably capture all of what students say. This situation is yet another reminder that practical considerations will influence what you can investigate in the classroom.

Considering available technology, your research plan can be divided into three interdependent aspects of data management:

1. What technology will you use to record your data?
2. What technology will you use to transcribe your data?
3. What technology will you use to analyze your data?

The first question applies to research that draws from primary data sources. The second and third questions are often addressed with one software program, though great variation exists in how many applications are used to conduct research in the classroom. Referring to past studies or consulting an expert in the area of your study is often the best first step in answering any of these aforementioned questions.

Furthermore, time must be factored in to learn how to use technology: Applications for transcription and analytic tasks typically have comprehensive instructional materials, and some software developers even run workshops for their software. It is important not to overlook the learning curve involved in developing a basic understanding of such tools.

A more detailed overview of recording and transcribing data recordings follows this section on practical considerations. The issue of analysis is, of course, addressed in subsequent chapters.

2.1.4 Ethics

The ethics of classroom discourse research is about using a "sense of what is good/bad or right/wrong" to establish "core principles along with ideas about ... the practice of research" (Hammersley & Traianou, 2012, p. 17). Engaging in the practice of research according to ethical principles presents a number of logistical challenges, as most empirical studies conducted in classrooms must pay special attention to who the research participants are (e.g., low- or high-risk students), how informed (or written) consent is provided, and whether the identities of students must be protected in publications, to name a few. These ethical considerations exist to protect the participants of your study; the concerns here are that your research participants are not exploited, do not feel manipulated, and are portrayed in a fair way.

Two important aspects of conforming to ethical principles are seeking advice and getting approval: an ethics committee and/or your supervisor will not only need to advise you on the extent to which ethical principles are being followed, but such people will also make the final decision on whether your research may be conducted. That is to say, classroom discourse research often requires you to demonstrate to an ethics committee and/or your supervisor that you will not harm your research participants during your study.

Seeking approval from a committee or a supervisor may require knowing what forms to complete for ethical consideration, who to ask for additional information, and how long the process will take. Furthermore, research participants will often need to give you consent before you can collect and analyze your data – obtaining consent is a complex task in itself, including knowing what information should be included in a consent form. For instance, how much information about your study that you should include in the consent form varies from one institution to another.

While the answer to this situation, along with other ethical issues, are far too complex to address in a section on logistical considerations, many excellent books have been published on the topic (e.g., De Costa, 2015; Heigham & Croker, 2009). These books should be consulted when planning and reflecting on your ethical role as a researcher, what relationship, if any, you should establish with your participants, and how data recordings and transcripts are dealt with during the dissemination stage, to name a few. A considerable amount of variation exists in how these ethical issues are addressed, so it is important to seek advice as soon as possible.

The variation that exists in how to address ethical issues is indeed complex (see the online recommendations provided by the British Association for Applied Linguistics), but one thing remains constant in the context of research ethics. That is, the process of seeking advice and approval must be factored in to your research plan, as much time is needed to determine whether your study follows expected rules of conduct. For example, an ethics committee must deal with potentially hundreds of ethical approval requests, and it is therefore not uncommon for this entire process to take several weeks or even months. In this sense, seeking ethical advice and approval is very much a time-sensitive logistical issue, and a situation that should remind you of the importance of good research planning.

2.1.5 Empirical issues

The logistical considerations discussed thus far, such as access, time, and resources, are intimately connected to what you plan on investigating in the classroom and how this task is accomplished. Put differently, empirical issues, such as your research questions and theoretical framework, are shaped by issues and situations that you may have little control over, such as how much money you can spend on recording and transcribing equipment and software. Additionally, deadlines are largely fixed, which often constrains the extent to which you can conduct a study that meets disciplinary expectations. For example, you may not have the time required to transcribe classroom data recordings according to the expectations of conversation analysts. The upshot is that adjusting empirical interests and objectives to reflect your personal circumstances is a natural part of doing classroom discourse research. That is to say, empirical issues are not just a reflection of your professional and analytic interests, but they must also account for the issue of feasibility. For instance, is it feasible – given your existing practical constraints – to answer your research questions?

Other questions that you may want to answer when considering how your personal circumstances influence how your carry out your study include the following:

1. Does your submission deadline make it feasible to answer your research?
2. Can someone provide feedback on your paper before submission?
3. Does your research question require specific recording technologies?
4. Is your research question best answered by examining a classroom?
5. Does your research question pose ethical approval challenges?
6. Does your research question require primary or secondary data?
7. Will/can your research participants give you informed consent?
8. How much data is necessary to address your empirical objectives?
9. How much time is needed to transcribe your data?
10. Can you pay for someone to help transcribe your data?

While this list of questions is by no means comprehensive, it should provide a sufficient foundation to devise a research plan according to practical considerations. After you have reflected on the important connection between empirical issues (e.g., your research interests and questions) and practical considerations (e.g., time and access), you can start thinking about how your data collection plan meets disciplinary, theoretical, or methodological expectations.

2.2 Collecting data

This section is relevant to readers that are conducting research using primary data. When conducting research using primary data, your analysis will be based largely on the records of spoken communication that you make or the written assignments that you collect. Yet it is important to keep in mind that your analysis can be strengthen by making classroom observations, which may include writing down notes of what is happening between the teacher and students when you are behind (and operating) a video recorder. That is, classroom observations (both participant and nonparticipant; cf. Chapter 7) are also data and should be considered when discussing data collection principles: Simply put, records and observations are both primary data. The current section deals with collecting "records," and more specifically recordings of spoken communication, as written discourse is far less complicated and will be addressed in relation to investigating texts (e.g., Chapter 5).

Before moving on to what it means to collect records of discourse (see also Meyerhoff, 2015; Wiggins, 2016), it is useful to think about data collection as a process of creating an archive or corpus of discourse examples. An archive of discourse examples should reflect your attempt to answer a research question or address an empirical objective. That is, only collect data that you know will help you complete your research project. For example, if you are interested in understanding how students construct an understanding of themselves as language learners, then it may be helpful to create writing assignments that encourage a reflection of identities (as opposed to recording teacher-fronted interactions). You could, of course, first collect data and then generate a research question or empirical objective (cf. Chapter 3), but even this situation requires establishing a general direction based on some research interests (cf. Chapter 1).

Furthermore, theoretical frameworks and methodological approaches possess unique data collection requirements, such as the expectation that corpus linguists will carry out their study using large data archives or the tradition in conversation analytic work to collect naturally occurring spoken discourse. Theoretical and methodological expectations vary widely in terms of what you are expected to do and produce in your research, and are indeed the reasons why there are so many chapters in the latter half of this book.

Notwithstanding the variation that exists in research expectations, there are a number of general principles that can be discussed before moving on to the more analytic-focused chapters of this book. These general principles will help you navigate the complex and complicated task of data collection, but should again reflect the empirical and pedagogical interests and ideas that you identified in the previous chapter. This section on general data collection principles is divided into three interrelated tasks: recording, managing, and making sense of your data sets.

2.2.1 Recording data

The equipment and software used to record classroom discourse will depend on your methodological approach and empirical questions. An ostensibly subtle or small change in a research question – say, changing your analytic focus from teacher to student talk – can have a significant impact on how you approach data collection. The upshot is that there is great variation in how data is recorded in classrooms, making it impossible to coherently identify all of the variables involved in this important stage of your research. Accordingly, this section maps out some aspects of data collection that will help you record data according to your research objectives. However, learning the nuances of data collection requires you to actually try recording classroom data.

The first set of variables worth considering relates to what is captured in your recordings. Will you be recording only the spoken communication? Is it necessary to capture what people are doing gesturally? Are you investigating online interactions?

2.2.1.1 Using a microphone

In most empirical situations where the researcher is recording a physical classroom, you will minimally need a recording device with a microphone capable of capturing audio. You should probably resist the temptation to use a mobile phone, as the microphones built into these devices are not designed to capture the nuances of multiparty classroom interactions. With that said, however, mobile phones are ubiquitous in today's world, and may offer a familiar way for your participants to go about their interactional business in the classroom in a "natural" way. If you are currently affiliated with a university, then your academic unit may be in possession of an audio device with a multidirectional microphone capable of capturing voices in all directions. A device purposefully built to record audio is, by and large, the preferred option when recording physical classrooms.

2.2.1.2 Using video recordings

Video recordings of physical classrooms should be approached in a similar way. That is, the audio quality of a video recording is a crucial aspect of whether your data recordings are "useable." For example, the extent to which you can accurately transcribe and disseminate the spoken exchanges of your participants determines the quality of your video recording. This is because the microphones built into video recorders typically do an adequate job at capturing the audio of the immediate spatial area, but if there are students in the back of the room participating in a discussion, then a device set up near the teacher in the front may not capture everything that is said during a whole-class discussion – the same challenges exist in informal settings outside of classrooms. These multiparty contexts generally require you to use an external microphone that can be placed away from (and in conjunction with) the main video-recording device.

Video recording classroom discourse presents a different challenge: how do you capture all of the "nonverbal" or embodied movements in a classroom? If you only have access to one video-recording device – a common situation for many classroom discourse researchers – then you must determine whether you should privilege the embodied movements of the teacher or students. In simple terms, do you point the recording device at the teacher or do you have it facing the students? If you plan on moving the camera back and forth between the teacher and students, then where in the classroom is the best position to do so? In most video-recording situations, whether in possession of one or more devices, a tripod should be used for picture stability and clarity. A tripod will also free your hands to make notes and accomplish any other fieldwork-related tasks. Finally, a wide-angle lens, if you have access to one, will result in superior data by capturing a more panoramic recording of the spatial environment. Standard lenses, conversely, tend to produce a narrower frame of recording. That is, close-up recordings will only capture the participants in the immediate vicinity of the device, which is often problematic when investigating whole-class interactions.

2.2.1.3 Recording online spaces

While classroom discourse research has a long tradition of recording and analyzing physical classrooms, it is now not uncommon to investigate teaching and learning in online settings. Recording online data is an exceptionally complex task (e.g., Smith, 2008), and indeed space in this book does not permit an adequate overview of relevant issues; yet, it is worth identifying a few basic issues that will help you determine what to consider when recording online data. Further information about recording online teaching and learning can be found in Lamy (2012), Levy (2015), and Smith (2012).

Recording online data entails less hardware demands in that external microphones and camcorders are not needed in most investigatory situations (a researcher may, however, wish to record the physical activity of computer users as they participate in online discussions; cf. Smith, 2012). With that said, capturing what is communicated and accomplished on a screen requires a high level of technical and software knowledge. A researcher needs to know what software applications exit, must weigh the strengths and weaknesses of each application, and of course is required to learn the software of choice. You must also consider a range of technical issues, including determining the ideal file format used after a recording is complete, deciding on how much of the screen or what window should be captured, determining whether it is necessary to superimpose a webcam stream (of you or any other user), annotating and time stamping the data, and presetting and fine-tuning the audio and video of the screen capture.

2.2.1.4 Testing your equipment and software

In all data collection situations from physical classrooms to online spaces, it is helpful, if not necessary, to test your recording equipment and software. The ideal situation is to test recording equipment and software at your site of investigation, which allows you to adjust your data collection plan according to unforeseen challenges, such as a spatial arrangement in a classroom that requires you to place a video recorder in a location that hinders your ability to address a particular empirical objective. That is, testing recording equipment and software at your site of investigation will help you determine whether your research question is feasible. If are unable to run tests at your site of investigation, then you should try recording discourse that resembles your analytic interests. For example, if you are interested in recording students complete oral tasks in a classroom, then you may find it helpful to record some of your friends or colleagues around a dinner table.

2.2.1.5 Planning learning activities

Apart from the technical and software knowledge needed to record data for research purposes, you will need to think about what the teacher and students (or participants) will be doing while going about the business of learning. That is, will you create a lesson plan that is strategically connected to your analytic focus or research question? Alternatively, will you simply record unplanned and naturalist interactions with no specific analytic focus in mind? The former approach requires thinking about the extent to which specific components of a lesson plan will lead to specific discourse outcomes, such as the discursive relationship between a collaborative component in a task and students negotiating for meaning (cf. L. Lee, 2008). Combing through the literature will help you identify studies that have already established important connections between a lesson plan and a particular type of discourse (e.g., Blake, 2011). The latter approach is often used when the goal is to allow your naturalistic recordings determine your analytic focus, as what the classroom participants do in and through their discourse is unplanned and may likely not relate back to a pre-identified empirical objective.

2.2.1.6 Determining how much

How much data you collect is an essential planning issue to address early in your research. Do you need to collect ten hours of classroom data or will one recording of a lesson be enough? Your methodological approach (e.g., qualitative versus quantitative), analytic focus (e.g., lexical collocations versus turn-taking patterns), institutional expectations (e.g., the guidelines established by your instructor), and your logistical constraints (see the beginning of this chapter) should all be factored in when answering such questions. Determining how much data to collect will also require you to see what other researchers are doing for similar-sized projects and seek advice from colleagues when devising your research plan.

Although a considerable degree of variation exists in how scholars collect data, and how much of it they will end up using in their analyses, there is one aspect of research that must be included in all plans to record spoken discourse. That is, the data that you collect, whether it is ten hours or one hour, will need to be transcribed. Transcribing time must be considered when identifying your data collection approach, as what you record and how you transcribe are inextricable aspects of doing classroom discourse research (specific transcription issues are discussed later in this chapter). So, any attempt to collect data must attend to whether there is enough time to transcribe some or all of it.

TABLE 2.1 Data collection plan

Data collection plan	Transcription time	Ideal project
1 hour of data recording	Minimally 1 day of transcribing	Course assignment
5 hours of data recording	Minimally 5 days of transcribing	Undergraduate thesis
10 hours of data recording	Minimally 10 days of transcribing	MA-level thesis
15 hours of data recording	Minimally 15 days of transcribing	Doctoral thesis

For example, a one-hour classroom recording of spoken discourse will generally take at least eight hours (or approximately one day) to transcribe with some resemblance of the actual talk and interaction. This approximate ratio provides a useful planning tool for determining whether your data collection goal is feasible given your time constraints and institutional expectations. Take, for example, the recording scenarios in Table 2.1 that provide time approximations for common data collection plans. The final column identifies the project that would be suitable for each data collection plan.

While the expectations of your instructor, supervisor, or institution will help you determine what is an acceptable amount of data to collect for your project, and their suggestions may indeed deviate from those in Table 2.1, these time approximations are a reminder that an overly ambitious data collection plan will not only require significant time and effort, but it also may not be necessary given what other researchers are doing for similar-sized projects. Furthermore, when doing discourse analysis, a general rule of thumb is that you should err on the side of less data and more transcription and analytic detail than the other way around (unless, of course, your research adopts corpus or quantitative approaches). This rule stems from the understanding that qualitative discourse analysts need not worry about issues of sample size and generalizability, as one of the overarching empirical objectives is to provide a deeper understanding of a particular context or phenomenon. Your data collection plan should thus include a number that is realistic, reflects institutional expectations, and allows you to answer your research question through deep and nuanced analytic observations.

2.2.1.7 Collecting written discourse

This chapter, and indeed this book, has thus far privileged the study of spoken communication over written discourse. This focus is a natural reflection of the literature on classroom discourse. Aspects of spoken communication, such as how teachers elicit answers from students, have long been the focal point of analysis in classroom discourse research. It is important, however, to resist the temptation to only associate classroom discourse with spoken communication. A great deal of classroom discourse is conducted in the written medium: Essays, online discussions, emails, text messages, and journals are just a few of the many facets of teaching and learning that should also be folded into a discussion of classroom discourse – empirical issues that are specific to studying written discourse will be addressed later in the book when applicable.

With that said, however, it is far less challenging to collect records of written discourse. Researchers need not worry about transcribing data, and the hardware and software requirements to collect (and analyze) written discourse are minimal. The upshot is, in most investigatory contexts, written records of teaching and learning are ready-made "transcripts," allowing researchers to begin analyzing their data quickly after assignments are completed. Nevertheless, data based on written discourses must still be "prepped" for analytic and dissemination purposes: Scanning paper-based assignments, organizing documents, and formatting texts for dissemination purposes are all time-intensive processes.

While written texts are important facets of teaching and learning that must play a more prominent role in the literature on classroom discourse, the logistical and planning challenges involved in recording spoken communication require much attention. To this end, the remaining chapter will continue to focus primarily on recording such data.

2.2.1.8 Using supporting materials

Teaching and learning are a multifaceted coordination of actions and practices, and thus simply collecting records of written discourse or only recording spoken communication will provide an incomplete picture of a classroom. In order to avoid this situation and provide nuanced descriptions of classroom discourse, it is often necessary to observe with your own eyes (and over multiple lessons) how your research participants go about the business of teaching and learning. This aspect of doing classroom discourse research may entail taking ethnographic notes (cf. Watson-Gegeo, 1988), collecting classroom materials (e.g., syllabi, lessons, and exercise sheets), and interviewing your research participants.

Another way of thinking about the usefulness of supporting materials is to remember that collecting data is not just about recording what is being communicated; collecting data is also about documenting the context in which classroom discourse unfolds. In other words, what teachers and students say and do in a classroom is based on a number of contextual factors (e.g., pedagogical goal, shared lesson, past experiences) that may not be "visible" in the classroom discourse that you record or collect. Capturing or documenting these contextual factors, and incorporating them into analytic observations, will improve the quality of your research (Rapley, 2008).

The upshot in this discussion of supporting materials is that you should bring a notepad with you into the classroom, discuss learning objectives with the teacher, pay attention to what is happening outside and beyond the frame of recording, and gather any documents that may help you remember (and better understand) your recordings or data records.

2.2.2 Managing data sets

After your recordings or records of classroom discourse have been collected, you will need to think about storing and organizing your data sets. This stage in the research process is often referred to as "archiving." Accessibility is the most fundamental issue to consider when archiving data. That is, you must create an archiving system so that your data sets can be easily located. You do not want to spend unnecessary time locating particular data sets while writing up your observations. The first step in creating an efficient archiving system entails using identifiable names for your stored recordings: date, recording time, and classroom context are commonly used markers for data sets (e.g., eslclass-9am-30MAY2019.mov).

The next step in creating an efficient archiving system entails bookmarking specific phenomena within your recordings. A straightforward, but somewhat archaic, way of doing this involves breaking your longer recordings into smaller segments of phenomenon that you will analyze later for your research project. For example, a one-hour recording of teacher-fronted discussion could be broken into 20 segments of students responding to questions (e.g., studentA-answer1.mov; studentB-answer2.mov; etc.).

A more advanced way of bookmarking involves using a transcription or data analysis program to tag specific moments in a recording that will be analyzed later. Such programs often allow you to avoid creating smaller files, which can hinder your ability to find specific discourse phenomena. However, programs designed for research purposes are often very expensive and all of them take a considerable amount of time to learn. Readers interested in using a program for transcription or data analysis purposes should incorporate practice time into their research plan.

In both archiving approaches, it is essential to back up your data. Data should be backed up on an external hard drive or using cloud storage. An additional security measure could be applied, such as storing your data in two file locations or protecting your files with a password.

2.2.3 Making sense of your data

The final aspect of data collection that should be factored in to your research plan is closely related to archiving. Knowing what to name your recordings, adopting an archiving system, and bookmarking specific discourse phenomena, all partly require you to identify the empirical objective for which your data will be used to address. Simply put, you need to have some basic understanding of what you would like to analyze before being able to organize or archive your data.

In order to do this – that is, make sense of your data – you must engage in preliminary data analyses. This may entail locating specific moments in your recording that you may want to transcribe in greater detail and investigate further. You could, in turn, present your initial observations to a small group of colleagues or even ask your research participants to comment on the preliminary observations. Getting feedback from such people is an excellent way of determining how to break your recordings into smaller segments of data that will be used to answer specific research questions. Once you have established a better understanding of your research objectives, you could make better sense of your data by presenting your work at a conference or seminar.

Whatever approach you use, it is important to remember that archiving and analyzing data are interconnected activities. Such activities are also closely related to transcription practices.

2.3 Transcribing your data

It is necessary to address what a transcript is before discussing the principles of transcribing classroom data. That is, understanding what a transcript is will help you determine what aspects of your recording can be transcribed into a document.

A transcript is a static record of classroom interaction. It can include anything from the prosodic features of talk to meta-commentary by the researcher. In addition to being a static record of classroom interaction, a transcript is a theoretical construct: What you transcribe reflects your empirical interests, theoretical framework, disciplinary traditions, and professional constraints.

A transcript is also reductional in that transcribing recordings of classroom discourse requires you to take an experience that is ephemeral and highly complex, and transform into a static object of texts and images. This process – referred to as "entextualization" (Bucholtz, 2007) and discussed in greater detail below – means that classroom discourse takes on new interpretations once they have been represented in transcript form.

Although this process of entextualization results in subjective transcripts, most discourse analysts embrace the highly interpretive nature of classroom discourse research. This openness to interpretation is evidenced in the variation that exists in transcripts (Bucholtz, 2007). The issue of variation, though not viewed as inherently problematic, is a reminder that transcripts are highly contextualized artifacts that require being cognizant of the relationship between your empirical interests and how your recordings of classroom discourse are transcribed.

To this end, the first theoretical issue to consider when transcribing your recordings of classroom discourse is *transcription detail*.

2.3.1 Open and closed transcripts

The discussion of transcripts has thus far established that transcribing classroom discourse is an inherently theoretical endeavor. That is, what ultimately ends up in a transcript is a reflection of the theories that guide your research. In practical terms, this means approaching the transcription process by reflecting on the relationship between your research questions and transcripts. Does your research question require you to produce detailed transcripts that include prosodic and interactional features or do your analytic observations depend on just the words spoken between the teacher and students?

Your answer to the aforementioned question is based on whether you will produce an open or closed transcript.

An open transcript requires you to put aside most of your beliefs regarding what is and what is not relevant in a recording of classroom discourse. The assumption here is that everything in a classroom recording is potentially relevant to your research question. An open transcript requires you to transcribe as much spoken and interactional detail as time and resources allow: this often entails transcribing audible breathing, pauses between utterances, embodied communication, overlapping talk, and hand gestures, to name a few. Creating an open transcript is sometimes an objective because the researcher does not have a specific research question in mind; in this case, the open transcript allows the researcher to generate research questions according to the classroom recording – this is referred to as *data-driven* research.

A closed transcript is typically created when you know precisely what your analytic focus is and understand what aspects of classroom discourse you need to transcribe in order to answer your research question. Closed transcripts only reflect your empirical objectives; put differently, features of talk and aspects of interaction that do not help answer your research question are not transcribed. This deductive process of transcribing according to specific empirical objectives often results in much less transcription detail than found in open transcripts.

When thinking about your own research, it is useful to view this discussion as a spectrum of transcription practice (see Figure 2.2).

For example, while the far-left end of the spectrum represents an attempt to transcribe every feature of talk and aspect of interaction, a classroom recording can never be fully captured in a transcript (Cook, 1990). Similarly, while the far right end of the spectrum entails being highly selective in the transcription process, as in the case when a corpus linguist is only concerned with investigating the spoken words of a lesson, even said research would benefit from understanding how utterances are produced and the ways in which they are situated within a larger interactional context. Where you place your transcript within this spectrum of transcription practices is ultimately based on both methodological considerations and logistical constraints. The upshot is, as noted previously, transcripts are theoretical constructs that are based on who you are as a researcher, what your interests are, and the time and resources that can be allocated to the transcription process. These transcription variables influence how you represent and transform recordings of classroom discourse, which is the topic of discussion in the next section.

FIGURE 2.2 Transcription detail

2.3.2 Representation and transformation

Transcribing requires you to make a number of representational decisions that will transform what the teacher and students have experienced during a lesson into a simplified account of classroom discourse. Such representational decisions include anything from important organizational issues, such as margin size, font type, and line spacing, to complex features of discourse, such as inhalations, laugh particles, voice amplitude, gestures, and gaze.

Such representational decisions present you – a concerned researcher of classroom teaching and learning – with a substantial task and responsibility. That is, how do you approach the transcription stage of your research knowing that not only is there a wide spectrum of discursive features that should be transcribed, but also your decisions will, to varying degrees of transformation, capture an experience that is somewhat removed from the original event as captured in the recording?

An important first step in addressing this question is to accept that compromises must be made, as a transcript possesses finite space. A recording of classroom discourse must be transformed into an interpretation of discursive features that must obey the spatial limitations of a letter- or A4-sized document; this simplified version of classroom discourse allows your transcript to be read again and again, which is a necessary part of doing research, though doing so potentially leads to new interpretations of the recording (see Silverstein & Urban, 1996).

Transcribing classroom discourse is fundamentally about managing the degree to which your transcripts simultaneously reflect your empirical interests and accurately represent the data. Multiple approaches exist in managing this task (see Jenks, 2013a); in this book, this task is divided into five overlapping aspects of transcribing classroom discourse: readability, granularity, accuracy, research agenda, and ethics.

The issue of readability is often overlooked during the transcription process; this is because researchers spend a considerable amount of time in isolation examining their data recordings, which makes it easy to forget that transcripts are largely created so that an academic audience can understand a past classroom event. Enhancing the readability of your transcript is accomplished by using a set of transcription conventions that transform a classroom recording into a legible document (see Section 2.3.3 for an overview of transcription conventions).

The systematic use of transcription conventions is related to the issue of granularity. Classroom discourse research often requires using nonstandard writing conventions, such as symbols and punctuation marks, to represent the rich and highly complex nature of teaching and learning. In other words, a transcript that only includes what has been verbally been said leaves out important discursive aspects of a lesson, such as the way rising or falling intonation accomplishes meaningful pedagogical actions (cf. Hellermann, 2003). Intonation and other discursive features of a lesson cannot be accurately transcribed using words and letters, but rather again requires adopting a system of nonconventional spelling approaches.

TABLE 2.2 Representational issues

Transcription issue	Practical considerations
Readability	Although a transcript is fundamentally a reflection of what has been said and done in a classroom recording, what ultimately ends up being transcribed will be read by other researchers or professionals. To some extent, your transcription decisions ought to consider the reading demands of these researchers and professionals.
Granularity	Your classroom recordings include an exceptionally wide range of discursive and interactional features that interface with teaching and learning practices. What transcription conventions will be used to represent such features and practices?
Accuracy	Transcription granularity is closely related to the degree to which a transcript accurately reflects a classroom recording. Compromises will need to be made while transcribing; what aspects of discourse must be included in order to answer your research questions?
Research agenda	A transcript is a research construct. It is as much a reflection of your disciplinary expectations as it is an accurate portrayal of a classroom event.
Ethics	Representational decisions are inherently political, as they are shaped by a number of human factors. A particular accent or dialect, for example, represents a cultural history that must be factored in when transcribing classroom discourse.

Granularity is related to accuracy. Specifically, the transcription issue is concerned with how much of your classroom recording is transcribed. Accuracy is about the type of discourse that ends up in your transcript. For example, a transcript may include not only aspects of spoken discourse, but also interactional features (e.g., turn-taking organization) and embodied actions (e.g., body movements). Although accuracy and granularity may seem like the same transcription issue, the two present different representational challenges. For instance, an accurate transcript may include everything that is said (i.e., what is said), but could omit the (highly granular) phonological features of such talk (i.e., how something is said).

The fourth row is related to how your disciplinary expectations shape what you ultimately transcribe. That is, a research agenda is about representing classroom discourse according to exogenous theories, methodologies, and ethical considerations. For example, a classroom discourse researcher interested in how students develop the English sound system may not transcribe embodied actions despite the importance of movements and gestures. In the same vein, a lesson that discusses sensitive topics, such as politics and religion, may require a researcher to omit much of what is said during a lesson.

Ethical considerations are centrally about protecting the interests of those individuals that your research is investigating. It is standard practice to conceal the identities of participants, which often requires using pseudonyms for teachers and students, place names, and other proper nouns. Excellent overviews of how to protect the identities of participants can be found on the websites of most professional research organizations.

A second important ethical consideration is related to whether, and how, you respect the cultural identities of those participants under investigation. The unique accents and dialects of teachers and students are steeped in cultural history, and thus how you represent such varieties is bound to ethical and political issues. For example, how much time should you afford to transcribing the discursive idiosyncrasies of your research participants? Your answer to this question should be shaped by the following transcription approaches: standardization and vernacularization (see Jenks, 2011, p. 19).

Standardization is the practice of using conventional spelling and grammatical constructions to represent the spoken words of your classroom recordings. This practice does not attempt to illustrate the unique speech varieties of your participants, but rather uses generic or standard constructions, such as the transformation from "I wanna know more" to "I want to know more" or "I ain't got the answer" to "I do not have the answer."

Vernacularization, on the other hand, uses nonstandard spelling, symbols, and punctuation marks to represent the talk of classroom teaching and learning. This practice, which is sometimes referred to as eye dialect or orthographic metonymy (see Bucholtz, 2000), attempts to capture the actual sound of a particular utterance, such as the representation of contractions like "wha'cha doin" (rather than "what are you doing"). A more technical approach to eye dialect is to use the International Phonetic Alphabet, but this requires careful training and practice.

Both standardization and vernacularization can be used in one transcript depending on what your empirical objectives are. In other words, any given stretch of communication in your recording can be transcribed using either standardization or vernacularization. For example, if there is a stretch of miscommunication stemming from the way a word is pronounced, then said problematic utterance could be transcribed using vernacularization, while standardization may be applied to the surrounding talk.

Yet, there are ethical and political implications to consider when selecting a particular transcription approach. Vernacularization can lead to problematic or stereotypical depictions of your participants. For example, using the International Phonetic Alphabet to transcribe a stretch of communication may encourage readers to view your students as deficient speakers. Although standardization shields participants from such depictions, conventional transcription approaches erase the unique cultural and linguistic features of speech patterns. That is, standardization homogenizes the participants of classroom discourse by erasing their idiosyncratic ways of speaking and communicating.

Table 2.1 demonstrates that transcription issues often work against each other. For example, a transcript that accurately represents spoken utterances, and includes the granular features of how such talk is spoken, will be more challenging to read than transcripts that omit such phonological information. Similarly, a legible transcript that omits the complex nature of classroom discourse is both less accurate and detailed. As with much of what has been discussed in this chapter, the transcription approach that you adopt will be shaped by the unique contextual factors of your research project.

2.3.3 Transcription practices

Transcribing classroom discourse requires understanding a number of theoretical issues, as discussed in the previous section. While theoretical issues, such as the empirical and political implications of representing talk in a particular way, are integral to producing transcripts, the act of transcribing is largely practice-based. That is, transcribing classroom discourse requires a significant amount of time sitting in front of a computer playing and replaying a recording, and inputting what you hear and see in a document.

To this end, the following discussion offers some basic steps that can be taken when you are ready to transcribe your data. As highlighted before, individual circumstances and constraints will shape how you approach the practice of transcription; therefore, the following steps are merely suggestions. You may deviate from this list or any other suggestions made in this section on transcribing.

The following list provides a simple five-step method for transcribing your classroom recordings. The list, which has been modified from Jenks (2011, p. 116), assumes that you have already collected your data.

1. Before transcribing anything, back up your data.
2. Create a file-naming system for your data and transcripts.
3. Playback your recordings; create a list of interesting phenomena.
4. Protect the identities of your participants; create pseudonyms.
5. Begin transcribing.

The first four steps are prerequisites to transcribing; they are essential for creating transcripts that can be tailored for your specific research objectives. The fifth step entails making basic organizational decisions, such as establishing the spacing of your margins, determining whether and how line numbers will be used, and deciding on the level of granularity and accuracy that you will achieve in your transcripts. These basic organizational decisions must be made before you start inputting words into a document, as changes to spacing and margin size will distort how the words and utterances on your transcript appear.

The actual practice of transcribing often begins at the orthographical level; that is, transcribing only the spoken words using conventional spelling allows you to focus on establishing the gist of a recording. If deemed necessary, you may then include the interactional (e.g., pauses) and prosodic (e.g., intonation) detail that brings your recording to life. Adding such detail often requires listening to a recording several times after the words and utterances have been transcribed. In other words, be prepared to listen to your recordings and revise your transcripts many times over: A transcript is an ever changing, always evolving document.

To this end, Cook (1990) speaks of the infinite detail that exists in a recording of spoken communication, making a transcript an inherently superficial representation of a human encounter. While transcripts can never fully represent what has occurred in a classroom, researchers can ensure that what is said and done in a recording is to some extent faithfully presented in a transcript. This attempt to be faithful to a recording can be accomplished by using a transcription system, which consists of a list of symbols and punctuation marks, to represent what and how a discursive event unfolds (for a more detailed overview of different transcription systems, see Jenks, 2011, p. 115).

Table 2.3 includes a list of ten commonly transcribed features of spoken communication as approached by conversation analysts – it must be noted that using

TABLE 2.3 Transcription conventions

Discourse feature	Convention	Transcription description
Overlapping talk	[ ]	You may transcribe overlapping talk between two or more interactants when it begins [and ends].
Timed pauses	(0.4) (.)	You may transcribe pauses when they occur within a turn and between turns. Pauses greater than two tenths of a second are represented in their numerical value. Micro pauses of less than two tenths of a second are represented as a period/full stop.
Falling intonation	.	You may transcribe a fall in pitch at the end of an utterance with a period/full stop.
Rising intonation	?	You may transcribe a rise in pitch at the end of an utterance with a question mark, which does not always represent a question. A comma may also be used for a slight rise in pitch (e.g., hello,).
Elongation	:	You may transcribe elongated talk. Adding more colons denotes longer speech (e.g., hello::::).
Abrupt stop	-	You may transcribe abrupt stops or restarts with a hyphen.
Loud talk	CAPITAL	You may transcribe an increase in voice amplitude with capital letters (e.g., HELLO).
Quiet talk	° °	You may transcribe speech that is quiet with degree signs on both sides of the talk.
Fast talk	> <	You may transcribe speech that is fast with a greater-than sign and less-than sign on both sides of the talk.
Slow talk	< >	You may transcribe speech that is slow with a less-than sign and greater-than sign on both sides of the talk.

conversation analytic transcription conventions in your transcripts does not require you to use conversation analysis. Any methodology – not just conversation analysis – can benefit from transcribing classroom recordings according to conversation analytic transcription conventions.

Transcribing your classroom recordings according to these conventions, which have been modified from Atkinson and Heritage (1984), provides an excellent way of depicting how a lesson unfolds in a classroom, and is also closely related to how teachers and learners co-construct meaning in classrooms.

PART II
Analyzing

3
CONVERSATION ANALYSIS

Part II of this book begins with a methodology that has, in recent years, popularized the study of classroom discourse. Specifically, this chapter provides a glimpse into how conversation analysis (CA) approaches classroom discourse. CA is often associated with the study of classroom discourse because much has been reported on the importance of interactional sequence and organization, such as the turn-taking mechanics of teacher-fronted lessons and repair strategies by students, in how teaching and learning are managed in classrooms. The common view that CA is the ideal methodology to investigate classroom discourse partly stems from the excellent work done by conversation analysts (e.g., Seedhouse, 2004). Although many approaches have been used to investigate classroom discourse in general (e.g., Rymes, 2015), and the organization of classroom interaction in particular (cf. Walsh, 2011), CA offers a set of methodological principles that can be easily applied to the study of teaching and learning.

Before discussing classroom discourse from a conversation analytic perspective, it is important to address some basic theoretical principles that underpin the work covered in this chapter. First, the term conversation implies spoken communication in real time between two or more interlocutors. In CA jargon, the terms *talk* and *interaction* (or *talk-in-interaction*) are typically used to refer to this interest in spoken communication. Conversely, as discussed in Chapter 1, discourse is a much broader theoretical construct that includes, but extends beyond, talk and interaction (the term discourse can be, but is not often, used as an analytic construct within CA circles). Furthermore, while CA has been, and can be, used to study written discourse (e.g., Jenks, 2014), this chapter focuses on the spoken interactions of teachers and students.

Second, a conversation analytic account of classroom talk and interaction requires you as a researcher to "take on" the perspectives of classroom participants. That is, rather than explain why *you* think a teacher or student is talking or interacting in a particular way, you must demonstrate in your analysis *how* such people are talking and interacting. In this sense, CA observations are based on how classroom participants reveal their understanding, and accomplish teaching and learning, in the turn-by-turn moments of a classroom. What turns accomplish, and how they are organized, are two examples of what CA investigates in the context of classroom teaching and learning. How these empirical foci are examined, and what they look like in research papers, are topics addressed in the following sections.

Finally, the aim of this chapter is to provide a concise, but more importantly an introductory, overview of a potentially useful methodology for your research. The chapter aims to provide a glimpse into what a CA study of classroom discourse entails, but as with all methodologies discussed in this book, developing good conversation analytic skills requires extensive reading and data analysis practice. Accordingly, this chapter (as well as subsequent chapters in Part II on selecting a methodology and topic) is organized largely around reading lists and reflective questions. That is, the methodologies covered in this book are discussed by providing guidance and direction, which will point you in the right direction while establishing an adequate base from which to carry out your research.

To this end, Table 3.1 identifies several publications that offer CA overviews; these publications provide more theoretical explanations of CA than offered in this chapter.

TABLE 3.1 Introductory publications on CA

Recommended publication	*Description*
Hutchby, I., & Wooffitt, R. (2008). *Conversation analysis.* Cambridge, UK: Polity.	A classic introduction to conversation analytic principles. The writing style is not accessible, but key issues are discussed logically and succinctly.
Markee, N. (2000). *Conversation analysis.* New York, NY: Routledge.	An older book publication on CA, but often referred to in classroom discourse research. Writing is easy to understand, and overviews are supported by many examples.
Psathas, G. (1995). *Conversation analysis.* Thousand Oaks, CA: Sage.	A short and accessible book on the theoretical foundations and methodological principles of CA. An excellent book for readers with little time to learn about CA.
Schegloff, E.A. (2007). *Sequence organization in interaction.* Cambridge, UK: Cambridge University Press.	A specialized book that focuses on turn-taking and turn organization. The writing style is perhaps the most difficult to follow out of the five books identified here, but the book is an essential read for anyone wishing to develop their analytic skills.
Wooffitt, R. (2005). *Conversation analysis and discourse analysis.* London, UK: Sage.	An excellent book for readers that wish to learn about CA while considering what distinguishes it from other discourse analytic approaches.

3.1 What can I investigate?

CA is interested in a number of empirical issues. Preference organization, epistemic stance, prosody in interaction, storytelling, action formation, and gaze are just some of the many empirical issues studied by conversation analysts (cf. Sidnell & Stivers, 2013). Although these empirical issues can be, and have been, analyzed within classroom settings, investigating gestures and other similar complex topics requires extensive overviews and supporting data examples. Readers interested in developing advanced analytic skills in these issues, such as embodied action formation, are encouraged to work closely with a colleague or supervisor that actively engages in CA research.

This chapter takes a different approach to answering the question of what to investigate. Rather than cover all of the possible empirical issues that can be, and have been, investigated within classroom settings, this chapter provides an introductory account of what CA can offer a researcher interested in classroom discourse.

The sections that follow achieve this aim by reviewing some of the more common classroom discourse issues investigated by conversation analysts. Namely, turn-taking, turn design, repair, and interactional competence are reviewed. Although turn-taking, turn design, repair, and interactional competence provide an accessible way into a discussion of CA and classroom discourse, readers should again familiarize themselves with the books identified in Table 3.1 of the previous section in order to develop a broader understanding of conversation analytic principles. With that said, a discussion of turn-taking, turn design, repair, and interactional competence will provide you with enough information to make informed decisions about how to use CA in a study of classroom discourse.

These four empirical issues are divided into subsections; each subsection includes practical tips to begin your research, while Section 3.2 provides a separate theoretical account of what you should consider when applying conversation analytic principles. This approach of empirical issues first and methodology second will provide a more comprehensible introduction to CA.

3.1.1 Turn-taking

A turn at talk or interaction, such as a verbal correction or hand gesture to participate in a discussion, is often part of a larger system of turns. That is, turns make up larger sequences of talk and interaction, such as an exchange between two students completing an activity. Classroom teaching and learning can be understood by looking at this turn-taking system. Take, for example, the following exchange between a teacher and her students in an advanced ESL classroom. For the transcription conventions used in CA, refer back to Table 2.3 in Chapter 2.

```
1    Teacher      what does foundational mean?
2                 (1.0)
3    Teacher      does anyone know?
```

```
4      Student A      does it mean beginning?
5      Teacher        close.
6                     (2.2) ((teacher looks around the class))
7      Student B      base=
8      Teacher        =yes. base or source. something important
9                     that influences other things
```

In CA, turn-taking research does not usually entail counting who says what and to whom. CA is also not concerned with looking at turns in isolation. Such concerns violate what CA views as central to how social interaction is organized. That is, a turn-taking system, such as the previous exchange between the teacher and students, is a means through which meaning is co-constructed. A turn is inherently meaningful, and meaning is embedded with turns. As a classroom lesson unfolds, turns allow teachers and students to jointly achieve pedagogical goals, make adjustments to clarify something uttered previously, and engage in important identity work, to name a few.

Turn-taking research in CA requires looking at how what is said in a current turn is based on a previous turn. For example, looking at line 7 in isolation only reveals that the student uses her turn to provide an answer. However, looking at what unfolds before and up to line 7 allows us to see that Student B treats the teacher's evaluation, pause, and eye gaze in lines 5 and 6 as an indication that a different answer should be provided. In other words, the answer provided in line 7 reveals a number of important classroom discourse issues, including Student B's understanding that the teacher is actively testing and evaluating the knowledge of the students.

Therefore, turn-taking in CA is, first and foremost, a system of meaning-making "tools" that allows teachers and students to engage in different classroom actions and practices. The "tools" used by teacher and students to co-construct meaning become empirical objects for conversation analysts. For example, a conversation analyst will use the turn-taking practices of classroom participants to understand the extent to which a teacher is able to fulfill her pedagogical objective.

The questions that follow offer some tangible examples of what a conversation analyst would ask when investigating a turn-taking system in general, and the previous extract in particular.

1. What can you say about the one-second pause in line 2? For example, how does the teacher respond to the momentary silence?
2. What is the teacher doing with her questions?
3. How is this exchange and activity organized according to turns?
4. Who is allocating all of the turns? What does this say about the turn-taking system?
5. How are the students contributing to this exchange? Does this say anything about the type of activity that the teacher is managing?

These questions can also be used to consider how to approach your own research. For example, if you have already recorded and transcribed your data, then it may be helpful to think about how students and teachers react or respond to pauses. Do the turns following pauses in your data tell you anything about the type of teaching and learning that is occurring? You may formulate your own research question for your project using the aforementioned empirical issues. Take, for example, the following research questions:

1. How are pauses used by teachers and students to demonstrate their understanding of learning activities?
2. What turn-taking patterns are used when teachers provide feedback to students?
3. How do students initiate a question during a teacher-fronted lesson?

If you have not recorded any data, then you can think about your experiences in the classroom as a student or teacher. How are turns used to accomplish different pedagogical goals? Do students have control over how turns are managed? If not, then why?

While these questions are helpful in understanding what conversation analysts examine in classroom settings, Table 3.2 identifies references that offer more concrete examples of what an analysis of turn-taking looks like.

When thinking about how to approach a study on turn-taking, it is also useful to think about how activities in the classroom (e.g., Mori, 2002), such as a teacher-fronted grammar lesson or a student-centered task, are often organized differently. For example, the types of questions asked during an activity that is led by a teacher may be different from what students ask each other when completing a collaborative task. Such differences are of importance to conversation analysts. The following are three related questions that may help you better understand the type of research that takes place using CA:

1. How do students display their understanding during whole-class activities?
2. What are the interactional features of teacher-fronted lessons?
3. How is misunderstanding co-constructed during online task-based learning?

These questions are all related to how teachers and students construct and allocate turns. The research questions also relate to how teachers and students organize their talk and interaction during a particular activity. As such, conversation analysts, when approaching the study of turn-taking, are centrally concerned with *sequence* and *organization*. A sequence, such as a brief explanation by a teacher or a debate between two students, is made up of an organization of turns. Conversation analysts are interested in what this organization looks like, and how classroom participants accomplish various things during sequences. Sequence and organization are also approached by conversation analysts by looking at specific aspects of an activity, such as when a teacher provides instructions, concludes a lesson, or takes attendance. Take, for example, the following opening sequence.

TABLE 3.2 Publications on turn-taking

Recommended publication	Description
Seedhouse, P. (2004). *The interactional architecture of the language classroom: A conversation analysis perspective.* Malden, MA: Wiley-Blackwell.	A must-read book for any student wishing to study the turn-taking mechanics of classroom teaching and learning. Although this book is based on many years of empirical research, the chapters provide excellent examples of how CA is used to study classrooms.
Seedhouse, P. (1996). Classroom interaction: Possibilities and impossibilities. *ELT Journal, 50,* 16–24.	This is a seminal investigation of turn-taking that argues that "real" conversations in classrooms are unattainable given the institutional roles of students and teachers. The publication is easy to follow, and offers examples of what an analysis of turn-taking should look like.
Wong, J., & Waring, H.Z. (2010). *Conversation analysis and second language pedagogy: A guide for ESL/EFL teachers.* New York, NY: Routledge.	The book offers an overview of how conversation analytic principles can help language teachers better understand their classrooms. In chapter 2, the authors focus on the relation between turn-taking and language teaching. Example transcripts help establish a better understanding of how turn-taking practices are examined.
Waring, H.Z. (2009). Moving out of IRF (initiation–response–feedback): A single case analysis. *Language Learning, 59,* 796–824.	This article examines how turn-taking practices are used to participate in a lesson. The study builds on existing classroom discourse work by showing how participants move in and out of the IRF sequence found in many classrooms.
Sert, O. (2015). *Social interaction and L2 classroom discourse.* Edinburgh, UK: Edinburgh University Press.	Although the book examines a number of discursive issues, the analyses provided by Sert are helpful in understanding how turn-taking can be studied from a conversation analytic perspective. In particular, chapters 2 and 3 provide introductory accounts of how conversation analytic principles are relevant to classroom teaching and learning.

```
1    Teacher      uhm, okay.
2                 (0.4)
3                 ((students shift their gaze to
4                 the front of the class))
5    Teacher      okay. are we ready?
6                 (1.1)
7                 ((students nod))
8    Student A    can I first ask a question?
9    Teacher      yes
10   Student A    do we have a quiz today?
11   Teacher      no.
```

```
12                     (0.1)
13      Teacher        okay, so what concepts did we go
14                     over last week?
```

Some of the issues within the opening sequence that would be of interest to a conversation analyst are formulated in the following questions:

1. How does the teacher begin the lesson?
2. How do students demonstrate their understanding that the lesson has started?
3. How do the classroom participants (both the teacher and students) jointly establish an understanding that a lesson is about to start?
4. What nonverbal or embodied actions are used to organize the opening sequence?
5. How does the teacher transition from the opening sequence to the lesson?

A number of observations can be made regarding the opening sequence in general, and the five questions in particular. The teacher begins the sequence with the discourse marker "okay," which often signals the beginning of an activity in many contexts (Schiffrin, 1987); the students orient to the discourse marker by shifting their gaze to the front of the class, demonstrating their understanding that the teacher is about to start the business of teaching and learning. The teacher, in line 5, uses a discourse marker and question to explicitly seek confirmation that the students are ready. Notice that the utterance in line 5 does not occur until after the students have shifted their gaze to the teacher: this sequential feature is an example of how the classroom participants are jointly establishing an understanding that the lesson is about to start. In addition to embodied movements being used to organize the opening sequence (cf. the gaze in lines 3–4), the teacher uses verbal communication to begin the lesson (cf. the discourse markers in lines 1 and 5). The teacher begins the lesson by asking what the students learned the previous week, marking the end of the opening sequence.

In sum, turn-taking is a central empirical issue for conversation analysts. This interest in turn-taking can be formulated in the following ways:

1. *Practice and action*: CA is concerned with how turns accomplish things, including co-constructing meaning. An action is a specific accomplishment, such as a clarification request or a confirmation check. A practice is a larger activity, such as teaching, opening a sequence, and explaining instructions. A practice may consist of a number of actions.
2. *Sequence and organization*: CA is concerned with how turns sequentially unfold during an exchange or within an activity, such as the beginning of a lesson.

Turns are used to carry out practices and actions. Practices and actions possess an internal structure in that they are often made up of a number of turns that unfold sequentially. A turn also possesses an internal structure. For instance, a turn may be short or long, comprising any combination of words, phrases, embodied movements, gaze, or pauses, to name a few. The internal composition or shape of a turn is a critical aspect of understanding classroom turn-taking systems, as how teachers and students jointly accomplish the task of teaching and learning is accomplished in and though what they do with turns (i.e., how they construct and allocate them).

3.1.2 Turn shape and placement

Understanding how teachers and students construct and allocate turns is approached by conversation analysts by looking at *turn constructional units* (TCUs). Although a turn may include grammatical units, such as clauses, lexical items, or even complete sentences, a TCU is not defined as such. That is, a TCU is not a grammatical unit: for instance, an ostensibly simple head node can make up an entire TCU.

Furthermore, a turn can be made up of a number of TCUs. We return to the first extract of this chapter, which is presented again here to demonstrate this point.

```
1    Teacher     what does foundational mean?
2                (1.0)
3    Teacher     does anyone know?
4    Student A   does it mean beginning?
5    Teacher     close.
6                (2.2) ((teacher looks around the class))
7    Student B   base=
8    Teacher     =yes. base or source. something important
9                that influences other things
```

In lines 1–3, the teacher asks two questions: "what does foundational mean?" and "does anyone know?" Each question represents a separate TCU. That is, in lines 1–3, the teacher constructs two TCUs. The two questions are not considered one TCU because the first question is followed by a pause, which indicates that the teacher is waiting for a response from the students. No response is given in line 2, so the teacher constructs another TCU in line 3 (in CA, lines numbers included in transcripts are NOT turns). Note also both questions are seeking the same information, but line 3 is a reformulation of the question uttered in line 1. Therefore, TCUs can perform the same action but have a different shape. Although the teacher is the only participant speaking in lines 1–3, she takes two turns at talk.

Furthermore, TCUs need not be complete sentences. In line 5, the teacher constructs a TCU of only one word. Similarly, the student in line 7 constructs a one-word TCU. Both TCUs are short, but each utterance accomplishes an important function in teaching and learning. For instance, the TCU in line 5 is an evaluation of a previous turn that lets the students know that they are incorrect, but "close" to the expected answer.

Central to an understanding of TCUs are *transition relevance places* (TRPs). That is, what counts as a TCU is dependent on when there is a TRP. TRPs are places within an interaction where a speaker change may occur. The previous example of the teacher producing two TCUs provides an excellent way into a discussion of TRPs.

```
1   Teacher    what does foundational mean?
2              (1.0)
3   Teacher    does anyone know?
```

Again, the teacher in line 1 constructs a TCU in the form of a question, which is followed by a pause. The question and pause signal a TRP, as the teacher, by soliciting an answer and giving students time to provide a response, creates a space for a change in speakership to occur: from teacher to student. The nonresponse by the students, and the follow-up question by the teacher, demonstrate that TRPs are not places where a speaker change must occur.

TCUs and TRPs are helpful in understanding *turn-allocation* practices: the shape of turns reveal how teachers and students engage in turn-taking practices. For example, the teacher's question in line 1 selects the next speaker by soliciting an answer from the class; the pause in line 2 indicates that the students are not willing or able at that particular time to provide an answer; and the second question in line 3 is where the teacher decides to self-select herself as the current speaker because the students do not provide an answer.

These three lines of interaction follow what conversation analysts have observed as prototypical turn-allocation possibilities in spoken communication (cf. Sacks, Schegloff, & Jefferson, 1974):

1. The current speaker selects the next speaker.
2. Someone listening self-selects as the next speaker.
3. No one listening self-selects; the current speaker continues speaking.

It is important to note that these possibilities are not turn-taking rules. Classroom participants can, for instance, speak in overlap or simultaneously. Understanding the basic shape and placement of turns can help you understand a number of classroom issues. For instance, the five reflection questions that follow require you to think about the relationship between TCUs, TRPs, and turn-allocation practices on the one hand, and classroom teaching and learning on the other.

1. What are the differences between the TCUs constructed by the teacher students?
2. What do these TCUs say about the role of the teacher (or student)?
3. How are pauses used to organize the lesson?
4. What type of questions are being asked by the teacher?
5. Why are the students' TCUs shorter than the teacher's?

TABLE 3.3 Publications on turn shape and placement

Recommended publication	Description
Lerner, G.H. (1995). Turn design and the organization of participation in instructional activities. *Discourse Processes, 19*, 111–131.	The study looks at speaker turn design by focusing on incomplete turn-constructional units. The author shows how an understanding of turn design can be used to approach pedagogical challenges.
Garton, S. (2012). Speaking out of turn? Taking the initiative in teacher-fronted classroom interaction. *Classroom Discourse, 3*, 29–45.	The study examines teacher-fronted lessons, but from the perspective of how students initiate participation. The author uncovers some of the interesting ways students engage in a lesson despite ostensibly few opportunities for them to interact.
Ziegler, G., Sert, O., & Durus, N. (2012). Student-initiated use of multilingual resources in English-language classroom interaction: Next-turn management. *Classroom Discourse, 3*, 187–204.	The study looks at the multilingual resources used by classroom participants to manage next turns. The authors specifically examine modified repetition, monolingual reformulation, and meta-talk about language.
Kääntä, L. (2010). *Teacher turn-allocation and repair practices in classroom interaction: A multisemiotic perspective.* Jyväskylä, Finland: Jyväskylä Studies in Humanities.	The author uncovers how turn-allocation practices are used to organize teacher-fronted classroom interaction. The study demonstrates that selecting the next turn by the teacher can be accomplished by using a range of embodied and semiotic resources.
Mortensen, K., & Hazel, S. (2011). Initiating round robins in the L2 classroom: Preliminary observations. *Novitas-Royal (Research on Youth and Language), 5*, 55–70.	The authors look at how classroom participants design their turns in a teacher-fronted activity. The analysis shows how turn design, turn-allocation practices, and the sequential boundaries of next turns feed into an understanding of classroom discourse.

In addition to these questions, Table 3.3 provides examples of how the shape and placement of turns are incorporated into studies of classroom discourse.

The publications in Table 3.3 are a few of the many studies that examine the shape and placement of turns in classrooms. Some of these studies are important to a larger understanding of classroom discourse, as they demonstrate that turns – whether short or long – are composed of not just spoken utterances, but also gestures, eye contact, and other embodied movements. In other words, TCUs are potentially multimodal units that are situated within an equally complex and dynamic turn-taking system.

One way of making an important contribution to the literature with your own research is to look beyond the spoken word and examine the multimodal resources used by teachers and students to organize and situate their turns in classroom discourse.

3.1.3 Repair

Repairs are important empirical issues in classroom discourse research, as troubles and challenges in comprehension and communication occur frequently in language teaching and learning. Before discussing how repairs are used to organize classroom discourse, a few definitions must be provided.

A repair is not the same thing as a *correction*. A correction occurs when a classroom participant, say a teacher, replaces an error or mistake, such as an ungrammatical utterance spoken by a student, with a correct alternative (Schegloff, Jefferson, & Sacks, 1977). The following extract provides an example of a teacher correction.

```
1    Student    his researches is very interesting
2    Teacher    you should say research
3               (0.3)
4    Teacher    we typically don't use research as a
                countable noun
```

Correcting a perceived mistake or error in speech is not the same thing as a repair. Although a correction is a type of repair, a CA understanding of repair is more general. Specifically, a repair occurs when a speaker addresses a trouble in communication (speaking or hearing); further, repairs do not always replace one utterance with another. Take, for example, the exchange presented earlier in the chapter:

```
1    Teacher       what does foundational mean?
2                  (1.0)
3    Teacher       does anyone know?
4    Student A     does it mean beginning?
5    Teacher       close.
6                  (2.2) ((teacher looks around the class))
7    Student B     base=
8    Teacher       =yes. base or source. something
                     important
9                  that influences other things
```

The teacher's response in line 5 is a repair. Note that the utterance "close" does not replace what the student has said in line 5 with an alternative response. Rather, the utterance "close" simply tells the student (and the class) that "beginning" is not the exact answer that the teacher is looking for. In CA, the proposed answer in line 4 is referred to as a *repairable* or *trouble source*. That is, line 4 is the beginning of the repair sequence in that the proposed answer is treated by the teacher as the source of trouble (in this case, understanding) in the lesson activity.

CA is interested in the organization of repair sequences, which includes where the trouble source is and what it looks like, and who and in what way the next speaker subsequently engages in a repair. Schegloff et al. (1977) identify four repair types that make up such sequences:

56 Analyzing

1. Self-initiated self-repair.
2. Self-initiated other-repair.
3. Other-initiated self-repair.
4. Other-initiated other-repair.

All repair types address two fundamental issues: who initiates the repair sequence and who repairs the trouble source. For instance, in a self-initiated self-repair, the speaker both signals that there is trouble and repairs the trouble source. Similarly, in other-initiated other-repair, a speaker other than the one responsible for the trouble source both signals and repairs.

While these repair types can be easily applied to contexts where there are only two speakers, classrooms are significantly more complex and dynamic. For example, in the next extract, three different classroom participants are involved in the repair sequence.

```
4      Student A    does it mean beginning?
5      Teacher      close.
6                   (2.2) ((teacher looks around the class))
7      Student B    base=
```

In this exchange, Student A is responsible for the trouble source. The teacher is the speaker that signals that there is trouble (i.e., other-initiation). However, Student B is the speaker that actually repairs the trouble source. While this type of sequence is common in classrooms, it is significant in a discussion of repairs because the example demonstrates that other-repairs can be accomplished by speakers that do not signal the trouble source in the first instance.

In CA, a key empirical issue is where repairs occur within larger sequences of talk. The following questions ask you to reflect on this issue of repair position:

1. How and why do repairs occur within the same turn?
2. How and why do repairs occur within a TRP?
3. How and why do repairs occur within the turn immediately following a repairable (i.e., the next turn)?
4. How and why do repairs occur after the next turn?
5. How and why do repairs occur many turns after a repairable?

While these questions explore the social and interactional features of repairs, it is important to also reflect on how and why corrections feature prominently in some classrooms. For instance, when is it necessary for classroom teachers to explicitly correct (as opposed to repair) a student's contribution to a lesson? Can we, as scholars of classroom discourse, say anything noteworthy about what types of student responses are most likely to be corrected? Are there aspects of a language that are particularly conducive to repair or correction sequences?

The publications listed in Table 3.4 attempt to answer some of these questions. As with the CA empirical issues presented thus far, the five publications identified

TABLE 3.4 Publications on repair

Recommended publication	Description
McHoul, A. W. (1990). The organization of repair in classroom talk. *Language in Society, 19*, 349–377.	A seminal investigation that looks into the ways in which self- and other-corrections are managed in classrooms. The author explores how classrooms help establish a preference for particular types of repair sequences.
Macbeth, D. (2004). The relevance of repair for classroom correction. *Language in Society, 33*, 703–736.	Another seminal investigation that examines repair sequences in classrooms. This study is particularly helpful in learning about the differences between repair and correction in classrooms.
Hall, J.K. (2007). Redressing the roles of correction and repair in research on second and foreign language learning. *Modern Language Journal, 91*, 511–526.	An important study that explores the instructional uses of repair and correction. In addition to providing excellent overviews of the repair and correction literature from CA and second-language acquisition (SLA) perspectives, the author puts forward a number of suggestions regarding the use of both analytic terms.
Seedhouse, P. (2007). "On ethnomethodological CA and linguistic CA": A reply to Hall. *Modern Language Journal, 91*, 527–533.	Seedhouse provides a response to the above study conducted by Hall (2007). Seedhouse offers an account of how the use of repair and correction differ according to how faithful a researcher is in adopting conversation analytic principles.
Liebscher, G., & Dailey-O'Cain, J. (2003). Conversational repair as a role-defining mechanism in classroom interaction. *Modern Language Journal, 87*, 375–390.	The authors examine how classroom participants use repair practices to deal with issues of meaning and linguistic form during content-based learning. The paper identifies how repair sequences in classrooms are different to mundane conversations.

in the table provide numerous examples of how to approach the study of correction (and repair) in the classroom, but developing conversation analytic skills require knowing how to apply the fundamental principles of CA to your data. To this end, it is important to refer back to the beginning of this chapter in general, and Table 3.1 in particular.

The final empirical issue discussed in this chapter is interactional competence, which shares many similarities with other well-established concepts used to investigate classroom teaching and learning.

3.1.4 *Interactional competence*

To be competent in something requires an ability to meet an established standard. In many contexts, standards are established by an outside or external community or organization. In the context of learning an additional language, for instance, notions of speaking competently are established by testing organizations, schools and universities, and speech communities. Such established standards do not reflect true competence levels, as they provide a narrow, and sometimes biased, snapshot of what an individual can do without considering the entire context in which a person is communicating.

Such narrowly defined standards create what Kramsch (1986) sees as a deficit approach to determining levels of competence. To address this problem, Kramsch (1986) introduces the term *interactional competence* to focus on what classroom participants actually do in and through the talk and interaction of classrooms. To this end, Young (2008, p. 101) provides a succinct definition: "Interactional competence is a relationship between the participants' employment of linguistic and interactional resources and the contexts in which they are employed."

In CA, interactional competence is a useful analytic category because it draws attention to the "resources" used by participants within a particular context. In other words, a focus on an "ability to use interactional resources, such as doing turn-taking or dealing with problems of understanding" (Wong & Waring, 2010, p. 7), allows the classroom discourse researcher to identify and track competence as a set of practices. Wong and Waring (2010, p. 8) identify four practices of particular relevance to conversation analysts:

1. Turn-taking practices.
2. Sequencing practices.
3. Overall structuring practices.
4. Repair practices.

These four practices, which have been discussed in previous sections of this chapter to varying degrees of detail, form what CA views as interactional competence. Classroom interactional competence can thus be viewed as an ability to use these interactional practices for the purposes of teaching and learning. Put differently, to be a good teacher or learner requires being competent at taking turns, soliciting responses, answering questions, and co-constructing meaning, to name a few (cf. Walsh, 2012).

Implicit in this definition of interactional competence is what drives much of the CA work done on classroom discourse. That is, CA views classroom teaching and learning as an interactional task that, when examined closely, is made up of a number of practices.

As competence is often presented in the classroom discourse literature as evidence of learning (Hall, Hellermann, & Pekarek Doehler, 2011), conversation analysts use interactional competence to answer a number of related questions:

1. How do turn-taking practices change over time?
2. How do students adapt their repair practices to demonstrate understanding?
3. How is learning made demonstrably relevant in and through classroom interaction?
4. What interactional resources are used to participate in learning activities?
5. How do students learn how to increase their participation in class over time?

In CA, learning and competence should not be used interchangeably, as they are bound to different theoretical assumptions. Learning is often conceptualized as a linear change over a period of time (e.g., Pekarek Doehler & Berger, 2016), moving a student closer to an idealized standard (Hall, 2018). The importance of change and time in learning is embedded in the way some of the previous questions are constructed. For instance, research questions 1 and 5 include an explicit reference to change over time (cf. Markee, 2008), which requires you to track learning from one state (e.g., unable to use a particular word) to another (e.g., able to use a particular word).

For competence, a study must demonstrate that a participant is able to accomplish something in the classroom according to an established standard, which typically does not require tracking a change from one state to another over a period of time. Competence provides a snapshot of what a student can do at a particular point in time during a classroom activity. For example, research questions 2 and 4 focus on how practices and resources are used to demonstrate learning, and take part in classroom activities. Competence may be discussed as a learning object, in which case a study would examine interactional practices and resources according to time and change, as discussed in the previous paragraph.

The exemplar studies listed in Table 3.5 discuss some of the issues related to examining interactional competence.

The studies in Table 3.5 demonstrate that interactional competence is an important facet of communication in many contexts, moves researchers away from deficit notions of language standards, can be used as pedagogical objectives in instructional materials, and is one of several important aspects of learning. Interactional competence may be examined as a learning object or as an ability to do something at a specific point in time.

3.2 What are the methodological considerations?

In this part of the chapter, the discussion shifts to the methodological issues that underpin the work done in CA. Specifically, this section frames CA studies of classroom discourse using the five methodological issues of classroom discourse reviewed in Chapter 1 (i.e., data collection, data presentation, type of analysis, level of analysis, and role of context; see Table 1.5). Again, this approach of first discussing what conversation analysts typically investigate in classroom discourse, and then reviewing the key methodological issues, will hopefully provide a more straightforward, albeit superficial, overview of CA.

To this end, Table 3.6 identifies the methodological issues that conversation analysts must attend to when carrying out an empirical investigation. The references included Table 3.6 provide a starting point for readers interested in conducting a study using CA, but do not in any way account for all of the methodological issues that may need to be taken into consideration.

CA is an approach to classroom data that is based on an emic perspective. Establishing an emic understanding of classroom data requires describing how

TABLE 3.5 Publications on interactional competence

Recommended publication	Description
Hall, J.K., Hellermann, J., & Pekarek Doehler, S. (2011). *L2 interactional competence and development*. Bristol, UK: Multilingual Matters.	A collection of papers that examines interactional competence using conversation analytic principles. The contributors uncover how interactional competence is developed in a number of learning contexts. This volume is an essential read for researchers wishing to examine interactional competence.
Kramsch, C. (1986). From language proficiency to interactional competence. *Modern Language Journal*, 70, 366–372.	Kramsch is often given credit for coining, or at least popularizing, the term interactional competence. The publication offers reasons for moving away from traditional notions of communicative competence, making it an important theoretical paper for conversation analysts to cite.
Barraja-Rohan, A.M. (2011). Using conversation analysis in the second language classroom to teach interactional competence. *Language Teaching Research*, 15, 479–507.	One of the first empirical studies to investigate how conversation analytic constructs, such as turn-taking, can be used in classrooms to teach interactional competence. Barraja-Rohan argues that CA can help students learn more effectively, and suggests that teachers should also consider how the methodology can lend itself to better teaching practices.
Pekarek Doehler, S., & Berger, E. (2016). L2 interactional competence as increased ability for context-sensitive conduct: A longitudinal study of story-openings. *Applied Linguistics*, 39, 555–578.	The authors examine interactional competence over time in the context of storytelling. Although the study is not based in a classroom, the observations made of storytelling are helpful for readers looking to see how learning is conceptualized and operationalized by conversation analysts.
Hall, J.K. (2018). From L2 interactional competence to L2 interactional repertoires: Reconceptualising the objects of L2 learning. *Classroom Discourse*, 9, 25–39.	Hall presents readers with her understanding of interactional competence as an object of learning. The paper attends to some of the misconceptions and misuses of the construct in previous studies. Hall argues that interactional repertoires is a more useful construct, as it captures the variable nature of language learning.

the research participants themselves engage in teaching and learning (for a more detailed account of emic perspectives, see Pike, 1967). This defining methodological principle of CA prevents analysts from interpreting and explaining classroom data from the researcher's perspective.

CA studies thus rely on naturally occurring data, which means rejecting experimental approaches to data collection that attempt to control how research participants behave and communicate. In other words, conversation analysts record classroom participants going about the business of teaching and learning in natural

TABLE 3.6 CA methodological issues

Methodological issue	CA considerations	Further reading
Data collection	CA asks researchers to collect data with no predetermined focus (cf. "unmotivated looking"). CA assumes that all micro discursive features are potentially interesting, so transcripts are exceptionally detailed. Accordingly, the amount of data that you collect is often less than other approaches.	Rapley, T. (2008). *Doing conversation, discourse and document analysis*. London, UK: Sage.
Data presentation	CA asks researchers to present data according to very specific transcription conventions. CA transcripts are expected to be exceptionally detailed. For CA, collecting, transcribing, and sharing data are all part of the analytic process.	Hepburn, A., & Bolden, G.B. (2013). The conversation analytic approach to transcription. In J. Sidnell & T. Stivers (Eds.), *The handbook of conversation analysis* (pp. 57–76). Malden, MA: Wiley-Blackwell.
Type of analysis	CA observations are largely descriptive. The analyst describes how classroom participants are engaging in teaching and learning, rather than explaining what may be happening. The interpretations of the researcher stem from the methods used by participants to makes sense of each other.	Psathas, G. (1995). *Conversation analysis*. Thousand Oaks, CA: Sage.
Level of analysis	CA observations are based largely on the micro details of talk and interaction. Macro issues are only discussed when made relevant by the classroom participants of your study.	Hutchby, I., & Wooffitt, R. (2008). *Conversation analysis*. Cambridge, UK: Polity.
Role of context	CA is concerned exclusively with the interactional and sequential context of classroom discourse. CA uses next-turn proof procedure and procedural consequentiality to attend to the interactional and sequential context.	Mandelbaum, J. (1990). Beyond mundane reason: Conversation analysis and context. *Research on Language and Social Interaction, 24*, 333–350.

settings. Although conversation analysts know that they will be collecting data in a classroom setting, the precise circumstance or contextual variable is typically unknown at the time of data collection. In other words, conversation analysts engage in what is called unmotivated looking, which entails collecting (and analyzing) data without the guidance of predefined empirical objectives. Mondada (2013) provides an excellent overview of CA data collection principles and practices, and should be read together with Rapley (2008).

CA presents classroom data by adopting a rigid transcription system, which is briefly discussed in Chapter 2 (see also Table 2.3). The aim of this transcription system is to transform the spoken and interactional elements of classroom discourse into a transcript that presents communication as accomplished by the research participants. The components of a CA transcript are identified as follows, and discussed in detail in Hepburn and Bolden (2013):

1. The structure and organization of the transcript (e.g., margin sizes, spacing, and font type).
2. The timing and sequencing of interactional practices (e.g., pauses between utterances and overlapping talk).
3. Ways of talking and interacting (e.g., voice amplitude, intonation).
4. Analysts notes (e.g., describing an event or episode).
5. Ways of doing (e.g., gesture and eye contact).

These dimensions of a transcript allow conversation analysts to focus on the micro details of talk and interaction. That is to say, CA engages in micro-level research. This interest in the micro is based on an understanding of context as a sequential environment that reveals how classroom participants co-construct meaning on a turn-by-turn basis. Although this understanding of context is the narrowest out of the four approaches discussed in this book, it allows conversation analysts to attend to the emic nature of classroom discourse. Wong and Waring (2010, p. 6) identify five analytic concepts that help conversation analysts examine classroom data; only three are particularly relevant to the present discussion:

1. Unmotivated looking.
2. Repeated listening and viewing.
3. Answering "why that now?"

Unmotivated looking, as discussed above in relation to data collection, requires analysts to first examine their data recordings with no set notions about what the research participants are doing and saying. Unmotivated looking is important to CA studies of classroom discourse because the ultimate aim is to provide an emic perspective to teaching and learning.

Unmotivated looking is based on the idea that specific empirical interests will form after repeated listening and viewing of data recordings. That is, conversation analysts are expected to listen and view their data recordings over and over again until a phenomenon is selected for further analysis. In fact, repeated listening and viewing of data occurs after a specific phenomenon is selected. One of the reasons for engaging in this repetitious exercise is to ensure that the analyst truly understands how the research participants themselves co-construct meaning. To this end, asking "why that now" helps analysts attend to an emic perspective in that the "now" refers specifically to the sequential moment within an interaction, such as a turn or a pause. Thus, the "why that now" question is not only a tool that conversation analysts use to investigate teaching and learning, but also an example of how they understand the role of context in classroom discourse.

3.3 Key terms, constructs, and people

This final section of this chapter identifies ten key terms, constructs, and people associated with CA. The operative term here is "associated," as some of the terms and constructs identified are used in other approaches, including those discussed in this book. Each entry is followed with a brief description or explanation. The first three entries are key scholars in CA. The next seven entries are terms and constructs listed in alphabetical order.

The justification for including ten entries is simple. The concise list provides an accessible, albeit superficial, overview of the different terms, constructs, and people that have shaped CA. In other words, the list does not represent all of the key terms, constructs, and people in CA, but the entries nonetheless capture the core ideas of, and thinkers in, the approach. Furthermore, all of the entries have not been discussed in detail in this chapter, and thus offer a different perspective of CA than provided in the sections before.

A more comprehensive understanding of the key terms, constructs, and people of CA can be developed by reading the references included throughout this chapter.

1. *Gail Jefferson* is one of the founders of CA. Gail Jefferson is responsible for creating the transcription system that conversation analysts use today. Her analytic work on side sequences, storytelling, and laughter are also particularly noteworthy.
2. *Harvey Sacks* is a founder of CA, but also the pioneer in the detailed and methodical study of spoken interaction. Harvey Sacks is responsible for many of the theoretical principles adopted in CA. His empirical work on storytelling by children, analytic categories, and joke telling continue to influence how CA is used.
3. *Emanuel Schegloff* is a founder of CA. He is responsible for much of the earlier empirical work done following the conceptualization of CA and is most recognized for his work on turn-taking practices, sequence organization, and overlapping talk.

4. *Ethnomethodology* is an approach to sociological inquiry that aims to understand how the research participant themselves makes sense of the world around them. It is a descriptive approach in that it only describes what people are doing and saying from their perspectives. The principles of ethnomethodology form the theoretical basis from which CA operates.
5. *Intersubjectivity* is a term used to describe how mutual understanding is achieved in and through discourse. The term is often used in CA to capture how actions and activities, such as providing instructions in a classroom, are jointly constructed. How classroom participants accomplish intersubjectivity is a central empirical interest in CA.
6. *Next-turn proof procedure* is an analytic tool that requires classroom discourse researchers to use the next turn of a speaker (e.g., a response to a question) as evidence of intersubjectivity.
7. *Procedural consequentiality* is a theoretical principle that suggests analytic observations, such as the observation that a group of students is not enthusiastic, must be consequential to – that is, made relevant in – the talk and interaction of the classroom participants.
8. *Recipient design* is a modification or adaption of talk and interaction that reflects the perceived needs, wants, or expectations of the audience. Conversation analysts are interested in recipient design, as it reveals how classroom participants work together to make sense of each other.
9. *Relevance* is related to how conversation analysts treat contextual issues, such as an emotional state during a communicative exchange (e.g., anger or happiness). The term refers to how teachers and students, through their talk and interaction with each other, establish that an aspect of classroom discourse is relevant to their activity at hand. For example, saying "I am angry" during a communicative exchange is an explicit way of making this emotional state relevant to the classroom participants.
10. *Socially distributed cognition* is a term often used (but not coined) by conversation analysts. It refers to the idea that cognitive states, such as a state of knowing or feeling, are distributed in and though talk and interaction. The term is commonly used in CA, as conversation analysts are dedicated to understanding how talk and interaction is used by classroom participants to achieve different actions and activities, including revealing cognitive states.

4
DISCOURSE ANALYSIS

The term discourse analysis (DA) leads to much confusion, as it is often used as a hypernym for all approaches that are concerned with discourse-level features and phenomena (for a discussion of different qualitative and quantitative approaches to DA, see Lazaraton, 2002). That is, DA is an umbrella term for discourse-based approaches, including pragmatics, interactional sociolinguistics, framing and positioning, and flow of discourse. To add to this confusion, DA is sometimes treated as a specific methodology with a unique set of assumptions about how to analyze discourse-level features and phenomena (e.g., Wooffitt, 2005).

In this chapter, DA is used primarily as a generic term to represent any approach that is concerned with how discourse is used in context. Classroom DA, as presented in this chapter, is thus an approach utilized to uncover how discourse-level features and phenomena, such as the direction a conversational floor takes during a lesson, are related to the organization and accomplishment of teaching and learning.

Such approaches, while diverse in theory and methodological principles, collectively stand in contrast to CA practices. DA, for instance, does not limit its analytic tool kit to the methodological principles discussed in the previous chapter, such as next-turn proof procedure and procedural consequentiality. Although a DA study of classroom discourse can make use of next-turn proof procedure, other methodological principles may be employed to answer research questions. CA and DA also differ in that the former is tailored to examine spoken communication, whereas the latter approach has a history of examining both writing and speaking.

DA is an interdisciplinary approach that has been taken up by researchers working in linguistics, education, sociolinguistics, pragmatics, philosophy, anthropology, and psychology, to name a few. Disciplines have their own expectations of what constitutes a DA study, though there are methodological principles shared by researchers, such as the belief that discourse indexes social issues that are not always

TABLE 4.1 Introductory publications on DA

Recommended publication	Description
Rampton, B., Roberts, C., Leung, C., & Harris, R. (2002). Methodology in the analysis of classroom discourse. *Applied Linguistics, 23*, 373–392.	A short journal article that reflects on the theoretical and methodological assumptions of several DA approaches to classroom discourse. The authors discuss the similarities and differences between DA approaches, and identifies the strengths and weaknesses of each methodology.
Jones, R.H. (2012). *Discourse analysis: A resource book for students*. London, UK: Routledge.	A great resource for students wanting to use DA for their research assignments or projects. The book covers a number of different approaches to DA, including mediated DA and corpus-assisted DA.
Brown, G., & Yule, G. (1983). *Discourse analysis*. Cambridge, UK: Cambridge University Press.	A short, accessible, and classic book on the different tools that can be used to investigate discourse. Although some of the content is a bit dated, the authors provide an excellent overview of DA for readers.
Gee, J.P. (2014). *How to do discourse analysis: A toolkit*. London, UK: Routledge.	Gee provides an easy-to-follow overview of the theoretical and methodological principles that form the bases of DA tools. Each chapter includes a list of suggested reading and reflective questions to help readers practice their analytic skills.
Tannen, D., Hamilton, H.E., & Schiffrin, D. (2015). *The handbook of discourse analysis*. Malden, MA: Wiley-Blackwell.	An excellent collection of chapters for readers that wish to get a comprehensive, but not an in-depth, understanding of the different DA tools that exist and how they differ from each other.

immediately visible when looking at surface linguistic forms. These shared methodology principles are discussed, in part, in the publications identified in Table 4.1. These publications also provide overviews of what DA is and how it may be applied to social contexts, such as classrooms.

The publications identified in Table 4.1 provide a more comprehensive overview of DA than offered in this chapter, and should thus be referred to if an advanced understanding of the approach is needed. With that said, the discussion that follows establishes a foundational understanding of DA, provides much needed direction for the novice researcher, and reviews empirical issues that could be investigated in a study on classroom discourse. Again, the goal here is to offer an easy-to-follow, no-nonsense account of DA for readers new to classroom discourse research.

Although it is customary to begin an introductory account of DA by reviewing theories and methodological principles, the following section first introduces four empirical issues that are commonly investigated with discourse approaches. This strategy of discussing empirical issues before theory and methodological principles will provide a more comprehensible introduction to DA.

4.1 What can I investigate?

DA is used to investigate a plethora of empirical issues ranging from spoken communication to written discourse. Furthermore, DA represents a number of different methodological approaches, such as mediated DA, multimodal DA, and critical DA (see Chapter 5). Take, for instance, the widely used introduction on DA by Brown and Yule (1983). In this book alone, DA is discussed as an approach capable of understanding the functions of language, sentences and utterances, reference, presupposition, implicatures, co-text, paragraphs and paratones, titles and themes, coherence and cohesion, scripts, schemes, speech acts, and many other issues. These empirical issues can be, and many have been, investigated in classroom settings.

Understanding how DA can be used to examine teaching and learning requires knowing that while scholars have different interpretations of how the approach should be utilized, researchers approach the study of classroom discourse from the same starting point: Classrooms are bound to a complex relationship between discourse actions and structures. Discourse analysts argue that an examination of such actions and structures reveals a great deal about teachers and students (for an example of how DA can be used to investigate classroom identities, see Menard-Warwick, 2008), and the ways in which they go about the business of teaching and learning (e.g., Markee, 2015). Discourse actions and structures shape, and are shaped by, reflective practices, recasts, learning strategies, language policing, task-based learning, online communication, and collaborative work, to name a few empirical issues.

Among these empirical issues, the chapter introduces four discourse phenomena that are commonly investigated in the DA literature: triadic dialogue (initiation–response–feedback (IRF)/initiation–response–evaluation (IRE) sequence), floor management, teacher questions, and discourse markers. These four empirical issues provide a sufficient foundation from which to apply DA to a study of classroom discourse.

4.1.1 Triadic dialogue: IRF/IRE sequence

A triadic dialogue is a feature of classroom discourse that occurs in most contexts where a classroom participant, usually the teacher, controls the flow of communication. Teachers commonly need to control the flow of communication, as they are responsible for either delivering new information to students or the medium of communication is also the learning objective.

Triadic dialogues are communicative exchanges that unfold in three turns: (I) initiation, (R) response, (F) feedback. Although classroom participants may deviate from this three-part exchange, triadic dialogues are a fairly rigid discourse structure of classrooms. The I, R, and F are based on a model of discourse that was developed by Sinclair and Coulthard (1975); their work, inspired by Halliday's (1961) rank scale framework, views classroom discourse as consisting of five ranks or levels: lesson, transaction, exchange, move, and act. The rank applicable to the present discussion is move, which is referred to in this section as turn. IRF sequences are a popular topic of investigation because they reveal a great deal about how teachers and students make sense of each other while engaging in the business of teaching and learning, as will be discussed later in this section.

Two general approaches can be taken when investigating IRF sequences. The first approach entails looking at what is accomplished with a particular turn, such as teacher feedback (F). For instance, Zemel and Koschmann (2011) attend to the ways in which teachers evaluate during the third turn, identifying the different strategies teachers use to deal with correct and incorrect answers during triadic dialogues. Indeed, Zemel and Koschmann (2011) refer to triadic dialogues as IRE sequences because the teachers in their data use the third turn or "slot" to evaluate rather than to provide feedback. It should be noted, however, that the term "feedback" covers a wider range of interactional possibilities, and thus IRF sequences are more frequently used in the classroom discourse literature.

The second approach entails analyzing turns as components of larger sequences, which is often done when identifying the organization of activities and lessons (e.g., how IRF sequences are used to organize grammar activities). In practice, however, most discourse analytic methods use both approaches when examining IRF sequences.

An IRF sequence typically begins with a teacher initiating a pedagogical agenda or conveying information that is relevant to a particular teaching objective. Take, for example, the following exchange where the IRF sequence begins with the teacher establishing an interactional agenda that is based on a book read by all students. In this example, the initiation turn is organized as a question.

```
1    (I)       Teacher     okay. we know that the book teaches
2                           us a lesson. what do you think that
3                           lesson is?
4    (R)       Student A   life is not easy?
5    (F)(I)    Teacher     yes. it could be. anyone else?
6    (R)       Student B   challenges are okay
7    (F)       Teacher     challenges are another way to think
8                           about the characters in the story.
9                           yes, especially in the beginning of
10                          the book. okay.
```

When analyzing classroom discourse from the perspective of IRF sequences, it is common practice to first categorize each turn according to the relevant move (I, R, F), which has already been done in the above example. When categorizing turns according to generic discourse analytic methods, it is important to note that multiple actions can be accomplished in the same turn. In line 5, for example, the teacher provides a feedback for the previous IRF sequence, but also initiates a new triadic dialogue.

Categorizing each turn allows the researcher to zoom out of the micro details of the talk and interaction (cf. conversation analytic principles), and focus on larger discourse structures, such as the issue of who is talking when and for how long during each triadic exchange. For instance, the beginning of the reading lesson consists of two IRF sequences: lines 1–5 and lines 5–10. Furthermore, the beginning of each IRF sequence includes a question, which allows the teacher to establish the direction of the lesson (see the topic of floor management in Section 4.1.2). It can also be said that students use the R turns (lines 4 and 6) to provide minimal responses, whereas the teacher appears to have more interactional space to talk during the I and F turns (lines 1 and 7–10).

The following five questions offer examples of what a discourse analyst may ask when investigating IRF sequences:

1. How does the teacher control the direction of the communication?
2. What can you say about the student turns in lines 4 and 6?
3. What actions are being performed by the teacher in lines 1–3 and 7–10?
4. What type of questions are being asked in lines 2–3 and 5?
5. In line 5, the teacher performs at least two actions. Can students do the same?

These questions can also be formulated into research questions:

1. How do teachers control the direction of the communication?
2. How do IRF sequences promote or restrict student participation?
3. How are teacher corrections made relevant during IRF sequences?
4. How are student mistakes made relevant during IRF sequences?
5. How do IRF sequences unfold in different pedagogical activities?

It would be helpful to have a transcript of classroom discourse of your own when thinking about the aforementioned research questions. If you do not have access to classroom discourse data, then use your experiences in the classroom as a student or teacher to reflect on the importance of these questions.

In addition to reflecting on the ten questions above, Table 4.2 provides examples of how IRF sequences are examined in different contexts.

When thinking about the significance of IRF sequences in classroom discourse, it is important to remember that much variation exists in what can be done within triadic dialogues. For instance, a close examination of any individual turn within an IRF sequence reveals classroom participants can perform a range of teaching or learning actions. The third turn (F) is one such example. Researchers show that third turns in triadic dialogues are organized in different ways.

```
1  (I)      Teacher     okay. we know that the book teaches
2                       us a lesson. what do you think that
3                       lesson is?
4  (R)      Student A   life is not easy?
5  (F) (I)  Teacher     yes. it could be. anyone else?
6  (R)      Student B   challenges are okay
```

```
 7  (F)    Teacher    challenges are another way to think
 8                    about the characters in the story.
 9                    yes, especially in the beginning of
10                    the book. okay.
```

While line 5 represents a single turn, the teacher's utterance can be broken into different actions or functions, including acknowledging what the student has previously said ("yes"), providing an evaluation ("it could be"), and moving away from said answer by seeking a response from a different student ("anyone else"). In lines 7–10, the turn evaluates ("challenges are another way to think about the characters in the story"), confirms ("yes"), unpacks the student's answer ("especially in the beginning of the book"), and ends with a discourse marker ("okay"), which is often used to signal the end or start of a new exchange (see Section 4.1.4).

Another noteworthy IRF issue that is worth reflecting on in relation to the above example is teacher questions. In lines 2–3, for instance, the teacher asks a

TABLE 4.2 Publications on IRF sequence

Recommended publication	*Description*
Wells, G. (1993). Reevaluating the IRF sequence. *Linguistics and Education, 5*, 1–37.	An older, but seminal, study that examines how classroom discourse, and more specifically classroom activities, are tied to an understanding of IRF sequences.
Waring, H.Z. (2009). Moving out of IRF (initiation–response–feedback): A single case analysis. *Language Learning, 59*, 796–824.	A conversation analytic study that looks at how classroom participants move in and out of IRF sequences. The study demonstrates that students are capable of creating new participation structures according to their particular learning needs.
Pryde, M. (2014). Conversational patterns of homestay hosts and study abroad students. *Foreign Language Annals, 47*, 487–506.	While most IRF studies are based on traditional classrooms, this investigation looks at communicative exchanges during homestays. The largely quantitative study reveals that hosts establish a controlling role in their conversations with their guests, leading to interactional patterns often seen in classrooms.
Zemel, A., & Koschmann, T. (2011). Pursuing a question: Reinitiating IRE sequences as a method of instruction. *Journal of Pragmatics, 43*, 475–488.	This conversation analytic study examines how teachers use the third turn of the IRF sequence to deal with particular answers from students. The study demonstrates that IRF sequences reveal much about how classroom participants co-accomplish teaching and learning objectives.
Miao, P., & Heining-Boynton, A.L. (2011). Initiation/response/follow-up, and response to intervention. *Foreign Language Annals, 44*, 65–79.	The authors examine how teachers use intervention strategies to monitor classroom learning within IRF sequences. The findings show that while IRF sequences are ostensibly rigid, there are many strategies that can be used in each turn of triadic dialogues.

display question (i.e., a question in which the teacher knows the answer), which leads to a minimal response by the student in line 4. When doing classroom discourse research, it is often good practice to reflect on how the teaching and learning would have changed had the teacher, in this case, asked a different type of question. For example, would a referential question (i.e., a question in which the teacher does not know the answer) in lines 2–3 lead to different responses?

Some additional questions that could be asked in relation to individual turns or specific actions within IRF sequences are identified for your reflection:

1. How are display and referential questions organized within IRF sequences?
2. What question types are used by teachers during whole-class discussions?
3. Are open-ended questions organized in the same way as yes/no questions?
4. How do teachers use the I in IRF to perform different actions?
5. How do students respond to corrections made by the teacher?

These five questions offer some direction when considering a study on classroom discourse that focuses on IRF sequences (for two studies that examine how individual turns function within IRF sequences, see also Y. Lee, 2007, 2008). The questions also point to several key features of IRF sequences that are helpful in understanding the significance of triadic dialogues:

1. IRF sequences can help researchers understand how teachers and students fulfill their classroom roles.
2. IRF sequences can help researchers determine the extent to which the discourse of a classroom matches the pedagogical goals.
3. IRF sequences can help researchers uncover the different discursive resources used to teach and learn.
4. IRF sequences can help researchers evaluate the quality of teaching and learning.
5. IRF sequences can help researchers map the discursive organization of classroom lessons and activities.

An empirical issue that is closely related to triadic dialogues is floor management.

4.1.2 Floor management

A floor, which is also referred to as a conversational floor, is a useful analytic concept for classroom discourse research, as it provides a holistic picture of how lessons are organized and accomplished. Before providing examples of what this may look like empirically, it is important to explain what a floor is.

A floor, according to Edelsky (1981, p. 383), is "a collaborative venture where several people" operate "on the same wavelength." In the context of classroom discourse, a floor is thus the discursive space that is occupied by teachers and students as they make sense of, and carry out, a lesson. The notion of a wavelength suggests

72 Analyzing

that classroom discourse is not just about a teacher establishing what to say and do, but additionally requires students to receive, interpret, and respond to such directives (Jones & Thornborrow, 2004).

A floor is often used in a more colloquial way to refer to who is currently speaking or participating during a lesson, as in "the student currently has the floor" or "the teacher allocates the floor to the student." However, a floor is not limited to who is talking during a particular lesson. A floor is also a discursive "psychological space" (Edelsky, 1981) in that classroom participants reveal their inner feelings and cognitive states in and through the completion of a lesson.

A floor also possesses discursive characteristics (e.g., informal versus forms, shorter versus longer turns, monologue versus overlapping talk) that reflect who the classroom participants are and their relationship with each other (e.g., students talking to each other versus a teacher providing directions). A floor can reveal how classroom participants determine a topic of conversation and what direction it takes (Simpson, 2005). Furthermore, a floor is shaped by the participatory expectations (Nofsinger, 1975) of classroom participants and how they fulfill these roles (Jenks, 2007).

Perhaps the easiest, but by no means the only, way of defining a floor is to think of it as a space with a self-contained topic of discussion. For example, it is not uncommon for students to be broken into smaller groups so that they can complete their respective tasks; in this case, each group represents a separate floor space. In other contexts, say in a whole-class discussion, there may be only one floor space, as a teacher may control who says what and when.

```
1     Teacher       okay. we know that the book teaches
2                   us a lesson. what do you think that
3                   lesson is?
4     Student A     life is not easy?
5     Teacher       yes. it could be. anyone else?
6     Student B     challenges are okay
7     Teacher       challenges are another way to think
8                   about the characters in the story.
9                   yes, especially in the beginning of
10                  the book. okay.
```

In this example, the teacher asks questions and the students respond when asked to do so. All of the interactants are discussing a book, and therefore the classroom is made up of one floor space. Counting the number of conversations unfolding in a classroom is an easy way of understanding the basic idea of a floor (again, a floor can be understood as a self-contained space where participants communicate). Take, for example, classrooms with two or more floor spaces, such as in the following example.

```
                FLOOR 1                              FLOOR 2
1   Student A   w[hat do we do    |                  (1.7)
2   Student B     [is this it     |Student D         ready?
3               (1.4)             |Student C         let's start here
```

```
4   Student B  okay I get it    |Student D  she said here
5   Student A  okay             |           (0.2)
```

The classroom discourse in this example can be viewed as having two floor spaces, as two groups of students are working on an activity that requires them to construct sentences using a map. Floor 1 and floor 2 possess different conversational directions (and structures), as each group has their own way of working out how to begin and complete the activity.

Yet, a floor is much more than a space; each floor space possesses a set of norms and expectations, which shapes how the discourse unfolds. That is, a floor is not only about who is speaking when, to whom, and on what particular topic (cf. Aukrust, 2008). The real empirical value in studying floor management is that it offers a different way of looking at the organization of classroom discourse. For instance, while IRF sequences present classroom discourse as a series of triadic exchanges, not all classrooms are organized as such (the previous example of two floors spaces is one such example). An understanding of classroom discourse that is based on a notion of floor allows researchers to ask the following questions about the two extracts presented in this section:

1. Who controls the floor?
2. Are participatory rights equally distributed in the floor?
3. What does the floor reveal about the activity being completed?
4. What interactional roles are required to participate in the floor?
5. How do students manage their ability or right to participate in the floor?

These questions point to several pedagogical reasons why it is useful to study classroom discourse from the perspective of floor management. Teachers and students often possess different interactional roles, and this key feature of classroom discourse can be uncovered by looking at floor spaces. For example, a teacher is, more often than not, the participant responsible for imparting knowledge to students. This responsibility creates interactional possibilities and constraints (e.g., IRF sequences) as a floor space unfolds, which helps researchers understand the larger issue of classroom roles and how the expectations of teachers and students influence the structure of lessons and activities. Understanding how teachers and students participate in a particular floor is useful in determining whether a lesson or activity is accomplishing, pedagogically speaking, what it set out to do (cf. Jenks, 2007).

The publications identified in Table 4.3 offer different examples of how the notion of a floor can be investigated. Not all publications are based in classrooms; nonetheless, the findings demonstrate how conversational floors help uncover important discursive issues, such as the institutional role of the participants.

The five publications are centrally interested in uncovering how floors are organized. But what does it mean to study the organization of a floor? The following questions offer some examples of what a researcher may ask when attempting to uncover how floors are organized:

TABLE 4.3 Publications on floor management

Recommended publication	Description
Edelsky, C. (1981). Who's got the floor? *Language in Society, 10,* 383–421.	Although this publication is not based in a classroom, it is often credited for establishing the theoretical structure from which investigations of floor management are based.
Jones, R., & Thornborrow, J. (2004). Floors, talk and the organization of classroom activities. *Language in Society, 33,* 399–423.	The study examines a number of floor-management issues and phenomena in classroom discourse. Critiquing the traditional view of floors as either speaking one at a time or all at once, the authors suggest that notions of tight and loose better capture floor-management behaviors.
Koole, T. (2007). Parallel activities in the classroom. *Language and Education, 21,* 487–501.	Although floor management is not explicitly referenced, the findings contribute to a better understanding of floors by showing that multiple activities are often being managed in a classroom with each one responsible for a different stretch of communication (i.e., classroom discourse entails multiple floors).
Marti, L. (2012). Tangential floor in a classroom setting. *System, 40,* 398–406.	The author shows in this classroom study that the ability to use two or more languages allows students to create side or tangential floors. In other words, floors are sometimes established according to the language spoken by the classroom participants.
Shepherd, M.A. (2014). The discursive construction of knowledge and equity in classroom interactions. *Linguistics and Education, 28,* 79–91.	This publication examines how taking the floor (i.e., participating in an ongoing dialogue) is dependent on how teachers solicit responses from students that actively or demonstrably seek to participate. The researcher argues that teachers must be cognizant of the equitable nature of their floor-management practices.

1. Who is talking and when?
2. How are the students participating and what are they talking about?
3. What are acceptable forms of participation and how are they managed?
4. Is it possible for students to establish their own floors?
5. What happens if students try to establish their own floor?

Asking questions about the structure or organization of a floor will lead to an interesting study of classroom discourse. Such questions can also be used to investigate other teaching and learning issues.

The following extract illustrates this point. The objective of the activity is for students to develop their ability to converse in English. The students are required to work their way through a map that is missing information. The missing information is incorporated into the activity because it is thought to encourage students to negotiate for meaning (Foster & Ohta, 2005).

```
1    Student 1    ehs. aech. eye. pea.((spelling ship))
2                 (0.4)
3    Student 2    that a sh- (0.2) oh yeah, (0.4) ship (2.8)
4                 and (.) next
5    Student 1    and then (0.4) the (0.9) mm plane (1.3)
6    Student 2    plane
7    Student 1    yeah
8                 (1.7)
9    Student 2    plane yeah (0.7) next
10   Student 1    and uhm (1.4) the mountain (2.0)
```

Although the objective of the activity is to promote spoken communication, the actual language produced in this task is stilted (Seedhouse, 1999): The exchange is marked with long pauses between utterances (lines 3, 5, 8, and 10) and one-word turns (lines 1, 6, and 7). Closer examination of the floor space reveals that the stilted nature of the communication stems from the interactional roles assigned in this activity. Both students are required to collectively navigate their way through a map, but this limits the contributions to short utterances based on landmarks.

As this example demonstrates, using floor management as a lens through which to understand classroom discourse allows the researcher to look at how an activity creates a unique set of interactional demands on students. Both researchers and teachers can use this understanding to evaluate whether an activity creates the type of learning and communication that is expected of students. For the map activity, for instance, the stilted language suggests that researchers and teachers should use a different task if the goal is to promote fluency and the production of extended turns.

4.1.3 Teacher questions

Researchers are particularly interested in how questions are used to accomplish teaching and learning objectives. This is because the way teachers ask questions in classrooms has a profound impact on how a lesson unfolds. Consider, for example, the following reflective questions:

1. What are the primary functions of teacher questions?
2. How do teacher questions ensure the success of a lesson?
3. How do teacher questions elicit different responses from students?

These questions collectively suggest that teacher questions are more than attempts to elicit information, but are additionally ways to achieve and adjust pedagogical objectives according to student understanding. Practicing teachers will be familiar with the ways in which questions influence the ability of students to comprehend and remember learning materials. Even readers that have only been in a classroom as a student will be able to reflect on how teachers facilitate dialogue and learning in and through questions. It may also be helpful to reflect on how learning is facilitated when students ask each other questions (for an earlier and seminal study on comprehension checks, clarification requests, and confirmation checks, see Varonis & Gass, 1985).

Being one of the most widely used discourse practices (Boyd, 2015), teacher questions have been investigated in the literature for many decades. However, teacher questions are often associated with other empirical keywords, such as elicitation (Koshik, 2002) and repair (Koshik, 2005). Readers interested in studying teacher questions should refer to such keywords when searching for relevant studies. Different keywords exist because teacher questions perform a range of pedagogical functions. Teacher questions are used to ensure comprehensibility, seek clarification, manage transitions from one exercise to another, assess the acquisition of content, determine how students are feeling or what they did outside of class time, and control the flow of interaction, to name a few. In other words, classroom teaching and learning is intimately connected to teacher questions.

In the interest of simplicity, this section will focus on two categories of teacher questions commonly investigated in the classroom discourse literature.

These categories, according to Farrell and Mom (2015, p. 851), can be classified into the following taxonomy:

1. *Echoic*:
    (a) comprehension checks, e.g., "does that make sense?"
    (b) clarification requests, e.g., "could you repeat that?"
    (c) confirmation checks, e.g., "do you mean this?"
2. *Epistemic*:
    (a) referential, e.g., "what did you do yesterday?"
    (b) display, e.g., "is research a countable noun?"
    (c) expressive, e.g., "how do you feel about the story?"
    (d) rhetorical, e.g., "how could I forget today's lesson?"

Echoic questions attempt to get students to repeat or confirm information or knowledge. Epistemic questions attempt to get information from students. The following reflective questions establish how echoic and epistemic questions shape classroom discourse:

1. Why does a teacher need to get a student to repeat information?
2. Why does a teacher need to confirm information already said by a student?
3. Why does a teacher need to get information from a student?
4. What are the pedagogical differences between confirming information and eliciting information?
5. What type of learning opportunities do confirming and eliciting questions offer?

Both questions types, and their pedagogical functions (i.e., confirming and getting information from students), provide a representative sample of what teachers do in classrooms to elicit responses, but there are other ways of approaching this empirical issue, including the classification of questions identified in Boyd (2015, pp. 383–384). Later in this section, Table 4.4 identifies studies that adopt other approaches to teacher questions. For now, we will focus on how a study of classroom discourse can be organized around echoic and epistemic questions. Specifically, this section explores how confirmation checks and display and referential questions contribute to a better understanding of teaching and learning.

The most rudimentary way of applying DA to a study of teacher questions (or any taxonomy of classroom practice for that matter) is to quantify the number of times a particular question occurs in your data. This quantification approach is based on the premise that the number derived from the statistical analysis, such as the total number of times a teacher performs a confirmation check or the average number of echoic questions asked per activity, will tell you something about classroom discourse. For example, if it is believed that clarification requests facilitate language learning (Ellis, Basturkmen, & Loewen, 2002), then knowing how many times a teacher performs such a question during a lesson may help researchers assess the quality of teaching.

A more nuanced approached to investigating teacher questions, however, requires at least examining how a particular question type is organized and what this organization says about its pedagogical function. This nuanced approach to classroom discourse is crucial to uncovering the complexities of teaching and learning, as the category that is assigned to an utterance may not provide a complete picture of what a teacher is trying to do (Nunn, 1999). The following extract illustrates this point.

```
1    Student A    the circus was funner
2                 (0.4)
3    Teacher      oh, the circus was more fun, was it?
4                 (.)
5    Student A    yes
```

The student in the beginning of this exchange constructs an ungrammatical utterance ("funner"). The teacher subsequently responds with a question, which on the surface appears to be a confirmation check ("was it?"). While knowing what type of question is being asked in line 3 is important, closer examination reveals that this utterance also reformulates the student's turn into a grammatical construction ("the circus was more fun"). This type of reformulation, which is commonly referred to as a recast (Lyster & Saito, 2010), provides an important pedagogical function in that it provides the correct alternative in a way that does not disrupt the flow of communication.

For the epistemic category, the two utterances that receive the most attention in the classroom discourse literature are referential and display questions. A referential question is a request for unknown information (i.e., the teacher does not know the answer to the question). A display question is a request for known information (i.e., the teacher knows the answer to the question). Asking students what they think about the weather is a type of referential question. Conversely, asking students to recall a particular grammatical rule is a type of display question, as the teacher presumably knows the grammar of the target language.

After correctly identifying an utterance as a display or referential question, a discourse analytic approach to referential and display questions could ask the following questions:

1. What is the shape or structure of the question?
2. What type of response does the question elicit?
3. What does the student response say about the pedagogical value of the question?
4. How does the question fulfill its pedagogical objective?
5. Does the question provide the interactional space for students to take long, extended turns?

Reflecting on these questions can help establish an appreciation for how teacher questions factor into classroom discourse in general, and the following two example excerpts in particular.

Referential question

```
1    Teacher       we have a quiz today. did you all study
2                  for it?
3                  (0.9)
4    Student C     a [little
5    Student A        [yes
```

Display question

```
1    Teacher       the story has a main character. what was
2                  his job?
3                  (.)
4    Student A     cooking. a chef.
```

The two questions both elicit information from the students, but closer examination using the five preceding questions reveals several noteworthy issues. First, looking at the structure of both questions does not provide much information. The referential example begins with a "did," and is therefore a yes/no question; the display example begins with a "what," and is accordingly an open-ended question. However, referential and displays questions can both begin with a "did" or a "what."

Second, the referential question elicits a minimal response, though this example demonstrates that yes/no questions can elicit more than two possible answers: The student in line 4 provides a more informative answer than offered in line 5. The display question requires a specific answer, but the possible variation that may exist in the responses from the students is greater than with yes/no questions.

Third, although the referential question is formulated as a closed-ended question, and will therefore elicit a minimal response, the teacher in this example can use the student responses to gauge the extent to which the class is ready for the quiz and make any pedagogical adjustments deemed necessary. Similarly, the display question allows the teacher to assess whether the students have completed their reading assignment and determine whether they remember key aspects of the book. Furthermore, the utterance in lines 1–2 allows the teacher to make future adjustments based on how the students respond to the display question.

Fourth, while the teachers' lessons plans are not included in these examples, some observations can be made regarding how the questions fulfill their pedagogical objectives. As discussed in the responses to research question 3, the teachers in both examples fulfill their basic pedagogical objectives by using questions to monitor and manage student learning. The referential question does this by determining the readiness of the students. The display question does this by assessing the knowledge of the students.

Fifth, the referential question elicits minimal responses, while students are given much more interactional space to respond to the display question. However, as alluded to above, this difference in interactional space provides an impartial account of the pedagogical functions of referential and display questions. Again, display questions can also be closed-ended constructions that elicit minimal responses. Moreover, referential questions are often said to be more pedagogically useful for teachers that wish to create a learning environment that encourages communication found outside of classrooms (Brock, 1986). The upshot is that all five questions are needed in order to establish a nuanced understanding of teacher questions.

The publications identified in Table 4.4 offer additional examples of how teacher questions can be investigated and represent the methodological and empirical diversity that exists in teacher question research. Referring to these publications will offer much needed direction for the novice researcher in what is possible in an investigation of teacher questions. The precise discourse analytic principles that shape the work accomplished in these publications, as well as what has been discussed in this section, are discussed later in this chapter.

4.1.4 Discourse markers

Discourse markers, such as *like* and *you know*, are utterances that "bracket units of talk" (Schiffrin, 1987, p. 31). According to Schiffrin (1987), a discourse marker functions as a "bracket" in that such utterances refer back or forward to something that was said or written within a communicative context. In this sense, discourse markers are "intra-sentential and supra-sentential" (Fung & Carter, 2007, p. 411): these markers occur within sentences or utterances but function at the discourse level, as they reveal how the surrounding talk or text should be interpreted.

Discourse markers are integral to how teachers and students co-construct meaning during a lesson. Before addressing how this aspect of classroom discourse

TABLE 4.4 Publications on teacher questions

Recommended publication	Description
Pun, J., & Macaro, E. (2019). The effect of first- and second-language use on question types in English medium instruction science classrooms in Hong Kong. *International Journal of Bilingual Education and Bilingualism, 22*, 64–77.	This study on teacher questions looks into whether language use – specifically English and Cantonese – factors into how teachers elicit responses from students. The researchers also examined how such language options, as well as correspondent questions, created different ensuing interactional patterns. The results suggest that the use of the L1 leads to more higher-order questions.
Boyd, M.P. (2015). Relations between teacher questioning and student talk in one elementary ELL classroom. *Journal of Literacy Research, 47*(3), 370–404.	The author looks at several aspects of question practices, such as typology, contingency, convergence-divergence, textual, extra-textual. The results show that while the teacher engages in varied questioning practices, the questions were largely based on student contributions.
Hu, G., & Duan, Y. (2019). Questioning and responding in the classroom: A cross-disciplinary study of the effects of instructional mediums in academic subjects at a Chinese university. *International Journal of Bilingual Education and Bilingualism, 22*, 303–321.	This study looks into whether instructional media and instructor background factors into how teachers elicit responses from students. The researchers argue that teacher questions and student responses are, by and large, simple in terms of their cognitive demands and syntactic constructions. The findings reveal that teachers in soft disciplines (e.g., humanities) typically constructed more complex questions than instructors in hard disciplines (e.g., engineering).
Ernst-Slavit, G., & Pratt, K.L. (2017). Teacher questions: Learning the discourse of science in a linguistically diverse elementary classroom. *Linguistics and Education, 40*, 1–10.	The authors examine the questioning practices of one teacher in a classroom of emergent bilinguals. The teacher in the study made use of a range of elicitation techniques, including higher-order, parlance, reflective, display, and managerial questions.
Farrell, T., & Mom, V. (2015). Exploring teacher questions through reflective practice. *Reflective Practice, 16*, 849–865.	In this study of university classrooms, the researchers explored the relationship between what teachers state as important pedagogical objectives and the questions that were asked to students to achieve such goals. The researchers argue that reflective practices help teachers ask better questions.

can be investigated, it is helpful to reflect on what discourse markers are and their pedagogical functions in classrooms.

Examples of discourse markers:

and, but, well, so, like, or, oh, okay, you know, I know, actually, if, now, yeah

1. When are discourse markers likely to occur during a lesson?
2. Can a single discourse marker perform multiple classroom functions?
3. Are teachers more likely to use discourse markers than students?
4. What pedagogical functions do discourse markers fulfill?
5. How do discourse markers facilitate communication?

These five questions collectively suggest that, like teacher questions, discourse markers function in the classroom in multiple ways. Indeed, discourse markers are largely examined as a pragmatic issue in the literature (Brinton, 2017), meaning that *and, but, so*, and other similar utterances do not possess syntactic meaning, but rather mediate communication between classroom participants. The pragmatic importance of discourse markers means that both teachers and students must be competent in constructing and interpreting such utterances so that they can maximize comprehensibility (Polat, 2011).

Brinton (1996, p. 37) provides an excellent overview of how these largely one-word utterances mediate communication between classroom participants by identifying the functions of discourse markers. In the interest of clarity, five of the nine functions identified by Brinton (1996, p. 37) are identified:

1. Discourse markers "initiate discourse, including claiming the attention of the hearer, and to close discourse."
2. Discourse markers "aid the speaker in acquiring or relinquishing the floor."
3. Discourse markers "mark a boundary in discourse."
4. Discourse markers "denote either new information or old information."
5. Discourse markers "repair one's own or others' discourse."

While these five functions do not comprehensively account for everything that discourse markers do in communication (see also Schiffrin, 1987), the list is helpful in establishing some of the empirical issues that can be investigated within this area of study. For example, functions 1 (initiate/close) and 3 (mark a boundary) demonstrate that a study of classroom discourse can look at how discourse markers are used to initiate a task or lesson.

```
1    Teacher    okay, let's get ready class.
```

The teacher in this example uses the discourse marker "okay" to mark a boundary in discourse, which is later revealed in the turn as the beginning of a lesson ("let's get ready class"). The turn, and discourse marker, collectively function to reorient the students' attention to the start of something new. In terms of sequential position, the discourse marker occurs in the beginning of the turn. According to Fung and Carter (2007), discourse markers frequently occur at the beginning of a turn, sentence, or utterance. Students can also use discourse markers to initiate turns.

1   Student   so. what should we do now?

In this example, the discourse marker allows the student to claim the attention of the teacher (function 1), allowing him to momentarily obtain the conversational floor (function 2). This turn by the student demonstrates that discourse markers and floor management can together represent a "single" focus in a study of classroom discourse. The example also shows that any given feature of classroom discourse is potentially multifunctional and can be approached from different methodological perspectives (e.g., for a CA study of discourse markers, see Hellermann & Vegun, 2007).

Discourse markers can, unlike the previous examples, occur at the end of a turn, sentence, or utterance.

1   Teacher   let's get ready class, okay?

Ending a turn with a discourse marker, such as "okay," helps the teacher to confirm whether the students have understood her previous directive, which is to get ready for class. Put differently, the discourse marker functions as a question, and ends a turn that marks the beginning of something new.

Discourse markers can also help classroom participants signal that something is wrong, such as in situations when a speaker self-repairs.

1   Student   we should focus on this word. I think. no,

In this example, the student expresses an opinion about what the group should focus on, but later expresses doubt ("I think") and finally rejects the original thought ("no"). In other words, the students use two discourse markers within a single turn to accomplish different pragmatic functions.

Some questions that could be asked in relation to the previous examples and functions include:

1. What discourse markers are used to initiate and end turns?
2. Are there discourse markers that are more successful in helping classroom participants gain control of the conversational floor?
3. How are discourse markers used to mark the beginning of a lesson?
4. What discourse markers are used to review old teaching material?
5. How do teachers use discourse markers to correct student mistakes?

In DA, the research questions that you ask should be guided by the belief that discourse, such as those pragmatic-based utterances discussed in this section, are shaped by, but also shape, classroom teaching and learning. For example, it is not enough for researchers to simply identify what discourse markers are used during a lesson. A researcher could additionally seek to understand whether there are discourse markers associated with particular activities, or if students and teachers use the same discourse markers for different teaching and learning purposes. The point here is that a DA investigation of classroom discourse ought to minimally accomplish two analytic objectives:

1. *Describe*, e.g., what discourse marker is being used? Where is it being used within a turn?
2. *Contextualize*, e.g., what is the pedagogical reason for using the discourse marker? How does the discourse marker help the student accomplish a learning goal?

The first analytic objective of describing a feature of discourse is an aspect of research that exists in all of the approaches discussed in this book. The second analytic objective of contextualizing the description part of the analysis is what makes DA unique. In contextualizing a discourse feature, a researcher is effectively identifying its pedagogical function. In other words, describing the functions of classroom discourse is a key feature of DA research.

Table 4.5 includes publications that offer examples of how a study of discourse markers can be approached using different discourse analytic approaches.

It is easy to overlook the importance of discourse markers, as they are short in construction and can be surrounded by long stretches of talk. Discourse markers are nonetheless not only omnipresent in classrooms interactions, but as the publications referenced in the Table 4.5 demonstrate, they also help teachers and students accomplish a range of teaching and learning objectives.

4.2 What are the methodological considerations?

In this part of the chapter, the discussion shifts to the methodological issues that underpin the work done in DA. Specifically, this section frames DA studies of classroom discourse using the five methodological issues of classroom discourse reviewed in Chapter 1 (i.e., data collection, data presentation, type of analysis, level of analysis, and role of context; see Table 1.5). Again, this approach of first discussing what discourse analysts typically investigate in classroom discourse, and then reviewing the key methodological issues, will hopefully provide a more straightforward, albeit superficial, overview of DA.

To this end, Table 4.6 identifies the methodological issues that discourse analysts must attend to when carrying out an empirical investigation. The references included in Table 4.6 provide a starting point for readers interested in conducting a study using DA, but do not in any way account for all of the methodological issues that may need to be taken into consideration.

TABLE 4.5 Publications on discourse markers

Recommended publication	Description
Fung, L., & Carter, R. (2007). Discourse markers and spoken English: Native and learner use in pedagogical settings. *Applied Linguistics*, 28, 410–439.	The authors examine how English speakers use discourse markers in pedagogical settings. Using corpora taken from different contexts, the findings suggest that discourse markers are used to organize communication and manage interpersonal relations.
Hellermann, J., & Vergun, A. (2007). Language which is not taught: The discourse marker use of beginning adult learners of English. *Journal of Pragmatics*, 39, 157–179.	Although this study of discourse markers utilizes conversation analytic principles, the observations provide readers with a detailed account of how "well," "like," and "you know" are situated within communication and used for different interactive purposes.
Polat, B. (2011). Investigating acquisition of discourse markers through a developmental learner corpus. *Journal of Pragmatics*, 43, 3745–3756.	Using a corpus of language-learning data, the author investigates the reasons why discourse markers are used in particular ways. The study is unique in that the development of discourse markers is analysed over a one-year period. The author comments that corpora are ideal sources of data for the study of language learning in general, and discourse markers in particular.
Chaudron, C., & Richards, J. (1986). The effect of discourse markers on the comprehension of lectures. *Applied Linguistics*, 7, 113–127.	An older, but seminal, study on discourse markers. The authors examine how the use of discourse markers in university classrooms aid in comprehension.
Müller, S. (2005). *Discourse markers in native and non-native English discourse*. Amsterdam, the Netherlands: John Benjamins.	One of a few book-length investigations of the use of discourse markers by native and non-native speakers of English. The publication situates a discussion of discourse markers within the field of SLA. Analytic chapters individually examine one discourse marker, such as "well," "you know," and "like."

Unlike CA, discourse analysts have a great deal of flexibility and choice in the methodological principles adopted for data collection and analysis. The most apparent difference lies in the type of data collected in DA studies of classroom discourse. Discourse analysts investigate both spoken and written discourse, and because their understanding of context is not limited to the sequential level (cf. Chapter 3), they also make use of synchronous (e.g., turn-taking in face-to-face communication) and asynchronous (e.g., an online dialogue taking place over many months) forms of communication. DA possesses analytic tools that can be used to collect and analyze data based on essays, monologues, presentations, discussion boards, and school documents, including learning materials, to name a few.

Discourse analysis **85**

TABLE 4.6 DA methodological issues

Methodological issue	DA considerations	Further reading
Data collection	DA, in contrast to CA, does not establish a set of guidelines regarding how to collect data. Being selective while collecting data is acceptable, as only those discourse features that help answer predefined research questions need to be collected. That is, predefined research questions determine, to a large extent, how a DA researcher collects data.	Jones, R.H. (2011). Data collection and transcription in discourse analysis. In K. Hyland & B. Paltridge (Eds.), *Continuum companion to discourse analysis* (pp. 9–21). London, UK: Continuum.
Data presentation	DA research draws extensively from both spoken and written discourse, and thus data presentation guidelines and transcription conventions vary considerably. Like data collection approaches, DA scholars present data according to the research questions being asked. Data presentation can fall anywhere between exceptionally detailed to decontextualized illustrations of language.	Edwards, J.A., & Lampert, M.D. (2014). *Talking data: Transcription and coding in discourse research*. New York, NY: Psychology Press.
Type of analysis	DA observations are descriptive, interpretive, and/or explanatory. The analyst describes and interprets the methods used by classroom participants to teach and learn. In some DA research, an analyst will also explain what readers should do with the data/findings.	Wetherell, M., Taylor, S., & Yates, S.J. (2001). *Discourse as data: A guide for analysis*. London, UK: Sage.
Level of analysis	DA engages in micro, macro, and meso analyses. Unlike CA, the macro level is discussed if a research question attends to such issues; meso issues do not require attending to how the classroom participants make connections between the micro and macro.	Hyland, K., & Paltridge, B. (2011). *Continuum companion to discourse analysis*. London, UK: Continuum.
Role of context	DA has a liberal interpretation of context. The facets of context that may influence discourse include not just the sequential environment, but also historical, institutional, political, and global issues, to name a few.	Gilbert, R. (1992). Text and context in qualitative educational research: Discourse analysis and the problem of contextual explanation. *Linguistics and Education, 4*, 37–57.

Furthermore, "unmotivating looking" is not a defining principle of data collection and analysis. That is, discourse analysts may isolate discursive features for data collection and analysis, ignoring other contextual variables. For instance, a study of student responses to teachers need not examine all of the talk leading up to, and following, such practices. In this example, an analyst may only need to examine the response turns with the aim of uncovering the discursive functions of such talk. This is because discourse analytic observations are not limited to one understanding of context, and the focus of analysis may be on anything from the forms and functions of spoken utterances to cohesive devices within and between texts.

Before collecting and analyzing data, it is acceptable in DA to possess assumptions and empirical interests about what is or is not interesting in a research setting, as discourse analysts have a wide spectrum of interpretations of what is important discursively and contextually in classroom teaching and learning. The role of context examined in DA studies may be based on language, communication, pragmatics, politics, or history, for example. What this variable interpretation of discourse and context means is that DA observations may not only be descriptive, interpretive, explanatory, or any combination of these analytic types, but also fall within any level of analysis from the micro to the macro. The multiple perspectives of context that exist within DA means that classroom discourse studies may examine anything from the sequential environment of communication to global and political issues.

4.3 Key terms, constructs, and people

This final section of the chapter identifies ten key terms, constructs, and people associated with DA. The operative term here is "associated," as some of the terms and constructs identified are used in other approaches, including those discussed in this book. Each entry is followed with a brief description or explanation. The first three entries are key scholars in DA. The next seven entries are terms and constructs listed in alphabetical order.

The justification for including ten entries is simple. The concise list provides an accessible, albeit superficial, overview of the different terms, constructs, and people that have shaped DA. In other words, the list does not represent all of the key terms, constructs, and people in DA, but the entries nonetheless capture the core ideas of, and thinkers in, the approach. Furthermore, all of the entries have not been discussed in detail in this chapter, and thus offer a different perspective of DA than provided in the sections before.

A more comprehensive understanding of the key terms, constructs, and people of DA can be developed by reading the references included throughout this chapter.

1. *Courtney Cazden* is a long-time contributor to classroom DA research. Her publications on the discourse of language teaching and learning have been cited extensively in many disciplines.
2. *Malcolm Coulthard* is an eminent discourse analyst, but is best known for his work on classrooms. His earlier work on the organization of classroom discourse continues to shape how research in this area is conducted.

3. *Ron Scollon* is an influential discourse analyst known for his work on intercultural communication, place, multimodality, and identity. His work on mediated DA continues to influence how scholars approach the study of communication.
4. *Frame* is a set of expectations that come with a particular discourse. For example, the word "OK" spoken by a teacher can frame classroom discourse in that it is commonly understood to represent an attempt to shift from one topic of discussion to another.
5. *Footing* is a term used to describe when classroom participants shift from one mode or way of communicating to another. Common footing examples in classrooms include switching from one language, lesson, pedagogical goal, or topic to another.
6. *Genre* is a set of language and communication features and patterns that are used for specific purposes. Genres of classroom discourse include a business report, email communication, informal conversations, and presentations. A genre possesses a specific pedagogical goal, and therefore has its own way of communicating.
7. *Recontextualization* occurs when an aspect of classroom discourse in one context is taken and used in another context, e.g., a teacher using the answers provided in a quiz in one week to create a discussion later in the month.
8. *Register* is a term used when teachers and students communicate in a way that distinguishes it from other forms of speech, such as when a classroom discussion shifts from social to academic talk. A register is often based on the established norms of a speech community.
9. *Reported speech* occurs when a speaker (or writer) uses the discourse of someone else to engage in some form of communication, such as reflecting on an experience or making an observation. Reported speech occurs in many classroom activities, such as report writing and academic presentations.
10. *Textuality* is the way classroom discourse is organized and how it is interpreted by the audience. The term is important in DA because it highlights that discourse is not just about linguistic features, but is also centrally dependent on human relations.

5
CRITICAL DISCOURSE ANALYSIS

The approaches to classroom discourse discussed thus far in the book are primarily concerned with the micro details of talk and interaction (i.e., discourse actions; see Chapter 1). However, classrooms are complex and dynamic spaces where discourse operates at multiple levels from the micro to the macro. Although talk and interaction are important areas of investigation in classroom research, teaching and learning practices are shaped, to varying degrees of influence, by a number of discourse structures, such as language policies, political systems, colonial histories, and neoliberal aspirations. How these larger discourse structures factor into, and can be investigated in relation to, classroom teaching and learning is the focus of the present chapter.

Critical discourse analysis (CDA) assumes that classrooms are not simply spaces where teaching and learning occur, but are also pedagogical spaces that index macro social issues and phenomena that transcend the immediately unfolding interactional context of classrooms. That is to say, a critical approach to classroom discourse entails unmasking "the hidden relationship between individual interaction in the classroom and the wider sociocultural and sociopolitical structures that impinge that interaction" (Kumaravadivelu, 1999, p. 479). CDA studies of classroom discourse include, but are not limited to, critical literacies (Vasquez, 2014), textbook discourse (Gray, 2010), neoliberalism (Chun, 2009), race and racism (Sayer, Martínez-Prieto, & Carvajal de la Cruz, 2019), discrimination (Rojas-Sosa, 2016), and power (Martin-Jones & Saxena, 1996).

Table 5.1 identifies publications that address the theoretical basis of CDA, and how this approach can be applied to classroom discourse.

The publications identified in Table 5.1 represent the diversity in theory and practice that exists in CDA. The first three publications are dedicated to reviewing principles and issues fundamental to CDA (Fairclough, 2013; van Dijk, 1993; Wodak & Meyer, 2015), and should thus be referred to when attempting to gain

TABLE 5.1 Introductory publications on CDA

Recommended publication	Description
Wodak, R., & Meyer, M. (2015). *Methods of critical discourse studies*. London, UK: Sage.	The editors bring together leading critical scholars to offer a discussion of what CDA is, how it can be used, and why it is an important methodology to examine social and political issues. Chapters cover a range of topics from a sociocognitive approach to corpus linguistics.
Fairclough, N. (2013). *Critical discourse analysis: The critical study of language*. London, UK: Routledge.	This book introduces Fairclough's interpretation of CDA by including his work over the last 25 years, covering a range of issues from ideology and power to language awareness in education.
van Dijk, T.A. (1993). Principles of critical discourse analysis. *Discourse & Society*, 4, 249–283.	The article establishes van Dijk's interpretation of CDA by looking at the social relations between elite groups, institutions, and society. The principles of CDA discussed are connected to a number of social issues, including race and racism.
Kumaravadivelu, B. (1999). Critical classroom discourse analysis. *TESOL Quarterly*, 33, 453–484.	An older, but seminal article that provides a framework for engaging in critical classroom discourse research. Using post-structuralism and postcolonialism as theoretical frameworks, Kumaravadivelu identifies principles that define critical work done in classrooms.
Rymes, B. (2015). *Classroom discourse analysis: A tool for critical reflection*. London, UK: Routledge.	Rymes presents classroom discourse research as a tool for teacher reflection and pedagogical development. The author identifies a number of approaches to classroom discourse that can be used to engage in such critical reflection, including framing and narrative analysis.

an in-depth understanding of what it means to be critical. The last two publications establish the practice of using CDA for examining classroom discourse (Kumaravadivelu, 1999; Rymes, 2015).

This chapter builds on the works identified in Table 5.1 by presenting CDA as a set of theoretical tools suitable for the study of classroom discourse. A practical overview of CDA will provide much needed direction for the novice researcher. Before discussing the core methodological issues of CDA, the following section introduces four empirical issues that are commonly investigated by critical scholars. This strategy of discussing empirical issues before methodological principles will provide a more comprehensible introduction to CDA.

5.1 What can I investigate?

Presenting examples of what CDA scholars investigate in classroom settings and contexts first requires explaining what the approach does *not* do. This explanation is needed, as the term "critical" is widely misunderstood in the literature.

The critical in CDA is not based on the colloquia or dictionary use of the term meaning "important" and "essential." That is to say, CDA observations and findings are not assumed to be more important or essential than those generated using other methodologies. For example, examining critical issues in the classroom should not be viewed as more important or essential than conversation analytic observations of teaching and learning.

Critical is also not about criticism, though some branches of CDA draw from the same theorists cited heavily in literary criticism (Foucault, 1984). Similarly, CDA is not in the business of criticizing, though its history of confronting social inequalities and systemic discrimination lends itself to such analyses (Luke, 2002). That is, it is natural to be critical, or to criticize, institutions that prop up hierarchies of oppression because doing so helps eradicate the very structures and systems that allow societal problems to exist in the first place. However, CDA studies of classrooms can be positive and transformative, looking at discourses that empower students to bring about change in their lives (cf. Orelus, 2016).

What, then, does CDA do? CDA is committed to improving societal issues and circumstances by investigating discourse. Although CDA is grouped together with other approaches in this book (e.g., CA, DA, and narrative analysis), it is more of a theoretical position: That is, critical scholars believe that discourse is not only an object of analysis, but it is also bound to social, historical, and political factors (Blommaert, 2005). Critical discourse analysts are not married to particular methodological principles, as they are primarily motivated by a need to understand the social, historical, and political aspects of discourse. Put differently, while some common methodological principles exist within CDA (see Section 5.2), critical scholars use whatever approach or tool that is at their disposal when attempting to improve societal issues and circumstances. CDA scholars are dedicated to improving the professional and personal lives of teachers and students.

This commitment to improve the lives of teachers and students can be approached by looking at a number of empirical issues, including power, language ideologies, neoliberalism, and racism.

5.1.1 Power

The power that exists in discourse has been discussed by scholars for many decades, leading to different interpretations of what it means to be powerful or powerless in educational contexts. The theoretical works of Foucault and Gramsci on power, for instance, have been applied to educational contexts in varying and diverging ways (e.g., Ball, 2013; Mayo, 2015). Rather than revisit the philosophical debates that exist in the literature on power (see, for example, Stoddart, 2007), this section offers a more practical overview of the subject and how it can be applied to classrooms.

To this end, power is defined as a social structure, such as the belief that there is only one way to speak the English language (Phillipson, 2009), that shapes how members of society, including teachers and students, understand themselves (e.g., identities) and manage interpersonal relationships (e.g., expert–novice dynamics).

In this sense, power is an organizational force that encourages individuals to communicate (and behave) in particular ways. That is, power helps establish norms and expectations within society. This does not mean, however, that individuals go about their lives perpetually under the control of power structures. The very act of being a member of society reinforces, but can also challenge, deeply rooted social norms and expectations. That is to say, power structures are not fixed, but can be difficult to reconfigure given the inequalities that exist in many domains of life.

Power is often created in and though a disparity of access. This access may be related to information, knowledge, cultural capital, or wealth, to name a few. Such disparities may be reinforced involuntarily or unilaterally (e.g., hegemony, domination, oppression); in other situations, disparities of access exist because of a mutual understanding, often a result of sedimented ideas passed along from one generation to another, between individuals and communities, such as in classrooms and the teachers and students that occupy such spaces. Social hierarchies are created when all individuals or communities do not have the same access to, say, information or knowledge.

For example, in classrooms, teachers and students do not have the same access to information and knowledge: Students attend schools to learn something from teachers. This disparity of access to information and knowledge partly contributes to a classroom hierarchy where teachers have more control (or power) than students. This power manifests in several ways, including controlling the flow of communication, assigning grades to students, and determining what is right and wrong. Other aspects of power that are visible in classroom discourse are included in the following reflective questions:

1. Other than information and knowledge, what are some of the reasons why teachers have more power than students?
2. Does power in classroom discourse facilitate or hinder teaching and learning?
3. Can students disrupt the power structures that exist in classrooms?
4. How does power shape what is included in, and the delivery of, teaching materials?
5. How can students establish themselves as more powerful members of classrooms?

One of the clearest examples of power manifesting in classroom discourse is the interactional exchanges that teachers and students have while managing a lesson. The IRF excerpt discussed in Chapter 4 (Section 4.1.1) is used to illustrate this point. While examining this example, it is helpful to think about how the I and F turns are connected to the power that the teacher possesses in this classroom.

```
1   (I)    Teacher    okay. we know that the book teaches
2                     us a lesson. what do you think that
3                     lesson is?
4   (R)    Student A  life is not easy?
```

```
5   (F)(I)   Teacher     yes. it could be. anyone else?
6   (R)      Student B   challenges are okay
7   (F)      Teacher     challenges are another way to think
8                        about the characters in the story.
9                        yes, especially in the beginning of
10                       the book. okay.
```

The IRF categorizations included in this example, as discussed in Chapter 4, are helpful in uncovering the pedagogical function(s) of each turn. This type of analysis has contributed much to current understandings of classroom discourse, and will continue to be a valuable analytic tool for future researchers.

A critical examination of triadic dialogues may also include such categorizations, but CDA takes this type of analysis a step further by seeking systemic or structural explanations for classroom discourse. Specifically, CDA understands that there are historically defined roles and responsibilities in classrooms that establish power imbalances between teachers and students. Thus, the triadic dialogue in the previous extract represents much more than a rigid turn-taking system; each turn is rooted in a hierarchy of power that results in interactional patterns that differ according to who is saying what and to whom.

For example, in the exchange in the previous excerpt, the teacher establishes the interactional agenda (lines 1 and 5). These I turns unilaterally establish what the students must say in subsequent turns. Although the students are expected to respond, their R turns return the floor to the teacher to provide feedback (lines 5 and 7). In this sense, there is little negotiation or co-construction of what is topically relevant and conceptually acceptable in this lesson. The students are expected to organize their responses according to what the teacher says, have little space to establish a new or different interactional agenda, and contribute to the lesson in quantitatively and qualitatively different ways than the teacher. In CDA, triadic dialogues are thus an outcome of an unequal distribution of participatory rights between classroom participants. The hierarchy of power that exists in classrooms, however, is often the result of a mutual, yet implicit, agreement between the classroom participants that the learning will be directed by the teacher.

Despite these normative expectations between classroom participants, it is not difficult to find examples of students reconfiguring triadic dialogues so that the communication is more evenly distributed. Often in such cases the teacher becomes the participant with less information than the students.

```
1   Teacher     your projects need to be submitted online
2               (2.4)
3   Teacher     the folder is.
4               (0.8)
5   Teacher     where is the folder?
6   Student C   you have to go back one page and,
7   Teacher     like this?
8   Student C   no. the back button and then there. it's
```

```
 9                    easier to do it from the homepage. the
10                    link is at the bottom of the page.
```

In this example, it is easy to see how access to information influences the communication between the classroom participants and the way turns are shaped. Unlike the first example, the student in the above exchange has information that the teacher does not. Namely, the student is knowledgeable of how to locate a particular folder located on a learning platform shared by all classroom participants. The student, in other words, is able to momentarily reconfigure the power structure in the exchange by offering assistance to the teacher. This reconfiguration is visible in the questions asked by the teacher in lines 5 and 7, which are both referential in nature (see Chapter 4). The new power dynamic is also visible in the contributions made by the student, which direct the teacher (lines 6 and 8–10) and provides feedback to her (the "no" in line 8).

The upshot in both extracts is that power equals classroom privileges and discursive rights. Power comes from having information that is not shared by all classroom participants, being socialized into the practice of respecting teachers and seeing them as important members of society, or believing that a particular learning objective, such as learning English, is necessary for career advancement, to name a few.

Power does not only operate within and across the turns taken by classroom participants. For example, power can be found in teaching materials, government-sponsored tests, the rules established at a particular school, the type of teachers employed in a particular country, or the omission of content from a lesson. These examples of power are reformulated into five reflective questions:

1. What cultural stereotypes are reproduced in teaching materials?
2. How do statewide tests marginalize or otherwise disadvantage minority students?
3. How is language policing a form of classroom power?
4. Do schools hire teachers according to their race or ethnicity?
5. How do textbooks promote cultural imperialism and hegemony?

It is sometimes difficult to think of how larger societal issues shape what teachers and students do in classrooms. To this end, each reflective question possesses a concrete societal issue that provides a starting point for readers attempting to adopt a critical perspective of classroom discourse: cultural stereotypes (question 1), marginalization (question 2), linguistic discrimination (question 3), racism (question 4), and imperialism (question 5). All five examples prop up power structures and hierarchies in societies, and can be the focus of analysis for a study of power in classroom discourse.

In addition to these five examples and questions, Table 5.2 identifies what other researchers have done to uncover the power dynamics of classrooms.

Table 5.2 is a reminder that power is a ubiquitous feature of classroom discourse, shaping in explicit and implicit ways how teachers and students make sense of each other and the ways in which they co-accomplish teaching and learning goals.

TABLE 5.2 Publications on power in classrooms

Recommended publication	Description
Candela, A. (1999). Students' power in classroom discourse. *Linguistics and Education*, 10, 139–163.	The author examines the discursive resources used by teachers to establish and maintain power. Candela argues that IRF sequences are not an accurate way of understanding who is in control during classroom discourse, as students can exert some power within triadic dialogues.
Brooks, C.F. (2016). Role, power, ritual, and resistance: A critical discourse analysis of college classroom talk. *Western Journal of Communication*, 80, 348–369.	Brooks investigates how shifts in authority shape the type of teacher-student interactions that unfold during a lesson. The author contends that teacher talk is inherently hegemonic, and thus important insights can be gained from investigating such power struggles.
Martin-Jones, M., & Saxena, M. (1996). Turn-taking, power asymmetries, and the positioning of bilingual participants in classroom discourse. *Linguistics and Education*, 8, 105–123.	The authors of this seminal piece look at the turn-taking practices of bilingual classrooms. The findings show that the medium of instruction creates different power dynamics in classrooms, such as the marginalization of support teachers when the instruction is delivered in English.
Manke, M.P. (1997). *Classroom power relations: Understanding student–teacher interaction*. Mahwah, NJ: Lawrence Erlbaum Associates.	A book-length publication on the ethnography of power relations in three elementary classrooms. The book offers a range of examples of how power relations manifest in classrooms, including how politeness markers are used to accomplish teaching objectives.
Ashton, J.R. (2016). Keeping up with the class: A critical discourse analysis of teacher interactions in a co-teaching context. *Classroom Discourse*, 7, 1–17.	Ashton examines how teaching and learning are managed in an inclusive classroom with disabled students. The findings show that the privileging of standard education in modern classrooms establishes a power structure where disabled students are marginalized and disadvantaged.

5.1.2 Language ideologies

Belief systems (i.e., ideologies) are an important aspect of classroom discourse, as the assumptions, feelings, and attitudes of teachers and students can be used to accomplish a number of empirical and pedagogical goals, such as designing context-sensitive learning materials, delivering teacher education, and doing holistic research that helps bring about change from the inside out. An ideology can include anything from a teacher's assumption about a particular teaching practice, such as explicit corrections, to students' attitudes towards the value of learning a language, such as English.

Given the plethora of beliefs that exists in classrooms, this section will focus on language ideologies so that the examples discussed are detailed and focused. Language ideologies are a useful belief system to focus on, as assumptions, feelings, and attitudes about the communication of classrooms often have a significant impact on how classroom discourse actually unfolds.

The study of language ideologies can benefit from Kroskrity's (2010) work on the subject (see also Kroskrity, 2015). His work is not only the theoretical inspiration for many studies of ideologies in and outside of classrooms, but it also offers an accessible way of carrying out a study of teacher or student belief systems. To this end, Kroskrity (2010, p. 192) contends that language ideologies are the "beliefs, feelings, and conceptions" about "structure and use." A structure is another term for linguistic feature, and includes, among other things, the morphosyntactic or phonological elements of a language. Examples of "use" include how individuals conduct themselves in and through a language system, such as the ways in which classroom participants manage a floor space. In other words, a language ideology is a belief, feeling, or conception about the linguistic features of, for instance, English, and how this language is used in context. This definition provides a useful starting point for the identification of language ideologies.

Language ideologies are expressed in speech or writing. A language ideology in both speech and writing may be located or expressed in a word, phrase, sentence/utterance, or extended stretch of discourse (Kroskrity, 2015). Some examples of words, phrases, sentences/utterances, and discourse that reference a language ideology are as follows:

1. "I **feel** like."
2. "**I am** a Chinese."
3. "British accent **is the best**."
4. "People in Hong Kong **trying so hard to mimic** British accent."
5. "**They just sound so unnatural** and **it seems to me they are very small-minded**."

These examples are part of a larger belief system expressed by one student. Before presenting this longer example, and discussing how it can be examined using CDA, it is helpful to reflect on the following questions:

1. How do feelings about a language influence the way teaching and learning occurs in classrooms? (cf. example 1)
2. How does the identity of a classroom participant shape the feelings or attitudes one may have of a language? (cf. example)
3. Can a positive attitude towards a language variety facilitate the learning of said language? (cf. example 3)
4. What do evaluative comments about a speech community say about the identity of a classroom participant? (cf. example 4)

5. Is it possible for an individual or speech community to own a language and what are the implications if so for teaching and learning? (cf. example 5)

As the five reflective questions demonstrate, a language ideology may interface with more than one teaching or learning issue. That is, a language ideology is often based on a system of interconnected classroom issues. For instance, the way a student self-identifies (question 2) will likely influence how she views the language for which the medium of instruction is taught (question 3). Attempting to understand how a student reflects on one learning issue will likely open up a discussion of other classroom issues.

The literature on language ideologies can be broken into two, sometimes overlapping, approaches to data collection. First, examples of language ideologies can be collected by asking teachers and students to reflect on their classroom discourse belief systems, such as in an interview, questionnaire, or focus group. Second, examples of language ideologies can be collected in a more naturalistic way as classroom participants engage in teaching and learning. Both approaches are suitable for a CDA study of classroom discourse (e.g., Mazak & Herbas-Donoso, 2014), as the deeper meanings that are expressed in a belief system are more important for a critical researcher than the means in which data are collected.

Therefore, if time to conduct research is limited, then it is recommended to opt for the first approach that directly asks classroom participants to discuss their language ideologies. One way of doing this in a more naturalistic way is to create assignments where students directly or indirectly reflect on their belief systems (e.g., Lee & Jenks, 2018). For teachers, this can be done by asking them to maintain a teaching diary (see Chapter 8).

The following example, which was presented above in five disparate parts, comes from an in-class assignment that asked students to talk about their relationship with the English language. It is recommended to use the five aforementioned reflective questions to guide the reading of the following passage in order to develop a greater appreciation of what CDA can offer a study of language ideologies.

> I am a Chinese, of course I have Chinese accent when I speak English. Sometimes I feel like a rebel and refuse to follow the trend that British accent is the best. When I hear people in Hong Kong trying so hard to mimic British accent, they just sound so unnatural and it seems to me they are very small-minded to define the real royal English as British English only.

Providing a critical perspective to this passage requires connecting the ideologies expressed by the student with some larger social or pedagogical issues. This is done by first establishing an *argument* or *position* for which the analysis of language ideology is framed. For example, reading the entire passage reveals that the student does not like the idea of Hongkongers mimicking British accents (e.g., "they just sound so unnatural and it seems to me they are very small-minded"). From this, the argument or position that can be made is the belief system expressed by this student disrupts the widespread assumption that language learners view their varieties of English as inferior.

This example analysis is driven by three questions:

1. What does the ideology express?
   - Hongkongers should not mimic British accents.
2. What discourse features support this observation?
   - "They just sound so unnatural and it seems to me they are very small minded."
3. What is the significance of this ideology?
   - The ideology disrupts the widespread assumption that language learners view their varieties of English as inferior.

A good critical analysis may entail adding further or additional arguments or positions. For example, the three questions can be addressed in the following ways.

1. What does the ideology express?
   - Hongkongers value their local accent.
2. What discourse features support this observation?
   - "Of course I have Chinese accent when I speak English."
3. What is the significance of this ideology?
   - Linguistic hierarchies, such as valuing British accents over Hong Kong accents, are not fixed and vary from one context to another.

A defining feature of CDA is the layers of arguments or positions added to an analysis. In other words, a single passage by one student expressing a belief system may provide the basis for several arguments or positions for a critical researcher. The three guiding questions presented twice for the student passage is one example of how this notion of "layers of analysis" can be put into practice. The publications identified in Table 5.3 provide further examples of how CDA can be applied to a study of language ideologies.

The publications in Table 5.3 represent a wide spectrum of data sets and methodological approaches, from spoken interaction to written discourse, and corpus linguistics to qualitative DA, respectively. Table 5.3 is a reminder that investigations into ideologies can be based on how teachers, students, and even family members view languages both in and outside of classrooms.

5.1.3 Neoliberalism

Neoliberalism, while defined and used in varied ways (Holborow, 2007), should, first and foremost, be viewed as an economic theory (Chomsky, 1999). To this end, neoliberalism is a critical theory that "proposes that human well-being can best be advanced by liberating individual entrepreneurial freedoms and skills within an institutional framework characterized by strong private property rights, free

TABLE 5.3 Publications on language ideologies

Recommended publication	Description
Martínez-Roldán, C.M. (2005). Examining bilingual children's gender ideologies through critical discourse analysis. *Critical Inquiry in Language Studies, 2*, 157–178.	The article investigates young students expressing their gendered ideologies in a second-grade Spanish–English bilingual classroom. The critical observations made in the study are based on sociocultural theory and feminist principles. The findings show that children are capable of exploring complex societal issues.
Mazak, C.M., & Herbas-Donoso, C. (2014). Translanguaging practices and language ideologies in Puerto Rican university science education. *Critical Inquiry in Language Studies, 11*, 27–49.	This investigation uses classroom observations and interviews to show that although science professors construct ideologies that prop up English as a dominant academic language, their actual communicative practices in classrooms look more like translanguaging.
Martínez-Roldán, C.M., & Malavé, G. (2004). Language ideologies mediating literacy and identity in bilingual contexts. *Journal of Early Childhood Literacy, 4*, 155–180.	The authors examine how a young Mexican American student expresses his beliefs about language, and explores the parents' view on the use of minority languages at school. The study is helpful in understanding how CDA can be used to critique educational systems in general, and bilingual classrooms in the United States in particular.
Subtirelu, N.C. (2015). "She does have an accent but …": Race and language ideology in students' evaluations of mathematics instructors on RateMyProfessors.com. *Language in Society, 44*, 35–62.	In this mixed-methods study, the author investigates how university students construct racialized language ideologies in relation to their Asian mathematics instructors. The study uses statistics and CDA to argue that Asian instructors are disadvantaged because dominant language ideologies view their varieties of English as problematic.
Lee, J.W., & Jenks, C.J. (2018). Aestheticizing language: Metapragmatic distance and unequal Englishes in Hong Kong. *Asian Englishes, 21*, 128–141.	The authors examine how university students explore their belief systems in relation to the languages spoken in Hong Kong: English, Cantonese, and Mandarin. The findings show that there is no monolithic language ideology in Hong Kong, and that university students have an uncomfortable relationship with the English language.

markets, and free trade" (Harvey, 2005, p. 2). In this sense, neoliberalism is the belief that governments should not be responsible for most domains of life, such as education and health care. Neoliberalism is an ideal vision of a society that operates according to free market principles: The belief, for example, that a school or university should be able to hire teachers according to their own interests (e.g., profit), and not what the government deems to be acceptable hiring practices (e.g., equal opportunities). Both individuals and institutions can participate in neoliberalism either through their belief systems or actions (Holborow, 2007).

Classroom discourse researchers use neoliberalism as a critical lens through which to understand how teaching and learning are shaped by free market principles. Before exploring how CDA may attempt to understand neoliberalism and classroom discourse, the following list captures, albeit in a superficial way, what neoliberalism is and how it can be applied:

1. Neoliberalism is fundamentally concerned with financial growth and wealth accumulation.
2. Neoliberalism promotes deregulation and privatization (for both individuals and institutions).
3. Neoliberalism can be identified in the actions of individuals and institutions.
4. Neoliberalism is a belief system that may (or may not) reflect what individuals and institutions actually do (see point 3).

CDA scholars are interested in neoliberalism because economic principles, such as deregulation and privatization, can have a profound impact on classroom discourse. Neoliberal discourses and ideologies can be found in teaching materials, government policy documents, school mission statements, the decisions made by parents to enroll their children at a particular school, and the language used in a classroom, to name a few examples. Neoliberalism is, in other words, present in many aspects of classroom discourse.

Take, for instance, the discourse of teaching materials. Studies have shown that neoliberalism is so interconnected with societal belief systems that economic principles can even influence how publishers develop teaching materials for classrooms. For example, Copley (2018) shows how publishers embed, perhaps unwittingly, political and economic messages into English-language coursebooks, such as the idea that students will live happy lives through consumerism (see also Chun, 2009). For a critical scholar, such embedded messages are important because neoliberal discourses can reinforce cultural hegemony in classrooms (Gray, 2010). In the same vein, Jenks (2018), in a study of the discourse of school hiring practices, shows how neoliberal ideologies encourage employers to hire instructors based on physical attributes rather than teaching qualifications (see also Jenks, 2017a). The upshot here is that neoliberalism offers a useful lens through which to examine classroom discourse.

The following questions provide additional opportunities to reflect on how neoliberalism may influence education and classroom discourse in particular:

1. What role does the government have in promoting educational success?
2. Do private institutions provide better education than state-run schools?
3. How can an economic system of a country influence the type of learning that occurs in classrooms?
4. Should all individuals within a society have the same access to education?
5. What aspects of classroom discourse are influenced by the need to generate income or profit?

Like language ideologies research, neoliberalism can be investigated by asking individuals to reflect on their economic belief systems (e.g., interviewing teachers with the five reflective questions above). Alternatively, neoliberalism can be investigated by collecting discourse examples in a naturalistic setting, which may include anything from the actual talk contained within a classroom to signs and advertisements in public spaces.

The example of neoliberalism presented in this section comes from an interview with a teacher reflecting on a job interview with a school that delivered English lessons over the phone. Note what the teacher's employer wanted to portray to their students and how this expectation is aligned with the school's business model.

> During my interview, the hiring manager made comments about how I had a "great English native speaker voice" and I was hired on a trial basis a few days later. When I next met the hiring manager to review the job requirements and lesson plans, they instructed me to tell students that I was a White female from California and showed me (what looked to be a stock photo of) a picture of a blond female with blue eyes that they would be sending to all of my students. Their justification was that it fit with the company's mission statement of employing only English native speakers.

Providing a critical perspective first requires understanding why the data excerpt is an example of neoliberalism, and then exploring how it is connected to a classroom issue. In this interview excerpt, for example, the teacher reveals that her previous employer wanted their students to believe that they are being taught by a "blond female" and that this expectation fits "the company's mission statement." The neoliberalism here can be understood as the school's desire to sell an image of instruction that maximizes their profit at the expense of the teacher's humanity (e.g., identity and emotional well-being).

One connection that can be made to classroom discourse is the expectation that is created (locally or globally) when schools engage in business practices that marginalize the individual (teacher). Namely, this neoliberal ideology, which conflates race and teaching, encourages students (and their parents) to believe that English teachers should possess certain physical characteristics, such as blond hair and blue eyes. Such expectations have significant consequences for how classrooms are structured and taught (cf. Kubota & Lin, 2006).

This example analysis demonstrates that economic issues are central to investigations of neoliberalism and classroom discourse. Many economic-related keywords can be used to conduct both a literature review and data analysis on neoliberalism, including profit, income, individualism, entrepreneurism, and capitalism, to name a few. Like many critical issues, it is also important to think about how neoliberalism intersects with other important social issues, such as race and racism as demonstrated in the previous interview except.

Table 5.4 identifies publications that will help readers better understand the multifaceted, systemic nature of neoliberalism.

In addition to providing representative examples of how to study neoliberalism and classroom discourse, the publications in Table 5.4 demonstrate that critical issues do not exist within a vacuum, but rather shape, and are shaped by, other important social issues, such as racism.

5.1.4 Racism

Racism is a popular topic of investigation for critical scholars, as it profoundly impacts the lives of individuals and communities. In recent years, critical scholars have shifted their attention to classrooms (e.g., Evans-Winters & Twyman Hoff, 2011), showing how racial categories and racialized discourses influence how individuals think about important teaching and learning issues (e.g., Charles, 2017). Before defining racism, and exploring how it factors into classroom discourse, it is necessary to establish what race is and why it is such a contested term.

Race is a category of identification (for an excellent overview of race and ethnicity, see Spencer, 2006). It allows people to assign individuals into distinct groups, such as Black, White, and Asian. Such categories are exceptionally problematic, as scholars have demonstrated that there are tenuous genetic reasons for grouping individuals according to race (Lewontin, 1972, p. 397). Simply put, race is not a valid genetic category of identification. Nevertheless, it seems that society, including teachers and students, cannot resist the temptation to group individuals according to race, which has been reduced over the decades to physical characteristics, such as skin color, body type, and facial morphology.

Racial classification turns into racism when the race of an individual is used for discriminatory purposes. For example, reducing the race of a community or culture into a single, negative behavior (e.g., "all Asians do …") is an example of racism. Racism is thus defined in this book as

> a belief, which manifests itself in a discursive act or social action, that privileges or disadvantages one ethnic or racial group; it creates essentialized images, often negative, of an entire population of peoples, and produces an unsymmetrical distribution of power between two cultural groups.
>
> *Jenks, 2017a, p. 24*

TABLE 5.4 Publications on neoliberalism

Recommended publication	Description
Chun, C.W. (2009). Contesting neoliberal discourses in EAP: Critical praxis in an IEP classroom. *Journal of English for Academic Purposes*, 8, 111–120.	Chun examines how a language program utilizes discursive practices to align itself with neoliberal ideologies. The findings, which are based on teaching materials and the program's website, are used to make a number of pedagogical suggestions for contesting neoliberalism in schools and classrooms.
Copley, K. (2018). Neoliberalism and ELT coursebook content. *Critical Inquiry in Language Studies*, 15, 43–62.	Copley examines coursebooks for English-language teaching. He argues that publishers align their teaching materials with neoliberal ideologies, such as the notion that language is a commodity.
Wilkins, A. (2012). Push and pull in the classroom: Competition, gender and the neoliberal subject. *Gender and Education*, 24, 765–781.	Wilkins explores how a neoliberal logic is embedded in classroom interaction. Using ethnographic tools, Wilkins argues that students are socialized into the worldview that their learning strategies must be designed to compete with others.
Warriner, D.S. (2016). 'Here, without English, you are dead': Ideologies of language and discourses of neoliberalism in adult English language learning. *Journal of Multilingual and Multicultural Development*, 37, 495–508.	Warriner investigates how neoliberalism is embedded in several classroom discourse artifacts, such as program documents, teacher comments, and student talk. The multiple data sources are used to show that neoliberalism creates a narrow and rigid set of institutional assumptions about how students must view and conduct themselves as learners.
Keddie, A. (2016). Children of the market: Performativity, neoliberal responsibilisation and the construction of student identities. *Oxford Review of Education*, 42, 108–122.	Keddie examines in this publication how a small group of primary school students talk about education and learning as neoliberal objectives. The findings demonstrate that neoliberalism is tantamount to good thinking, leading to fixed ways of conceptualizing successful learners and learning.

This definition of racism identifies two key empirical issues. First, racism is a belief or an ideology. Second, racism can lead to consequences, such as a discriminatory action or decision. The five statements that follow provide examples of the first empirical issue (i.e., racism as a belief system). After reading these five fictitious statements, it is important to think about what the consequences are of possessing such beliefs (i.e., the second empirical issue).

1. Caucasians are the best English teachers.
2. My Asian teacher has an accent.
3. English is best taught by native speakers of the language.
4. Asian students are hardworking but lack creativity.
5. African Americans do not speak standard English.

CDA studies of racism are committed to investigating how ideologies similar to these five statements manifest in classroom discourse. In an early and seminal publication on race and racism, for example, Amin (1997) explores the racial assumptions that exist in Canadian classrooms regarding what an English teacher ought to look like and who qualifies as a "proper" speaker of the language. Amin's (1997) exploratory work is important, as it demonstrates that racialized discourses, such as "only White people are real Canadians," not only exist, but such belief systems also disempower teachers that come from marginalized communities.

Amin (1997) and other similar investigations (e.g., Appleby, 2013) show that issues of race and racism are relevant to classroom discourse, and much work is needed to create equitable teaching and learning spaces for all teachers and students. CDA approaches issues of race and racism like other critical issues. Race and racism can be investigated by asking individuals to reflect on their belief systems (e.g., using the fictitious statements above to organize interviews with students or teachers). Alternatively, race and racism can be investigated by collecting discourse examples in a naturalistic setting, such as the discussions that may take place when students watch a video that explores issues of race and racism

The example of racism presented in this section comes from the neoliberalism example: the interview with a teacher reflecting on a previous employment situation. It is useful to revisit this excerpt, as doing so establishes that any given classroom discourse example may possess a number of critical issues worth investigating. The example is also reminder that one critical issue, such as neoliberalism, may influence another, such as race. When revisiting this example, try to think about what impact the racialized ideology has not only on the teacher, but also on teaching and learning in other contexts.

> During my interview, the hiring manager made comments about how I had a "great English native speaker voice" and I was hired on a trial basis a few days later. When I next met the hiring manager to review the job requirements and lesson plans, they instructed me to tell students that I was a White female from California and showed me (what looked to be a stock photo of) a picture of a blond female with blue eyes that they would be sending to all of my students. Their justification was that it fit with the company's mission statement of employing only English native speakers.

Adopting a critical perspective requires using a theory that allows the researcher to establish an understanding of the discourse that extends beyond the superficial level. In this example, a superficial account of the discourse is limited to what the teacher is reflecting on (rather than how the reflection is connected to some critical issue). Moving beyond the superficial level requires adopting a critical perspective, yet CDA does not privilege any particular framework so long as it allows the researcher to make these deeper connections. The notion of White normativity will be used to demonstrate how this is done.

White normativity is a critical theory that argues cultural norms and expectations are sometimes based on notions of Whiteness (Nakayama & Krizek, 1995). For example, White normativity could be the practice of hiring only teachers that have white skin because it is believed that such people are the best educated. White normativity, and thus Whiteness, is a structure of power that normalizes the physical characteristics and cultural practices of White individuals and communities while exoticizing and marginalizing groups from other cultures (e.g., ethnic minorities in the United States).

To this end, the application of a critical theory may look like the following: White normativity allows us to see that notions of teaching competence are not limited to work experience and education background. The request made by the employer for the teacher to lie about her physical features is based on, but also circulates, the belief that a White teacher with blue eyes is tantamount to being a native speaker of English. Therefore, White normativity helps us move beyond the simple fact that the teacher is reflecting on her past experience with an employer and center on the racialized ideology that drives the business decision to sell an image of Whiteness.

A key feature of CDA is the practice of adding critical perspectives on top of the one provided in the first instance. This can be done by folding the previous account of neoliberalism into the analysis of racism just provided.

Some questions that can be asked in relation to this discourse example in particular, and racism in general, are as follows:

1. How do racial ideologies privilege some teachers while marginalizing others?
2. How are teaching practices shaped by racialized discourses?
3. How do student backgrounds influence the way a teacher manages classroom instruction?
4. How can teachers provide equitable learning opportunities in classrooms?
5. How does racism intersect with other critical issues, such as neoliberalism or power?

As an empirical issue, racism is understood as a system of discrimination: an act or a thought that discriminates one race from another. Critical scholars are primarily interested in the type of discrimination that reinforces existing power dynamics or social hierarchies. For example, a CDA scholar may wish to investigate how English-only policies (i.e., a racialized ideology) marginalize language minorities in the United States (e.g., Wiley & Lukes, 1996). Other research example topics are included in Table 5.5.

The publications in Table 5.5 focus on the intersection of language and race, which is perhaps the most relevant focus for readers of this book. However, racism is an empirical issue that has been investigated by scholars working in many disciplines. Readers interested in studying race or racism within classrooms will find it helpful to begin their review of literature with the keyword "critical race theory" (Haney López, 1994), as this framework has relevance to scholars working in most disciplines.

TABLE 5.5 Publications on racism

Recommended publication	Description
Godley, A.J., & Loretto, A. (2013). Fostering counter-narratives of race, language, and identity in an urban English classroom. *Linguistics and Education, 24,* 316–327.	The authors investigate how a classroom teacher encourages her students to create narratives that complicate and counter racialized discourses and ideologies. The authors reveal what identities and experiences are important to counter-narratives, and argue that all classrooms need such instruction.
Shin, H. (2015). Everyday racism in Canadian schools: Ideologies of language and culture among Korean transnational students in Toronto. *Journal of Multilingual and Multicultural Development, 36,* 67–79.	In this ethnographic study of Korean study abroad students, the author explores how learner identities and learning experiences are shaped by race, class, language, culture, and citizenship. The high school students in this study talk about how they cope with marginalization in an English-speaking country. The author concludes with a number of suggestions for scholars working on similar racial issues.
Chang, B. (2013). Voice of the voiceless? Multiethnic student voices in critical approaches to race, pedagogy, literacy and agency. *Linguistics and Education, 24,* 348–360.	Critical approaches to race are used in this publication to understand how ethnic minority students makes sense of their identities and experiences in and outside of classrooms. The findings demonstrate the utility in critical approaches in distinguishing between important social constructs, such as race, language, and culture.
Taylor, L. (2006). Wrestling with race: The implications of integrative antiracism education for immigrant ESL youth. *TESOL Quarterly, 40,* 519–544.	The author examines the learning experiences of 30 immigrant high school students. The investigation looks at the students' understanding of race and racism, and how such concepts shape their own learning identities. The author argues that such issues are important to classroom learning.
Liggett, T. (2014). The mapping of a framework: Critical race theory and TESOL. *Urban Review, 46,* 112–124.	While this publication is not an empirical study based in a classroom, the author explores how critical race theory can be applied to such work. The author contends that critical race theory is a useful framework for uncovering the subtle ways language and race shape classroom teaching and learning.

5.2 What are the methodological considerations?

In this part of the chapter, the discussion shifts to the methodological issues that underpin the work done in CDA. Specifically, this section frames CDA studies of classroom discourse using the five methodological issues of classroom discourse reviewed in Chapter 1 (i.e., data collection, data presentation, type of analysis, level of analysis, and role of context; see Table 1.5). Again, this approach of first discussing what critical discourse analysts typically investigate in classroom discourse, and then summarizing the key methodological issues, will hopefully provide a more straightforward, albeit superficial, overview of CDA.

To this end, Table 5.6 identifies the methodological issues that critical discourse analysts must attend to when carrying out an empirical investigation. The references included in Table 5.6 provide a starting point for readers interested in conducting a study using CDA, but do not in any way account for all of the methodological issues that may need to be taken into consideration.

CDA is an approach to classroom discourse that is concerned with improving society through the analysis of critical issues. A number of theoretical frameworks are used to accomplishment this goal, including most notably post-structuralism and postmodernism (see McNamara, 2012). Although there are no established guidelines regarding how to collect and analyze critical data, in recent years, some CDA scholars have adopted quantitative approaches to "validate" their observations, such as corpus tools (e.g., Baker, 2012).

Despite these more recent attempts to adopt so-called objective measures, CDA research collects and analyzes data according to a range of methodological principles. CDA is concerned with both spoken and written discourse, and as such, data presentation guidelines and transcription conventions vary considerably.

In terms of data analysis, CDA observations are often interpretive and explanatory, as critical scholars conduct research because they wish to improve society in some way. Macro-level issues make up most of what CDA investigates, but this interest is often accomplished by examining micro discursive features, such as turn-taking practices.

The role of context in CDA is open to many possibilities. Spatial, institutional, linguistic, sequential, historical, political, and communicative issues are some of the contextual variables that make up CDA research. In other words, CDA does not possess a monolithic understanding of context, as what is ultimately included in an analysis is based on a larger desire to improve a situation or help a particular speech community.

Furthermore, CDA makes a number of unique theoretical assumptions about classroom discourse. These assumptions are outlined in Kumaravadivelu (1999, pp. 472–473) in relation to language classrooms, and paraphrased here as a list of five ideas that are applicable to a wider range of teaching and learning contexts:

1. Classroom discourse is socially constructed, politically motivated, and historically determined.
2. A classroom is not a secluded, self-contained minisociety; it is rather a constituent of the larger society.
3. Classroom discourse lends itself to multiple perspectives.
4. Classroom discourse should promote critical engagement among discourse participants.
5. Teachers need to develop the necessary knowledge and skills to observe, analyze, and evaluate their own classroom discourse.

TABLE 5.6 CDA methodological issues

Methodological issue	CDA considerations	Further reading
Data collection	CDA, in contrast to CA, does not establish a set of guidelines regarding how to collect data. Being selective while collecting data is acceptable, as only those discourse features that help answer predefined research questions need to be collected. That is, predefined research questions determine, to a large extent, how a CDA researcher collects data.	Rau, A., Elliker, F., & Coetzee, J. (2018). Collecting data for analyzing discourses. In U. Flick (Ed.), *The Sage handbook of qualitative data collection* (pp. 300–313). London, UK: Sage.
Data presentation	CDA research draws extensively from both spoken and written discourse, and thus data presentation guidelines and transcription conventions vary considerably. Like data collection approaches, CDA scholars present data according to the research questions being asked.	Meyer, M. (2001). Between theory, method, and politics: Positioning of the approaches to CDA. In R. Wodak & M. Meyer (Eds.), *Methods of critical discourse analysis* (pp. 14–31). London, UK: Sage.
Type of analysis	CDA observations are descriptive, interpretive, and/or explanatory. However, CDA analyses are often interpretive and explanatory, as critical scholars conduct research because they wish to improve society in some way.	Janks, H. (1997). Critical discourse analysis as a research tool. *Discourse: Studies in the Cultural Politics of Education, 18*, 329–342.
Level of analysis	CDA engages in micro and meso analyses, but for many studies, the aim is to uncover how macro issues shape classroom discourse. A primary objective is to bring about change, transform lives, and improve a situation, and thus, macro-level analyses are the topic of many CDA investigations.	Talib, N., & Fitzgerald, R. (2016). Micro–meso–macro movements: A multilevel critical discourse analysis framework to examine metaphors and the value of truth in policy texts. *Critical Discourse Studies, 13*, 531–547.
Role of context	CDA has a liberal interpretation of context. The facets of context that may influence discourse include anything from the sequential environment to historical issues, though there is a tradition of privileging the latter (as well as political issues).	Hart, C. (2011). *Critical discourse studies in context and cognition.* Amsterdam, the Netherlands: John Benjamins.

108 Analyzing

These five assumptions suggest that CDA research must establish connections between what happens in the act of teaching and learning (e.g., micro issues) with issues of relevant the world outside of classrooms (e.g., macro issues). Put differently, CDA research demonstrates how important societal issues manifest in classrooms (i.e., meso-level analyses). What these important societal issues are vary from one context or region to another, but may include colonialism, domination, oppression, alienation, neoliberalism, and discrimination, to name a few. Readers interested in how such larger societal issues shape classroom discourse should explore the empirical possibilities that CDA offers.

5.3 Key terms, constructs, and people

This final section of the chapter identifies ten key terms, constructs, and people associated with CDA. The operative term here is "associated," as some of the terms and constructs identified are used in other approaches, including those discussed in this book. Each entry is followed with a brief description or explanation. The first three entries are key scholars in CDA. The next seven entries are terms and constructs listed in alphabetical order.

The justification for including ten entries is simple. The concise list provides an accessible, albeit superficial, overview of the different terms, constructs, and people that have shaped CDA. In other words, the list does not represent all of the key terms, constructs, and people in CDA, but the entries nonetheless capture the core ideas of, and thinkers in, the approach. Furthermore, all of the entries have not been discussed in detail in this chapter, and thus offer a different perspective of CDA than provided in the sections before.

A more comprehensive understanding of the key terms, constructs, and people of CDA can be developed by reading the references included throughout this chapter.

1. *Norman Fairclough* is a founder of CDA. He is known for this three-dimensional model of critical analysis, which includes text analysis, processing analysis, and social analysis. His work on critical discourse studies has been taken up by scholars working in many disciplines.
2. *Teun van Dijk* is a notable discourse analyst and influential contributor to CDA. He is known for his work on power, racism, and elitism. Teun van Dijk publishes widely in the area of CDA, and is responsible for the conceptualization and management of several key journals that specialize in critical studies.
3. *Ruth Wodak* is a key contributor to CDA. She is responsible for developing the discourse-historical approach that sees discourse as a social practice. Her introductory book publications on CDA are widely used in university classrooms.
4. *Activism* is a position taken by an individual or group to bring about political and social change. CDA scholarship is committed to activism. Activism is part of being critical.

5. *Critical pedagogy* is a teaching approach that uses classrooms as spaces for the resistance of domination and hegemony. Many CDA studies of classroom discourse are based on the principles of critical pedagogy.
6. *Hegemony* is the ideology of a dominant group (e.g., country, political party, ethnic group) forced onto others in less powerful positions. CDA scholarship evolved from a desire to understand hegemonic forces in society.
7. *Intertextuality* is the process of one text incorporating the discursive features of another. In classrooms, for example, students often use the learning ideologies of their parents (e.g., "you must study harder to get into a good university") to manage their interactions with teachers. In classroom textbooks, it not common for learning materials to take on larger political discourses, such as neoliberalism and capitalism.
8. *Postcolonialism* is a theoretical framework commonly used by critical scholars to understand how colonialism (i.e., domination and hegemony) manifests in the lives of modern-day society, including in classrooms.
9. *Postmodernism* is a set of philosophical ideas taken up by many critical scholars. A central idea is the rejection of grand (or dominant) narratives (or ideologies). A grand narrative relevant to classroom discourse is the belief that English must be acquired in order to get a good job.
10. *Post-structuralism* is a set of philosophical ideas taken up by many critical scholars. Post-structuralism rejects binary oppositions, such as native and non-native speaker. A central idea is that all meaning (including terms developed and disseminated in research) is socially constructed and therefore open to multiple interpretations.

6
NARRATIVE ANALYSIS

The first two approaches to classroom discourse (i.e., CA and DA) introduced in the previous chapters are, by and large, used to examine participation data. Data based on participation concern what teachers and students do in the act of teaching and learning. CDA, the approach discussed in the previous chapter, has a history of using both participation and reflection data. Analyses based on reflection data look at the ways in which teachers or students discursively express their thoughts on teaching or learning. Narrative analysis, the methodology introduced in this chapter, is primarily concerned with reflection data (for a reminder of data types, see Chapter 1).

Narrative analysis is the study of narratives. A narrative is a genre of discourse that transforms an experience or belief system into any combination of utterances, words, texts, talk, and interaction. Narratives transcend time and space by transforming past events and experiences into the here and now. Furthermore, the experiences and beliefs expressed through narratives have a structural organization, including a beginning, middle, and end. Additionally, a narrative is sometimes referred to as a story; as such, narratives are made up of storytelling practices that can be traced to unique cultural norms and practices (Cremin, Flewitt, Mardell, & Swann, 2016).

In classroom discourse research, narrative analysis is a lens through which to understand the experiences and ideologies of teaching and learning as articulated by teachers and students, or those individuals engaged in practices related to teaching and learning (e.g., tutors, self-directed learners). Narratives are an important empirical topic because they provide a window into the minds of teachers and students, linking what they think about important teaching and learning issues with what happens in classrooms.

Narrative analysis is, like other approaches discussed in this book, taken up by researchers working in many disciplines. Conversation analysts may examine a particular structural component of narratives (Norrick, 2000), discursive psychologists investigate how stories reconstruct past events and emotional states (S. Taylor, 2010), education scholars look at how teachers reflect on their teaching practices (Johnson & Golombek, 2002), and anthropologists are interested in how cultural histories are passed down from one generation to another through storytelling (Agar, 1980).

Such disciplines have their own expectations of what constitutes a narrative inquiry, though there are methodological principles shared by researchers, such as the belief that narratives must be understood as a social practice in and of itself. Table 6.1 identifies several publications that provide introductory accounts of narrative analysis from perspectives ranging from sociolinguistics to applied linguistics.

The publications identified in Table 6.1 represent the diversity in theory and practice that exists in narrative analysis. The first two publications are dedicated to exploring the basic methodological and empirical issues that are related to narrative analysis (De Fina & Georgakopoulou, 2008, 2019), and are thus helpful for readers

TABLE 6.1 Introductory publications on narrative analysis

Recommended publication	*Description*
De Fina, A., & Georgakopoulou, A. (2019). *The handbook of narrative analysis*. Malden, MA: Wiley-Blackwell.	This updated handbook on narrative analysis brings together leading scholars to share what is and can be done with the methodology.
De Fina, A., & Georgakopoulou, A. (2008). Introduction: Narrative analysis in the shift from texts to practices. *Text & Talk, 28*, 275–281.	De Fina and Georgakopoulou provide an editorial introduction to a special issue on narrative analysis. The editors discuss, among other important methodological issues, the need for scholars to examine the here and now of narratives: that is, what can be said about narratives as social practice?
Barkhuizen, G. (2014). Revisiting narrative frames: An instrument for investigating language teaching and learning. *System, 47*, 12–27.	Barkhuizen explores how narratives frames, which he defines as a template for storytelling, can be used as a research tool to understand teaching and learning. To this end, Barkhuizen provides a list of the strengths and weaknesses of using narrative frames for empirical purposes.
Benson, P. (2014). Narrative inquiry in applied linguistics research. *Annual Review of Applied Linguistics, 34*, 154–170.	Benson establishes why narrative analysis is a valuable methodology in the study of language and communication. The article offers a number of helpful theoretical justifications for using, and methodological principles associated with, narrative analysis.
Pavlenko, A. (2007). Autobiographic narratives as data in applied linguistics. *Applied Linguistics, 28*, 163–188.	Pavlenko offers a slightly different, and more specific, account of narrative analysis by looking at personal narratives constructed by second-language learners. The article reviews the literature in this area, establishes how researchers can carry out such work, and provides recommendation for researching narratives from multiple perspectives.

interested in establishing a broad understanding of how the approach can be used according to different perspectives. The last three publications are shorter journal publications that focus on specific teaching and learning issues (Barkhuizen, 2014; Benson, 2014; Pavlenko, 2007), and should therefore be read for concrete examples of how narrative analysis can be used to study classroom discourse.

This chapter builds on the publications identified in Table 6.1 by presenting narrative analysis as a set of tools capable of understanding the discourses that exist in classrooms. A practical overview of narratives will provide much needed direction for the novice researcher. Before discussing the core methodological issues of narrative analysis, the following section introduces four empirical issues that are commonly investigated in this body of work. This strategy of discussing empirical issues before methodological principles will provide a more comprehensible introduction to narrative analysis.

6.1 What can I investigate?

Narrative analysis is used to investigate a plethora of empirical issues ranging from stories told in face-to-face contexts to reflective diaries written in classroom settings. Furthermore, narrative analysis is associated with a number of different methodological approaches, such as membership categorization analysis, CA, and CDA. Take, for instance, the comprehensive introduction edited by De Fina and Georgakopoulou (2019). In this book alone, narrative analysis is presented as an approach capable of examining gendered identities, family relationships, social practices, genres, time and space, cognition, and socialization. These empirical issues can be, and many have been, investigated in classroom settings.

Understanding how narrative analysis can be used to examine teaching and learning requires knowing that while scholars have different interpretations of how the approach should be utilized, researchers address spoken or written storytelling from the same starting point: classrooms are complex spaces that, while intricately organized according to discourse actions and structures, are profoundly shaped by sociocultural issues that are not immediately visible in what teachers and students do and say as they engage in teaching and learning.

Narrative scholars argue that this type of reflection data reveals a great deal about teachers and students, and the ways in which they think about the business of teaching and learning. Among the many empirical issues that can be investigated using reflection data (see Barkhuizen, Benson, & Chik, 2014; Benson, 2014), this chapter introduces four areas of investigation that are commonly studied in the narrative analysis literature: identities, teacher cognition, reflective practices, learner diaries. These four areas of investigation provide a sufficient foundation from which to apply narrative analysis to a study of classroom discourse.

6.1.1 Identities

Like many of the empirical issues discussed in this book, identity is a construct that can be defined in varied ways and studied using a number of different perspectives.

An identity can be studied as a biological (e.g., male and female), cultural (e.g., Chinese and British), or social construct (e.g., gender and class). Identities are multifaceted and co-dependent, meaning one identity construct (e.g., American) may shape the formation of others (e.g., masculine male). Identities, often thought of as fixed constructs, are however performative (Warren, 2001), fluid (Makalela, 2014), and context-dependent (Richards, 2006). Simply put, identities have varying degrees of saliency (Stryker & Serpe, 1994). What this means in practice is an individual can reveal, accentuate, hide, or even change an identity in order to achieve a particular goal. For example, being a fan of a basketball team has benefits in some contexts (e.g., showing affiliation with other fans of the same team), but an individual may wish to play down or even renounce this identity in other situations (e.g., talking to fans of a rival team).

Classroom identities, such as expert, novice, student, and teacher, also vary in terms of saliency and can be used to perform social actions. Such identities are important to an understanding of classroom discourse, as they can help explain how or why teaching and learning (or the belief systems associated with such practices) are organized in a particular way (Richards, 2006). Furthermore, identities are an important topic of investigation because they often change alongside an individual's development as a teacher or student (Benson, 2014). For instance, language learner identities typically reflect proficiency levels, and thus any development seen linguistically will potentially have a significant impact on how an individual self-identifies.

Bamberg and Georgakopoulou (2008, p. 385) provide a practical framework for approaching the study of identities from a narrative analysis perspective; their framework breaks down the analytic process into five steps (for a different useful approach to identity research, see Bucholtz & Hall, 2005):

1. Who are the "characters" and their relations?
2. What is the interactional accomplishment of the narration?
3. What is the research setting in which the narrative took place?
4. How is the interaction between the characters managed?
5. What identities are being constructed within the narration?

Bamberg and Georgakopoulou (2008) organize this five-step framework into three levels of analysis (i.e., positioning levels 1–3); however, in the interest of clarity, this section will focus on how to apply these five steps to classroom discourse. The following example is part of a larger in-class assignment that required students to reflect on, or tell a story about, their relationship with the English language.

> There is a guy looking at me in a strange way. He puckered up his lip and saying, "Again, another fake ABC, why can't she speak in Cantonese?" ... Since then, I try to speak in English in typical Hong Kong style.

Step 1 requires the researcher to identify the narrator and the individuals (or characters) that are identified in the narration. In this example then, Sandy is the student telling a story about an encounter in a public space with a stranger (i.e., the two characters are Sandy and the stranger).

Step 2 requires explaining what is being accomplished in and through the narrative. The excerpt above is taken from a short essay written by Sandy. The essay is written to fulfill an assessment requirement for a module that Sandy is taking. Thus, the main audience is the instructor, and the content of essay, including this data example, is organized in such a way to demonstrate an understanding of the teaching materials covered during the semester. Sandy's account of a bad experience fulfills this module requirement, but it also demonstrates a heightened awareness of the social pressures that exist in Hong Kong to speak particular languages in specific ways.

Step 3 requires explaining the research setting. As mentioned previously, Sandy is telling this story because of an assignment that she was set. Sandy was enrolled in a university class about language and culture. The instructor, who was also the researcher, asked students to talk about their relationship with the languages spoken in Hong Kong. Student were introduced to a number of theories that explore the intersections of nation, culture, and language. Therefore, Sandy was both trained and primed to write about her experiences with using multiple languages.

Step 4 requires explaining how the characters are interacting and what is being achieved through the interaction: Sandy is recounting an ostensibly bad experience where a stranger's reaction to her so-called standard English encouraged her to later speak in a more localized way. The use of "fake ABC" (American Born Chinese) and the rhetorical question "why can't she speak in Cantonese" are confrontational and disparaging, as Sandy does not invite the stranger to comment on her English and the assumption that she is faking her accent dismisses the possibility that Hongkongers can speak other varieties of English (Jenks & Lee, 2016).

Step 5 requires exploring how the characters develop an understanding of themselves and the world around them in and through the narrative. Sandy's narrative establishes that identities associated with the English language are closely tied to proficiency levels, ethnic background, and local expectations. For Sandy, possessing a high level of proficiency in English can potentially alienate her from other local Hongkongers. Sandy's language identity is thus not merely performed through the ability to use a particular variety, but it is also co-constructed by others.

Some reflective questions worth addressing in relation to Sandy's experience in particular, and identities and narratives in general, are:

1. How do social encounters shape identities?
2. Are identities important to teaching and learning?
3. Should classrooms be used to encourage self-reflection?
4. How is learning connected with the identities formed outside of classrooms, such as a student's ethnic identity?
5. In what ways can teachers foster the formation of student identities in classrooms?

Classroom teaching and learning are already challenging endeavors, and indeed much has been written about what can be done to help teachers and students meet their particular goals. Often what gets lost in such discussions is the role identities have in classroom teaching and learning. Teachers need to possess pedagogical skills and experience, but they must also know how the technical aspects of their work fit within an understanding of themselves as teaching professionals. Similarly, students must be able to acquire, remember, and apply new information, but their identities as learners (e.g., confident versus timid) will also have a major role in how they engage in the act of learning.

Narratives provide spaces for teachers and students to develop an awareness of how their identities shape classroom teaching and learning. The publications listed in Table 6.2 offer concrete examples of how narratives can be used to investigate classroom identities (see also Barkhuizen, 2016).

In classroom settings, narratives are often constructed in essays and other written assignments. However, narratives can also be constructed through speech in educational contexts (e.g., Hyon & Sulzby, 1994). Some care must be paid to what type of data will be collected when using narratives, as time and other logistical challenges will need to be considered during the research process. Furthermore, when locating relevant studies on identities, it is important to note that not all research uses narrative analysis as a keyword. Studies may also use diary studies, autoethnography, life history, and narrative inquiry (Barkhuizen et al., 2014).

6.1.2 Teacher cognition

Teacher cognition deals with what teachers think about their professional lives and pedagogical practices (Borg, 2006). In more simple terms, teacher cognition is about "what teachers know, believe, and think" (Borg, 2003, p. 81). In this sense, teacher cognition may include what teachers think about themselves as professionals, or in other words, their identities. What teachers know, believe, and think is important to classroom discourse, as "teachers' practices are shaped in unique and often unpredictable ways by the invisible dimensions of teachers' mental lives" (Kubanyiova & Feryok, 2015, p. 435). Teaching practices are, in other words, an extension of teacher cognitions. Furthermore, in teacher education, much has been written about the developmental benefits of getting trainee teachers to explore their cognitions in general (e.g., Barnard & Burns, 2012), and teaching philosophies in particular (e.g., Crookes, 2015).

In classroom discourse research, teacher cognition can be investigated as a discourse unto itself. That is, teacher cognition is a type of discourse (e.g., a teacher reflecting on her teaching practice in a diary) that can be examined outside of a classroom, as again the "mental lives" of teachers are inextricably tied to what is said and done in classrooms (Kubanyiova & Feryok, 2015). Classroom discourse researchers are also interested in how teacher cognition interacts with teaching practices. This particular research focus can be approached by either looking at how teacher cognition manifests in classroom discourse or examining what teachers know, believe, or think in relation to teaching practices. For example, the way an instructor responds to a mistake is often directly related to teacher cognition: said

TABLE 6.2 Publications on identities

Recommended publication	Description
Norton, B., & Early, M. (2011). Research identity, narrative inquiry, and language teaching research. *TESOL Quarterly, 45*, 415–439.	The authors use narratives to explore how their identities as researchers manifest in the investigation of language teaching in Uganda. The findings identify a number of researcher identities relevant to the investigation, including international guest, teacher educator, and team member.
Bathmaker, A.M., & Harnett, P. (2010). *Exploring learning, identity and power through life history and narrative research*. London, UK: Routledge.	The contributors of this 12-chapter edited volume explore different approaches to narrative analysis and identity research, as well as offer a range of findings related to classroom identities. The book covers topics ranging from the ethics of narrative research in educational contexts to using images to portray life histories and identities.
Tsui, A.B.M. (2007). Complexities of identity formation: A narrative inquiry of an EFL teacher. *TESOL Quarterly, 41*, 657–680.	Tsui studies how a teacher negotiates his professional identity over a six-year period. The findings show that teacher identity formation is a complex process that incorporates several domains of life, including the personal and professional.
Watson, C. (2006). Narratives of practice and the construction of identity in teaching. *Teachers and Teaching: Theory and Practice, 12*, 509–526.	Watson follows the negotiation of professional identities by one teacher. The findings show how the teacher constructs professional identities in relation to behavior management. The author contends that narratives are important resources for teacher development.
Fitch, F. & Morgan, S.E. (2003). "Not a lick of English": Constructing the ITA identity through student narratives. *Communication Education, 52*, 297–310.	This study examines how undergraduate students ascribe identities to their instructors (namely, international teaching assistants). The narratives show that international teaching assistants are often identified in problematic ways, including as foreigners. The authors contend that narratives can help researchers address the misconceptions of teachers that students often possess.

teacher may avoid correcting mistakes during a lesson because doing so is believed to give students the freedom to develop on their own. This type of belief system, and its relation to teaching practice, are the types of issues investigated by classroom discourse researchers.

Examining the knowledge, belief systems, and thoughts of teachers can be done by asking questions, getting them to keep a written journal, or observing how they engage in teaching practices. In narrative analysis research, all three forms of data elicitation are used (e.g., Barkhuizen et al., 2014), but the former two are the most commonly adopted. In recent years, teacher cognition scholars ask their research participants to complete a narrative frame (Shelley, Murphy, & White, 2013), which is a writing template for teachers to help them think about their professional lives and pedagogical practices (Barkhuizen & Wette, 2008). The way a researcher collects teacher cognition data is important, as it is often difficult for teachers to think about, reflect on, and especially critique their mental states and cognitive positions.

Teacher cognition research covers many domains of teaching and pedagogy, though there are several fundamental issues that represent the bulk of what is done in the literature, including the content of what teachers think and how such thoughts develop over time. According to Borg (2003, p. 81), these empirical issues can be formulated into research questions, for example:

1. What do teachers have cognitions about?
2. How do these cognitions develop?
3. How do they interact with teacher learning?
4. How do they interact with classroom practice?

Many domains of work and personal life shape what teachers know, believe, and think, including formal training in pedagogy, educational background, personal belief systems, student learning needs, personality type, and institutional demands. Readers are encouraged to think about how their own life experiences influence what they know, believe, and think about classroom teaching and learning. Borg (2003, p. 82) makes this reflection exercise simple by identifying four domains of professional life that shape teacher cognitions:

1. *Schooling,* e.g., formal teacher training.
2. *Professional coursework,* e.g., weekend teaching workshops.
3. *Contextual factors,* e.g., student developmental needs.
4. *Classroom practice,* e.g., dealing with disciplinary issues.

The framework created by Borg (2003) details the ways in which teacher cognition is shaped by, but also shapes, schooling, professional coursework, contextual factors, and classroom practices. While it is important to explore the mutually informing nature of Borg's framework, for the purpose of this introduction, these four domains of professional life can simply be used as a starting point when thinking about how to begin a narrative study on teacher cognition. In other words, any combination of schooling, professional coursework, contextual factors, and classroom practice can be used to create a list of questions or writing prompts for data collection. The following five questions provide examples of what can be asked to research participants (namely, in-service, practicing teachers) within the domain of schooling:

1. Did you learn any memorable pedagogical theory at university?
2. Did your ideas about teaching change while at university?
3. Why did you enroll in your teaching program at university?

4. How has your schooling at university shaped your teaching practice?
5. Has your schooling at university challenged your belief systems about teaching?

It is important to note again that teachers may have a difficult time reflecting on their professional lives and pedagogical practices; therefore, it may be necessary to provide some scaffolding help with these questions. For question 1, for instance, it may be helpful to provide a list of common pedagogical theories for teachers to consider. Similarly, identifying a list of common teacher belief systems may help research participants answer the last question.

After collecting teacher cognition data, it is necessary to begin thinking about the analysis. The theoretical framework and methodological principles adopted to do this will vary according to what teachers say or write. Psycholinguistic theories may be helpful to analyze how teachers reflect on issues of grammar and linguistic development, while critical theories are ideal for cognitions dealing with issues of discrimination or marginalization.

The following narrative offers an example of what teacher cognition data may look like, and how it can be interpreted using narrative analysis.

> I have noticed, especially through my pursuit of the Russian language, that a certain level of simplicity, organization, and structure is necessary in the classroom. This is absolutely crucial because it removes any superfluous and confusing aspects in the learning process. With my experience in L2 acquisition, I have come to the conclusion that learning a new language is confusing, but this confusion can be removed with the right outlook.

This data example is a smaller excerpt from a teaching statement: a short piece of writing that establishes what teachers know, believe, and think. The teacher responsible for writing this teaching statement was enrolled in a module that introduced a number of pedagogical theories, allowing said instructor to comfortably establish a number of positions about her teaching.

While narrative analysis does not require using a particular set of methodological principles (Barkhuizen et al., 2014), most scholars begin their analyses with a *thematic reading* of the data.

A thematic reading of the above excerpt involves reading what the teacher has written several times with the goal of uncovering ideas and themes specific to the data. A distinct theme in this short excerpt is the teacher's attempt to formulate a teaching belief according to her experience learning a second language. The teacher contends that language teaching should be simple, organized, and structured, as learning can be "superfluous and confusing."

A narrative scholar can then decide on what particular theory or relevant literature to use to interpret the data (e.g., Johnson & Golombek, 2011). That is, the next generic step in a narrative study of teacher cognition is to conduct an *interpretive reading* of the data. To this end, the author of the teaching statement demonstrates empathy by connecting her own struggles learning a language with how she views the role of the teacher (e.g., removing confusion). Much has been written about the role of empathy in teacher development and teaching practice, including the ability to understand students from diverse cultural and linguistic backgrounds (Boyer, 2010; McAllister & Irvine, 2002). Furthermore, language awareness is an important resource for teachers, as it allows them to create lessons that reflect authentic needs and challenges (Andrews, 2001). For this teacher, good teaching requires possessing learning experiences that are similar to what students face in classrooms.

The previous two paragraphs offer an example of how to formulate a narrative analysis of teacher cognition based on thematic and interpretive readings of the data. In Table 6.3, the publications offer similar examples with even greater analytic detail.

The publications identified in Table 6.3 establish the role teacher cognition plays in professional development. Through narrative analysis, a researcher is able to uncover the complex ways in which teachers know, believe, and think, and use such information to both reflect on important pedagogical issues and grow as professionals, which is the topic of discussion in the next section.

6.1.3 Reflective practices

Reflective practices are similar to teacher cognition in that both are concerned with the discourses that teachers construct when speaking or writing about professional and pedagogical issues. However, reflection is a more focused discourse that pertains to the "thoughts" and "feelings" of "recent experiences" (Kennison & Misselwitz, 2002). Classroom participants engage in reflective practices because there is an underlying assumption that something in the past could be improved, such as a teaching encounter with a student or a missed opportunity to learn important information during a lesson. Reflective practices are also a discursive resource for classroom participants to engage in unfocused and ongoing self-development. The underlying motivation for engaging in such reflection is the belief that all teachers and students have room to grow.

Thus, the impetus in all reflective practice, whether it is focused or unfocused, is to learn and grow. The discourses that are constructed as a result of reflection can be used for a number of teaching and learning issues, such as addressing a specific weakness in one's teaching or attempting to develop into a more confident language learner. The ability to learn or grow in and through reflection, however, requires acknowledging, analyzing, and addressing (Dewey, 1933): Classroom participants must acknowledge and describe the "problem," they must then be able to critically analyze said problem, and finally address the problem so that learning or growing occurs.

In classroom discourse research, reflective practices can be investigated by looking at how teachers or students acknowledge, reflect, and change. For instance, a study of reflective practices may examine how students talk about their challenges in learning new content. Such reflective discourses may occur in a classroom, as students talk to each other about their learning challenges. Alternatively, reflective discourses may occur outside of a classroom, such as when a student keeps a learning

TABLE 6.3 Publications on teacher cognition

Recommended publication	Description
Johnson, K.E. (2015). Reclaiming the relevance of L2 teacher education. *Modern Language Journal, 99,* 515–528.	Johnson explores how teacher cognition can be used in teacher education programs to develop training materials that are more sensitive to the needs of student teachers. The study is unique in that it addresses how teacher educators and student teachers can work together to enhance professional development.
Borg, S. (1998). Teachers' pedagogical systems and grammar teaching: A qualitative study. *TESOL Quarterly, 32,* 9–38.	Borg investigates how grammar teaching is managed according to teachers' pedagogical beliefs, educational background, and professional experiences. Borg argues that grammar teaching can be enhanced by focusing on what teachers know, believe, and think.
Barnard, R., & Burns, A. (2012). *Researching language teacher cognition and practice.* Bristol, UK: Multilingual Matters.	This collection of teacher cognition studies provides many examples of how different methodologies can be used to uncover what teachers know, believe, and think, including narrative frames and oral reflective journals.
Moodie, I., & Feryok, A. (2015). Beyond cognition to commitment: English language teaching in South Korean primary schools. *Modern Language Journal, 99,* 450–469.	In this study of four primary school teachers in South Korea, the authors examine how a commitment to language proficiency helps said instructors develop into competent professionals. The authors contend that a commitment to professional development is influenced by the positive and negative experiences of teachers.
Zembylas, M. (2005). Beyond teacher cognition and teacher beliefs: The value of the ethnography of emotions in teaching. *International Journal of Qualitative Studies in Education, 18,* 465–487.	Zembylas investigates how the narratives of one teacher over a three-year period are based on emotional experiences. The findings show that emotional states and teaching practices are reflexively connected. The study is useful in exploring how a focused analysis of one teacher over an extended period can yield detail that is often lost in short-term investigations of teacher cognition.

diary. Classroom discourse researchers are also interested in how reflection evolves over time and interacts with teaching and learning practices. The upshot here is that reflective practices are classroom discourses that are talked, written, or acted into being, providing researchers with a range of empirical possibilities.

Reflective practices can be examined by meeting with classroom participants on a daily, weekly, monthly, or even yearly basis. The aim in such meetings is to facilitate reflection by helping classroom participants identify areas of teaching or learning that require improvement. The precise schedule and duration of such meetings will depend on what research questions are being asked. Journals and diaries are also commonly used to collect and analyze reflection discourse, but such methods require the researcher to monitor what is being written because classroom participants may struggle to write about topics that can be used for professional or empirical purposes. It is important to note that reflective practices can be done in many ways: individually, collectively, while speaking, in writing, systematically, and unplanned, to name a few. While teachers and students have multiple resources to engage in reflective practices, classroom discourse researchers must create the conditions necessary for individuals to engage in critical reflections.

Reflective practice research covers many domains of classroom discourse. In teacher education, for example, reflective practices are used to train pre-service teachers. The teaching input that student teachers receive instructing them on how to engage in reflective practices can shed light on how pedagogical theory is incorporated into classrooms over time. Of course, the actual reflections produced by student teachers are discourses that play a central role in how classrooms are organized. In student development, reflective practices are used by students to identify, monitor, and address classroom issues that influence the learning process. The discourses that students construct in their reflections can help scholars and teachers design learning materials that better reflect the unique challenges of a classroom.

Reflective practices can also be understood by thinking about when reflection occurs, what type of information is used to assist in this practice, and who (if anyone) is responsible for assisting in the process. These issues are formulated in the following reflective questions:

1. How can reflection be used to anticipate problems before they happen?
2. How can reflection be used *in situ*, as problems arise during a lesson?
3. How can classroom participants better inform themselves with information to engage in reflection?
4. When can reflection be used to promote learning and growth?
5. How can classroom participants identify problems or areas for improvement without the help of others?

Questions of when, what, and who help researchers conceptualize reflective practices by uncovering what aspects of reflection will represent the focus of analysis in an investigation of classroom discourse. In other words, these five questions represent what type of reflection data will be collected. As a potential researcher of reflective practices, it is also important to think about what to ask research participants. Will you focus on how teachers engage in reflective practices or are students your primary interest? The following sample questions, with some modification, can be used to collect data from either teachers or students:

1. Is there anything about your teaching (or learning) that you think you can improve?
2. Why do you think that this area needs improvement?

3. What are other teachers (or students) doing in this area of teaching (or learning)?
4. What can you do to improve this area of teaching (or learning)?
5. How will this area of teaching (or learning) improve yourself as a teacher (or student)?

All five of these questions deal with one area for improvement. In other words, all five questions can be asked to one classroom participant about one teaching or learning issue, as each question addresses a specific stage of reflection: acknowledging, analyzing, addressing. Again, being able to learn or grow in and through reflection involves classroom participants acknowledging that a problem or an area for improvement exists (questions 1 and 2), analyzing the situation (questions 2–4), and addressing how learning or growth can occur (questions 4 and 5).

The following data excerpt helps establish how a narrative analyst approaches reflection discourse that is loosely based on the five questions above.

> I always work hard to make sure the classroom setting is a safe learning environment for all. If students do not feel safe in a classroom, whether it is emotionally, physically, or socially, their learning ability will greatly decrease, if not shut down all together. It is important to me that my students, as well as their parents, other teachers, administrators, and people in the community see me as someone they can trust, someone who will be fair and nondiscriminatory.

This data excerpt can be analyzed using the same two-level approach adopted in the previous section on teacher cognition. To this end, in this reflection, the teacher does not identify a problem or area for improvement necessarily, but she does nonetheless reflect on an issue that is important for her teaching: creating a safe and trustful classroom environment. The thematic reading of the data excerpt is the teacher's desire to establish a sense of safety and trust with her students. The next step is to provide an interpretive reading of the data. To this end, much has been written about the importance of safe classrooms, and the emotional benefits of creating spaces that allow students to explore their learning without fear of shame or ridicule. This interpretive reading of the data is supported by a number of empirical studies, including investigations that demonstrate how discursive resources, such as humor, are helpful in developing students' interactional competence in classrooms (Pomerantz & Bell, 2011). An actual investigation of reflective practices would require further interpretive observations, for example drawing from other studies and theoretical positions. For now, the discussion will move on to how researchers create opportunities for classroom participants to engage in reflective practices.

Designing a study on reflective practices requires creating opportunities for classroom participants to reflect. To this end, Farrell (2003, p. 17) identifies the following five elements of reflection that can promote reflective practices for teachers (for student reflection, refer to Section 6.1.4 on learner diaries):

1. Provide different opportunities for teachers to reflect through a range of different activities.
2. Build in some ground rules to the process and into each activity.
3. Make provisions for four different kinds of time.
4. Provide external input for enriched reflection.
5. Provide for low-affective states.

The first element, which includes group discussions, classroom observations, journal writing, and feedback from co-workers, aims to provide systematic and diverse opportunities for reflective practices. A study on reflective practice only needs to incorporate one of these activities, but having different options for your research participants can result in richer data. The second element is important for data collection and analytic purposes, as rules (or guidelines) help classroom participants reflect longer and more critically. The third element is related to when your research participants will be asked to engage in reflective practice: Researchers ought to think about the individual time classroom participants need to reflect, how long it will take to complete a particular reflection activity, the long-term time it takes to develop into competent reflective practitioners, and the time needed to provide support and input to said individuals from a researcher or co-worker (cf. Farrell, 2003, p. 17). The fourth element, which is related closely to the issue of time, is based on the understanding that classroom participants need support and input from more experienced and knowledgeable reflective practitioners. A study of reflective practice must ensure that classroom participants have the resources to create reflective discourses. Finally, the fifth element relates to the emotional demands of opening up, and critically reflecting on, one's problems, weaknesses, and other areas for improvement. Collecting reflection data is a process that requires an understanding on the part of the researcher that the research participants are engaging in emotionally challenging tasks when reflecting.

The publications identified in Table 6.4 are helpful in establishing an understanding of how reflective practices can be examined as classroom discourse, including giving examples of how a researcher can provide opportunities for reflection.

Although the five publications in Table 6.4 represent a small portion of the literature on reflective practices, the authors draw from a number of disciplines when exploring the role of reflection in teacher and student development. Indeed, the reflective practices literature spans multiple disciplines, covers numerous methodological principles, and makes use of many theoretical principles. Therefore, readers new to reflective practices will find the publications by Akbari (2007) and Loughran (2002) the most helpful in the first instance, as both authors identify the key theoretical areas in reflective practices research.

6.1.4 *Learner diaries*

A learner diary is a discursive record of a student's view of classroom experiences and events. Traditionally, learner diaries are recorded by hand or in a written

TABLE 6.4 Publications on reflective practice

Recommended publication	Description
Walsh, S. (2006b). Talking the talk of the TESOL classroom. *ELT Journal, 60,* 133–141.	Walsh examines how teachers develop an understanding of classroom discourse using reflective practices. The study is unique in that the research participants use recordings of their own classroom dialogues to engage in reflection.
Walsh, S., & Mann, S. (2015). Doing reflective practice: A data-led way forward. *ELT Journal, 69,* 351–362.	The study explores the ways in which reflective practice can be improved using different analytic tools. The authors contend that teacher reflection must be collaborative and data-driven, and that reflective practices only work with resources that support critical thinking.
Akbari, R. (2007). Reflections on reflection: A critical appraisal of reflective practices in L2 teacher education. *System, 35,* 192–207.	Although not an empirical study, this publication critically reviews the literature on reflective practices, and offers suggestions for researchers looking to continue this line of work. The review is useful for readers interested in establishing a broad understanding of reflective practices.
Hobbs, V. (2007). Faking it or hating it: Can reflective practice be forced? *Reflective Practice, 8,* 405–417.	Hobbs investigates the discursive challenges of asking teachers to engage in reflective practice, arguing that the need to be open and critical of one's professional practice can lead to being less honest. The publication offers a number of suggestions that will improve the use of reflective practice in teacher education.
Loughran, J.J. (2002). Effective reflective practice: In search of meaning in learning about teaching. *Journal of Teacher Education, 53,* 33–43.	Loughran explores the nature of reflection, suggesting that issues of time and experience are important to engaging in meaningful reflective practice. The author identifies how reflective practice can be improved.

document, though social media and online communication provide resources for spoken records as well. Learner diaries are useful for understanding classroom discourse, as these records help students develop an understanding of themselves as active participants of learning, provide spaces to voice important experiences and concerns, allow diverse opportunities to engage in communication outside of class time, and offer a safe environment for self-reflection and exploration.

Many theoretical motivations exist for maintaining a learner diary and all stem from the idea that learner diaries are developmental tools for students: Written or spoken records of learning establish structure for students, enhance critical thinking, develop metacognition, and help learners become more independent and active participants of the learning process.

In one of her seminal publications on learner diaries, Bailey (1991, p. 87) establishes the reasons why it is important to engage in this type of research:

> Diary studies allow us to see factors identified by the learners which we, as researchers and teachers, may not consider to be variables worth studying. The lack of researcher control over variables, which is seen as a problem in experimental science, is viewed as a strength of the naturalistic inquiry tradition … One strength of the diary studies to date is that they reflect the "real-world" conditions under which the data were collected.

Learner diaries are a form of classroom discourse, as they are introspective accounts of the learning process. As such, learner diaries reveal information about classroom teaching and learning that may be typically hidden in a communicative exchange that occurs during a lesson (e.g., Schumann & Schumann, 1977). Furthermore, learner diaries, like reflective practices, can be used to improve classroom teaching and learning by uncovering the gaps that may exist between predetermined learning objectives and how students deal with such expectations. In other words, learner diaries help teachers enhance pedagogical practice by creating teaching materials that are sensitive to the needs of students. Thus, the discourses that are constructed through learner diaries benefit several aspects of classroom teaching and learning, and are resources for both students and teachers.

When using learner diaries to collect classroom discourse data, it is important to establish (1) how much structure will be built into the reflection process, (2) the focus of the reflective discourses, and (3) whether there will be a dialogue component. These aspects of learner diaries can be illustrated as three separate spectra of discourse possibilities as follows:

1.	Structure:	free reflection	|-------|	scheduled reflection.
2.	Topic:	unfocused	|-------|	predetermined.
3.	Dialogue:	public	|-------|	private.

As the first issue illustrates, the structure incorporated into learner diaries can be located on a spectrum anywhere from free to scheduled reflection. Free reflection does not require learners to make entries into their diaries at specified times and for a set duration. That is, learner diaries structured on free reflection entail students writing or speaking about their learning experiences whenever they feel that it is important to do so. Free reflection creates less pressure to produce reflective discourses, gives students the freedom to reflect whenever they want, and encourages meaningful diary entries. However, with free reflection, researchers cannot know for certain whether their research participants will reflect to the extent that is needed for empirical purposes. In other words, learners may write or speak very little with free reflection, leaving the researcher scrambling for other ways to collect data.

In scheduled reflection, learners are required to make entries into their diaries at specified times and for a set duration. That is, learner diaries structured on scheduled reflection entail students writing or speaking about their learning experiences even if they feel that there is nothing significant to discuss. Scheduled reflection pressures students to produce reflective discourses, which may limit or hinder critical reflection. However, scheduled reflection allows researchers to control (to some extent) the amount of classroom discourse data that is collected through learner diaries.

The second spectrum addresses to what extent learners will be asked to write or speak about particular aspects of their learning. Unfocused diaries allow learners to write or speak about any topic. Learners may wish to reflect on their identities, feelings, belief systems, struggles learning new content, or recent successes. Like free reflection, unfocused reflections give learners the freedom to reflect on any aspect of their learning that they feel is important. Unfocused diaries, however, are not recommended for researchers that wish to examine a particular aspect of classroom discourse, such as student identities, as learners will likely talk about a range of topics and not just one. Conversely, asking learners to reflect on a predetermined topic will ensure that systematic analytic observations of a single phenomenon can be made across many entries (or even student diaries), which is a critical aspect of a research paper. With that said, predetermined topics may be considered less authentic, as the researcher controls to some extent what the learner discusses.

The third spectrum, which deals with whether learner diaries have an audience (usually a teacher), shows that the reflective discourses that are produced by learners can be considered as public or private. The most radical public diary is open to all classroom participants, giving them the opportunity to read and comment on each journal entry. With that said, most public learner diaries have one audience member: A teacher provides feedback or supportive comments so that a learner can evolve into a more critical reflective practitioner. While many learner diaries are written with no intended audience and are therefore private, when used for research and dissemination purposes, reflective discourses become public because they will be read and analyzed by an academic audience. The feedback and comments provided by a teacher (or class of students) can also be used for analytic purposes, creating new empirical possibilities in narrative research.

Structure, topic, and dialogue are helpful in determining what type of, and how much, classroom discourse data will be collected using learner diaries. It is important to remember that reflection discourses vary from one student and learner diary type to another. Incorporating ground rules and focus gives researchers some control over what type of classroom data will be collected. If time is not a logistical constraint, then free and unfocused reflections over several weeks or months will provide rich and diverse data that may be used for many future publications. Yet, most researchers have deadlines that require working efficiently and with few disruptions. To this end, some deductive approaches, such as scheduled reflections, ought to be used to maintain some control over the research process.

The following two journal entries provide examples of what a learner journal looks like and how it can be analyzed. The data excerpts come from a study that examines how language learning evolves over time and across different communicative events. The learner diary is focused and free, as the journal entries were not scheduled, but limited to aspects of the Korean language and language learning.

> August 25, 2013
>
> Learned that month is 월 /wol/ – and that you just put the number in front, so Feb. is the second month: 이월 (literally 2 month).
>
> August 26, 2013
>
> Just wanted to try to remember month in Korean, so I stopped what I was doing (transcribing some data) to think of the word. Success. But will I remember in a week???

Such journal entries provide introspective details to the learning process. The use of action words, such as "learned," "wanted," and "remember," is an indication that the learner experiences developmental gains. Learner diaries are also helpful in uncovering the challenges of learning a language; for instance, the learner claims to have "learned" a new word, but a day later, expresses his desire to "remember." Much has been written about why such reflective discourses are important to classroom discourse research (Schmidt & Frota, 1986), and how this information can be used to enhance teaching and learning (Helm, 2009).

Table 6.5 identifies several publications that will help readers expand their knowledge of learner diaries, and establish a better understanding of how journal entries can be analyzed using different analytic approaches, including narrative analysis.

The publications in Table 6.5 demonstrate that learner diaries can be conceptualized in multiple ways, leading to different empirical possibilities for classroom discourse researchers. Learner diaries, like all of the empirical issues discussed in this chapter on narrative analysis, are windows into the experiences and belief systems of teachers and students. Such reflective discourses contribute to a better understanding of how teaching and learning unfold in classrooms, and thus learner diaries will continue to form an important part of the classroom discourse literature.

6.2 What are the methodological considerations?

In this part of the chapter, the discussion shifts to the methodological issues that underpin the work done in narrative analysis. Specifically, this section frames narrative analysis studies of classroom discourse using the five methodological issues of classroom discourse reviewed in Chapter 1 (i.e., data collection, data presentation, type of analysis, level of analysis, and role of context; see Table 1.5). Again, this approach of first discussing what narratologists typically investigate in classroom

TABLE 6.5 Publications on learner diaries

Recommended publication	Description
Schmidt, R., & Frota, S. (1986). Developing basic conversational ability in a second language: A case study of an adult learner of Portuguese. In R.R. Day (Ed.), *Talking to learn* (pp. 237–326). Rowley, MA: Newbury House.	In this seminal study based on a learner diary, one of the authors explores his experiences learning Portuguese in Brazil over a five-month period. The author/learner maintains a systematic and focused diary, detailing the kind and amount of language used during this period. The study provides an excellent example of how a researcher can study his or her own learning experiences and turn a diary into a publication.
Hirano, E. (2008). Learning difficulty and learner identity: A symbiotic relationship. *ELT Journal, 63*, 33–41.	The study uses diaries with other research methods, such as interviews, to examine how identity and learning challenges influence each other in complex ways. The study helps establish the ways in which learner diaries provide insights into the learning process that are overlooked or unseen with other research methods.
Helm, F. (2009). Language and culture in an online context: What can learner diaries tell us about intercultural competence? *Language and Intercultural Communication, 9*, 91–104.	Helm explores how learner diaries can be used to better understand intercultural learning in online environments. The study is unique in that it offers a discussion of the ways in which quantitative tools can be adopted with narrative analysis.
Engin, M. (2011). Research diary: A tool for scaffolding. *International Journal of Qualitative Methods, 10*, 296–306.	In this diary study, the author explores how reflective discourses help her transform into a more competent researcher. Using a sociocultural theory of learning, the author investigates the ways in which learner diaries provide important scaffolding support.
Carson, J.G., & Longhini, A. (2002). Focusing on learning styles and strategies: A diary study in an immersion setting. *Language Learning, 52*, 401–438.	The authors investigate the learning styles and strategies adopted by a language learner as revealed in her diary entries. The findings show that for this particular learner, learning styles remain constant while her strategies varied over time. The study provides an example of how analytic instruments can be used to analyze diary entries.

discourse, and then reviewing the key methodological issues, will hopefully provide a more straightforward, albeit superficial, overview of narrative analysis.

To this end, Table 6.6 identifies the methodological issues that narratologists must attend to when carrying out an empirical investigation. The references included in Table 6.6 provide a starting point for readers interested in conducting a study using narrative analysis, but do not in any way account for all of the methodological issues that may need to be taken into consideration.

TABLE 6.6 Narrative analysis methodological issues

Methodological issue	Narrative analysis considerations	Further reading
Data collection	Narrative analysis is not a monolithic approach to classroom discourse, but it does require scholars to collect data over an extended period of time (researchers do not agree on the precise amount of data that is needed). Furthermore, data must be collected in a naturally occurring environment where the research participants can freely explore their lived experiences.	Barkhuizen, G., Benson, P., & Chik, A. (2014). *Narrative inquiry in language teaching and learning research*. London, UK: Routledge
Data presentation	Narrative analysis draws from spoken and written discourse. The analytic methodology used to study the narrative will determine how the data are presented. For example, if CA is used to examine a narrative, then the researcher is expected to follow conversation analytic transcription conventions.	Jung, D., & Himmelmann, N.P. (2011). Retelling data: Working on transcription. In G. Haig, N. Nau, S. Schnell, & C. Wegener (Eds.), *Documenting endangered languages: Achievements and perspectives* (pp. 201–220). Berlin, Germany: Mouton de Gruyter.
Type of analysis	Narrative analysis can be descriptive, interpretive, and/or explanatory. The analytic methodology used to complement the study of narratives determines what type of analysis is used.	Holstein, J.A., & Gubrium, J.F. (2012). *Varieties of narrative analysis*. London, UK: Sage.
Level of analysis	Narrative analysis constructs micro, meso, and macro observations. However, the process of collecting narrative data is a type of discourse that requires attention to the immediate (or micro) context in which the data is collected.	Maitlis, S. (2012). Narrative analysis. In G. Symon & C. Cassell (Eds.), *Qualitative organizational research: Core methods and current challenges* (pp. 492–511). London, UK: Sage.
Role of context	Narrative analysis has a liberal interpretation of context, but there is an expectation that narratives must be treated as a situated activity in and of itself. That is, context is related to when and how the narrative is recorded, and what the storyteller reports in the actual narrative.	Bamberg, M., & Georgakopoulou, A. (2008). Small stories as a new perspective in narrative and identity analysis. *Text & Talk, 28*, 377–396.

Narrative analysis is an approach to classroom discourse that is concerned with stories of teaching and learning. The approach is concerned with what is said during stories and how narratives are told. Narrative analysis draws from both spoken and written discourse data, and is adopted in a number of disciplines, including psychology, sociology, literary analysis, education, and cultural studies.

As such, narrative analysis is not a monolithic approach to classroom discourse. For example, narratologists are presented with different methodological challenges depending on whether they are conducting an ethnography, adopting conversation analytic principles, or utilizing statistical measurements. Classroom data may include short reflections written during one reflection period; alternatively, studies may wish to investigate how classroom participants evolve over time as expressed in their stories. Despite such variation, many narrative studies of classroom discourse are based on naturally occurring data.

Narratives can be examined using any one of the approaches discussed in this book. As such, a narrative study of classroom discourse may be descriptive, interpretive, or explanatory, and may focus on issues ranging from the micro to the macro. Similarly, the role of context in classroom discourse will vary according to the methodological tools used. A narratologist may, for instance, examine how students express critical issues in their stories of learning. This critical focus is based on a particular set of assumptions about what stories reveal to researchers, such as the belief that narratives are historical artifacts that contain meaning beyond the immediate context of the storytelling. Conversely, conversation analysts view stories as self-contained instances of talk that cannot be examined beyond the context of such narratives.

Although much analytic variation exists in narrative research, Barkhuizen et al. (2014, p. 89) identify three methodological issues that all scholars must attend to when examining stories in classroom discourse research:

1. Rigor.
2. Trustworthiness.
3. Generalizability.

Narrative research is rigorous when it is both comprehensive and systematic. What this means in practice is open to interpretation, but rigor is generally achieved when researchers adopt a methodological framework that clearly establishes the parameters for which data is collected and analyzed (narratologists must also later explain said methodological framework in their research reports). The methodological framework may be a novel approach to data collection and analysis, or based on an established analytic approach, such as CA, DA, or CDA. Adopting, and then later establishing and explaining, a methodological framework is crucial to rigor, as it allows readers to understand the extent to which a researcher is being systematic and analytic in data collection and analysis.

Trustworthiness refers to the degree to which narrative data are accurate representations of the human experience. As with all data types, narratives are situated activities that are temporally and spatially detached from the human experience.

Narratologists can maximize the trustworthiness of their data by allowing research participants to reflect on their experiences as honestly and accurately as possible. For example, it is important to be transparent about any influence a researcher may have on what is being discussed in a story. A teacher has a great deal of power over students, and must be mindful of how this dynamic may play out during data collection. Research participants should not feel pressured to write on a particular topic, nor should they feel obliged to omit information in their narratives for fear of punishment or ridicule.

Generalizability is a traditional scientific construct that refers to the extent to which something said or written in a narrative can be applied to other contexts. Although there is great variation in how narratives are examined, in classroom discourse research, most studies ignore the urge to make grand observations by celebrating the individual experience through detailed and nuanced description.

6.3 Key terms, constructs, and people

This final section of the chapter identifies ten key terms, constructs, and people associated with narrative analysis. The operative term here is "associated," as some of the terms and constructs identified are used in other approaches, including those discussed in this book. Each entry is followed with a brief description or explanation. The first three entries are key scholars in narrative analysis. The next seven entries are terms and constructs listed in alphabetical order.

The justification for including ten entries is simple. The concise list provides an accessible, albeit superficial, overview of the different terms, constructs, and people that have shaped narrative analysis. In other words, the list does not represent all of the key terms, constructs, and people in narrative analysis, but the entries nonetheless capture the core ideas of, and thinkers in, the approach. Furthermore, all of the entries have not been discussed in detail in this chapter, and thus offer a different perspective of narrative analysis than provided in the sections before.

A more comprehensive understanding of the key terms, constructs, and people of narrative analysis can be developed by reading the references included throughout this chapter.

1. *Michael Bamberg* is a notable qualitative research scholar and key contributor to the study of narratives. He is founding editor of the international journal *Narrative Inquiry*. His work on narrative analysis is dedicated to the teaching and promotion of this important approach to classroom discourse.
2. *Anna De Fina* has written extensively on the topic of narrative analysis. Her work on narrative analysis is partly based on developing the approach into a robust set of methodological principles. She is also known for her research on discourse and identity.
3. *Catherine Riessman* is the author of numerous books and journal articles on narrative analysis. Her work on narrative analysis is based on a range of empirical issues, such as gender, family relationships, and life stories.

4. *Indexing* refers to when a speaker or writer uses discourse to signal meaning beyond what is explicitly hearable or visible in the speech or text. In classroom discourse, teachers and students often use words and text to index or signal identities and ideologies.
5. *"Lived experienced"* is a phrase used by qualitative researchers in general, and narrative analysis scholars in particular, to highlight how discourses represent the experiences and knowledge of those classroom participants under investigation. It is a phrase that signals to the reader that the author views discourse beyond the linguistic level. That is, discourse is a human experience.
6. *Narrative frame* is a teaching method that requires students to construct narratives based on their lived experiences. Narrative frames are story templates that prompt students to write about specific feelings or experiences. This method is an effective way of collecting data on narratives.
7. *Narrative space* is the environment from which a story is constructed. Narrative spaces are, in other words, the places and people that make up a story. Two levels of space exist in narratives: the space(s) created within a story and the space of the actual storytelling event.
8. *Other* is a term used to identify the similarities and differences between two individuals or groups (e.g., the Self versus the Other; Americans versus Koreans), and to situate conditions of sameness and otherness within this binary. Narratives are often based on reflections of the Self and the Other.
9. *Positioning* refers to when a narrator positions the Self within a larger, more complex set of social conditions and stories. Positioning is a story within a story.
10. *Self* is a term used to identify the similarities and differences between two individuals or groups (e.g., the Self versus the Other; Americans versus Koreans), and to situate conditions of sameness and otherness within this binary. Narratives are often based on reflections of the Self and the Other.

PART III
Understanding and reporting

7
CLASSROOM ETHNOGRAPHY

The four approaches introduced in this book offer different conceptualizations of, and ways of examining, classroom discourse. CA, DA, CDA, and narrative analysis, while not an exhaustive list of approaches that can be used to investigate classroom discourse, collectively span a wide spectrum of empirical interests and cover many teaching and learning issues. Although these approaches are equipped with analytic tools that identify the discursive features of teaching and learning, they were not conceptualized to provide rich and detailed accounts of classrooms from multiple perspectives. Put differently, CA, DA, CDA, and narrative analysis are not in the business of providing detailed contextual descriptions of classrooms unless such accounts are directly relevant to their respective analytic interests.

Detailed contextual descriptions of classrooms are potentially useful for any researcher looking to describe and understand the discursive features of teaching and learning because the classroom is a space that is exceptionally complex in that it can be characterized from multiple perspectives, including the social, political, institutional, historical, linguistic, and cultural.

Accordingly, the discourse of teaching and learning represents only one of many perspectives that can be taken to describe and understand classrooms. Classrooms are exceptionally complex and thus warrant ethnographic descriptions. In other words, to truly understand the discourse in classroom discourse, a researcher needs to know, among many contextual issues, what lessons are being taught during the time of data collection, why such materials are used, who the students are, and the institutional challenges present at the school or place of learning. With that said, however, any of the methodological approaches discussed in the previous chapters can be used to complement a classroom ethnography.

This chapter introduces ethnography as a way of providing rich and detailed contextual descriptions of classrooms. In so doing, the aspects of research discussed in what follows provide a foundation from which you can better explain the

TABLE 7.1 Publications on ethnography

Recommended publication	Description
Mehan, H. (1979). *Learning lessons: Social organization in the classroom*. Cambridge, MA: Harvard University Press.	Although this publication is several decades old now, the book is a key text in the literature for its contribution to what classroom ethnography can reveal about teaching and learning. The book is a must read for any scholar looking to develop a deep understanding of how to conduct classroom ethnography.
Antón, M.M. (1996). Using ethnographic techniques in classroom observation. *Foreign Language Annals, 29*, 551–561.	The author provides a short, but very practical, account of how to engage in ethnographic descriptions. Much of the discussion is based on five steps to doing classroom ethnography.
Erickson, F. (2010). Classroom ethnography. In P. Peterson, E. Baker, & B. McGaw (Eds.), *International encyclopedia of education* (pp. 320–325). Oxford, UK: Elsevier.	In this short but very insightful publication, the author establishes the boundaries to which classroom ethnography is defined. That is, Erikson provides an easy-to-follow discussion of what constitutes classroom ethnography, identifying specifically five theoretical principles that make up this type of research.
Toohey, K. (2008). Ethnography and language education. In K.A. King & H. Hornberger (Eds.), *Encyclopedia of language and education* (pp. 177–187). New York, NY: Springer.	Toohey attends to the historical developments of ethnography in language education research. In addition, the author reviews the important contributions made in this line of research. The publication is helpful for readers attempting to establish a broad understanding of classroom ethnography.
Atkinson, P., Coffey, A., Delamont, S., Lofland, J., & Lofland, L. (2007). *Handbook of ethnography*. London, UK: Sage.	The editors bring together experts in the field of ethnography to discuss various aspects of engaging in ethnographic inquiry. Although the book is not dedicated to classroom discourse, the contributors offer helpful advice for prospective ethnographers. Collectively, the contributions span issues ranging from the empirical to the philosophical.

contextual variables that shape your research setting. Before reviewing the core principles and objectives of classroom ethnography, it is helpful to direct readers to some of the publications that can be used to supplement the issues covered in this chapter. To this end, Table 7.1 identifies publications that offer introductory accounts of ethnographic tools.

The publications identified in Table 7.1 collectively provide an advanced understanding of ethnography. Readers with more than a basic understanding of classroom ethnography should refer to these. For the more novice reader, the discussion that follows establishes a foundational understanding of classroom ethnography by reviewing the key issues and tools related to this line of research.

7.1 Purpose and principles

Ethnography is an approach to studying classroom discourse, but also a method for explaining or "writing up" your research (see Chapter 8). Classroom ethnography is an approach to studying teaching and learning, as it is based on a set of theoretical and methodological principles, such as the belief that classrooms are complex and dynamic spaces bound to cultural values and practices. As an approach that is dedicated to detailed and nuanced descriptions of classrooms, ethnography is naturally written to capture such detail and nuance. As much as possible, the writing of ethnographers must bring their readers into the classroom.

Ethnography evolved from anthropology (Watson-Gegeo, 1997), which is a discipline that has a history of transforming the unfamiliar (e.g., a remote tribe) into the familiar (e.g., universal family practices). This history of transforming phenomena into the familiar is visible in the word "ethnography," which means writing (-graphy) about people (ethno-). The aim of ethnography is to write about people from their perspectives (rather than from the researcher's point of view). How an insider perspective can be achieved is a topic of discussion later in this chapter.

Classroom ethnography approaches the research task by taking something that is familiar (e.g., classrooms) and turning it into something complex and strange (e.g., uncovering the complex ways a teacher asks questions). As Erickson (2010, p. 322) contends, classroom ethnographers "need to strangify the familiar in order to see it." This position is based on the idea that familiar things look mundane and uneventful, compelling researchers to overlook phenomena that may indeed be critical to an understanding of classroom discourse. For example, a teacher asking questions may, at first glance, appear to be a straightforward task: a teacher asks a question and a student responds. However, closer examination using multiple methods and over extended time periods (two common features of classroom ethnography) may in fact uncover "strange" things, such as a complex relationship between the linguistic construct of teacher questions and student responses (e.g., Boyd, 2015).

Classroom ethnography is broadly about establishing direct contact over an extended period of time, either as an active participant or passive observer, with your research participants and setting. An example of an active participant is a researcher that is also teaching students that are the object of study. An example of a passive observer is a researcher that is not teaching, but is rather sitting in the back of a class taking notes and recording the lesson. Establishing direct (and sustained) contact is necessary because classroom ethnography aims to provide, as mentioned before, detailed and nuanced descriptions of teaching and learning.

Detailed and nuanced observations are often associated with ethnographic descriptions. However, an ethnographic description is not a generic term, but is rather bound to an expectation to faithfully capture a classroom and its participants. For example, it is not enough to simply observe a classroom for one day, as this will only provide a superficial understanding of the research participants and setting. It could even be said that the most detailed ethnographic description of a classroom will fall considerably short in capturing all of the nuances of teaching and learning, and the logistics that go into the research process.

So, what then constitutes a classroom ethnography? According to Erikson (2010, p. 322), there are five characteristics of classroom ethnography that must be considered:

1. Long term.
2. Context focused.
3. Classroom participants.
4. Activities and actions.
5. Ideologies and identities.

Classroom ethnographies are long-term (longer than a two-week period) projects that seek to closely observe and detail the routine activities and practices of teaching and learning (1). Ethnographic descriptions attend to, with great detail, the contextual variables and dimensions that shape, and are shaped by, teaching and learning (2). Classroom ethnographies also seek to describe all of the participants involved in teaching and learning, and uncover, among many things, their rich stories, histories, and relationships with each other (3). The activities and actions of the classroom are completely analyzed (4), and the ideologies and identities of classroom participants are treated as complex and evolving (5).

Good ethnographic descriptions do not approach these five characteristics as disparate research components. In other words, the five characteristics of classroom ethnography do not represent isolated research tasks that are reported in different sections of a research paper. An ethnographer should attempt to weave together all of the five characteristics into a coherent set of observations, describing and interpreting the stories, histories, relationships, and activities, to name a few, of a classroom and its participants. Watson-Gegeo (1988, p. 576), a scholar that has for many years promoted ethnography in classroom discourse research, provides a similar interpretation of what it means to engage in ethnographic inquiry:

> The ethnographer's goal is to provide a description and an interpretive-explanatory account of what people do in a setting (such as a classroom, neighborhood, or community), the outcome of their interactions, and the way they understand what they are doing (the meaning interactions have for them).

How ethnographers achieve this goal is the topic of discussion in Sections 7.2 and 7.3.

7.2 The importance of context

A fundamental issue in classroom discourse research in general, and classroom ethnography in particular, is the role of context in teaching and learning. Context is the circumstances that inform classrooms and form classroom discourse. In ethnography, perhaps the most important circumstance that informs language and communication is culture. Context, like culture, should not be taken for granted when investigating classroom discourse, as there are myriad variables that influence why teaching and learning occurs in a particular way. For example, contextual variables include anything from a historical event that occurred many decades prior to a lesson but still influences how a teacher imparts knowledge to the micro, sequential communicative exchanges between students while they are co-constructing an understanding of an activity.

All good classroom discourse research attempts to understand the role of context in teaching and learning, but approaches vary considerably in what is meant by context and how it is incorporated into an analysis. Take, for example, the four research approaches presented in this book. In CA investigations of classroom discourse (see Chapter 3), context has a very specific meaning: it refers primarily to the turn-by-turn moments that teachers and students create in the pursuit of meaning-making (Kasper, 2009). Conversely, in CDA investigations of classroom discourse (see Chapter 5), context includes a wide range of variables: In addition to acknowledging the importance of sequentiality, critical scholars see context as including variables that may not be explicitly visible in the communicative exchanges between teachers and students, but nonetheless important in and to classroom discourse, such as power dynamics in societies and institutions (Blommaert, 2001). Context also has a liberal meaning in DA and narrative analysis, but what is ultimately acknowledged and included in a classroom investigation varies according to the analytic tools adopted.

While scholars seem to enjoy debating what theory or approach is the most suitable for understanding the role of context in teaching and learning, all classroom discourse research is inherently flawed when it comes to accounting for contextual variables. This is because the existential gap between what scholars attempt to report and what actually happens discursively in a classroom is exceptionally wide. Specifically, what researchers describe in their research reports will never mirror what participants actually do while dealing with contextual issues, such as discussing a lesson or giving a presentation. Like transcribing spoken communication (see Chapter 2), classroom ethnography can never fully capture what occurs in classrooms because discourse is infinitely complex and variable (cf. Cook, 1990).

Despite this uncontroversial statement, the underlying assumption in the literature is that context is a straightforward facet of research. However, as Edwards and Mercer (1989, pp. 91–92) remind us,

> Things are not so convenient. Although the investigators might have the luxury of access to recordings and transcripts, the participants themselves, like the referees whose decisions are examined in television's slow-motion replays, must rely on what they perceive, understand, and remember at the time … But, the fact that the investigator's recourse to context was only, in the first place, made in an effort to understand the communications of the

participants leads to the conclusion that this apparent luxury of a privileged vantage point could be illusory. Context is not concrete for the observer, but intersubjective for the participants.

This quote suggests that there are two realities when researching classroom discourse. First, the process of researching classroom discourse transforms an actual teaching or learning event into a reality that is seen through the lens of a researcher. This lens is constrained by the researcher's personal biases, theoretical subjectivities, and logistical challenges. It is natural, though not unproblematic, that what is reported in a research paper is different than what is actually experienced in a classroom. What is actually experienced in a classroom is, as the quote above contends, an "intersubjective" endeavor that requires negotiating a host of social, communicative, institutional, psychological, curricular, and emotional variables that can never be accurately and collectively represented in a research paper. In other words, research on classroom discourse belies the nuances of teaching and learning by flattening context into a static, observable report.

Yet, there are a number of methods that can be used to gain some insight into participants' viewpoints, gain a deeper understanding of context, and as a result construct a more accurate representation of classroom discourse. Many of these methods are discussed and reviewed in the publications identified in Table 7.1 (see also Woods, 2005). For the purposes of this introductory discussion, this chapter will present three aspects of classroom ethnography that help researchers develop a deeper understanding of context: doing fieldwork, writing field notes, and constructing thick descriptions.

7.2.1 Doing fieldwork

Fieldwork, which is a key requirement of ethnography, is a framework for studying classroom discourse as a complex space for teaching and learning. It is a framework, and not a method, as researchers can use a range of tools (e.g., interviews, observational checklists, archival work) to study classroom discourse. To this end, "doing fieldwork" should not be confused with "field notes." The latter is a method or tool (see Section 7.3.2) that can be used to engage in fieldwork, whereas the former is a larger set of ideas about how to get the most contextual information out of a research setting.

Thus, fieldwork should be thought of as an experiential framework that is used in research to meet the objectives of ethnographic inquiry. Fieldwork allows ethnographers to construct detailed accounts of teachers and students, and be faithful (as much as possible) to the role of context in teaching and learning, which are again key principles of classroom ethnography.

Fieldwork requires a researcher (whether an active or passive participant) to be the primary person collecting data and making observations. That is, fieldwork requires being in a classroom, taking notes if necessary, operating recorders if such devices are used, and observing teaching and learning as it unfolds during a lesson.

Fieldwork does not entail delegating important research tasks to an assistant or supervisee, which is a common approach with other methods. Ethnographers are in the field actively listening and watching lessons, and are constantly reflecting on their role, again either as an active or passive participant, in the research process. An assumption exists within fieldwork that researchers have some level of influence over how teachers and students behave. Unlike other approaches (e.g., experimental or quantitative studies), where there is an assumption that researchers are able to (and should) control biases, fieldwork embraces the messiness of classroom discourse and sees it as a natural part of real teaching and learning. Furthermore, for some ethnographers, an important part of doing fieldwork is attending to how personal subjectivities, such as a researcher's teaching philosophy, may have shaped what was observed and how it was analyzed.

Finally, not all fieldwork leads to ethnography. That is to say, fieldwork can be approached in many ways, and conducted to complement non-ethnographic observations, such as conversation analytic findings. However, ethnographic fieldwork is bound to a core set of ideas. For instance, Pole and Hillyard (2016, p. 10) identify five objectives to fieldwork that are compatible with ethnography:

1. Observe and experience at first hand what is happening.
2. Examine the significance of events and activities, beliefs and rituals (including the mundane and the ordinary) to people involved.
3. Examine the ways in which activities and events, beliefs and rituals relate to each other and to the participants in the location.
4. Look for the significance and meaning of social behavior.
5. Look below the surface of events and activities, beliefs and rituals for patterns and theories that can begin to explain social life in ways that go beyond the particular fieldwork location.

These objectives summarize the first few paragraphs of this section, but it is worth mentioning again that fieldwork in ethnography should be used as an opportunity to gain a much deeper understanding of the setting and participants than what is typically the case with other methodologies or approaches. It is typically not enough to visit a classroom for a short period of time (e.g., two weeks), using one methodological tool to understand classroom discourse. This type of study, while acceptable within many disciplines, cannot be considered ethnographic.

To this end, Eriksson and Kovalainen (2016, p. 156) identify a number of guidelines for readers interested in conducting a study of classroom discourse according to ethnographic tradition. They contend that ethnographers should do the following:

1. Collect a variety of information from different perspectives and different sources.
2. Use observation, open interviews, and site documentation, as well as audio-visual materials such as recordings and photographs.
3. Write field notes that are descriptive and rich in detail.

4. Represent participants in their own terms by using quotations and short stories.
5. Capture participants' views of their own experiences in their own words.

These five guidelines are all based on the belief that classrooms are complex sites that can only be fully understood by collecting more than one type of data (1), utilizing a range of methods (2), detailing the inner workings of a classroom that are difficult to capture with audio- or video-recording devices (3), relying on participant-based accounts of teaching and learning (4), and giving teachers and students a voice in the research process (5). Although there is no monolithic way of conducting fieldwork, making some effort to address all of these suggestions will bring you closer to your research setting and participants. In short, the best way to establish a comprehensive understanding of your research context is to make use of multiple empirical tools and adopt varied perspectives. To this end, the next two sections offer practical overviews of how to develop a better understanding of, and write detailed accounts that accurate portray, your research setting and participants: field notes and thick descriptions.

7.2.2 Field notes

Field notes are notes written "in the field," and represent a type of ethnographic data in that they are used to capture many of the complexities that exist in classroom discourse. Like recording devices that capture most of what is in frame, field notes are written from the conceptual and spatial viewpoints of the ethnographer, recording what is believed to be important to teaching and learning. Unlike recording devices, however, field notes can record behavior and phenomena to which understanding requires more than visual processing, such as the general mood of a class. Furthermore, field notes allow ethnographers to observe and record behavior and phenomena that are not in the frame of recording devices.

Field notes are often used to complement the data collected with recording devices, and are rarely used as the only form of data collection (again, ethnographic inquiry encourages researchers to use multiple methods). Put differently, field notes should almost always be used to complement other classroom data (unless an ethical issue discourages any other form of data collection). This complementary role is common in most recent ethnographies, as advancements in recording technology allow ethnographers to capture rich and detailed classroom data. Nonetheless, taking notes in the field is a legitimate form of data collection that leads to unique and important observations of teaching and learning.

Field notes may include any level of specificity from unfocused to focused, as illustrated in Figure 7.1.

When devising a fieldwork plan, ethnographers think about the extent to which their field notes should focus on a specific classroom participant (e.g., a problematic student) or a particular teaching issue (e.g., teacher engagement). Such focused

FIGURE 7.1 Types of field notes

notes are typically written in situations where the ethnographer has already visited the research site, and has some understanding of the research participants.

Field notes may also aim to provide impressionistic accounts of classroom teaching and learning. Such unfocused notes are often written in situations where the ethnographer either has no predetermined empirical objective or has never visited the research site. Unfocused notes are also written to capture the general characteristics of a lesson or class. Writing impressionistic notes will result in data that will help contextualize data collected using other methods, such as a recording device. In fact, whether they are focused or unfocused, field notes are contextualization tools that help researchers explain their primary data.

Impressionistic note-taking can be more challenging, as it requires knowing what type of notes will be of value later in the analysis and writing up stages of research. Some questions that may be asked to write impressionistic notes include:

1. What is the date and time of the field visit?
2. What is the general mood of the class?
3. What is the lesson about?
4. What type of communication is occurring?
5. What are your thoughts about the teaching and learning?

Impressionistic observations help establish a general understanding of a classroom, and may help researchers later identify more specific issues to investigate. Conversely, in focused field notes, what is written down is based on predetermined empirical goals. That is, focused field notes are based on specific behavior or phenomena; what is observed and written down in focused field notes may also help confirm a priori assumptions or test predetermined ideas (Fife, 2005).

In participant-based ethnography, where the researcher is either the teacher or actively involved with the teaching and learning, field notes provide a convenient way of logging critical events, issues, or phenomenon while managing other classroom tasks.

In addition to contextualizing primary data, Emerson, Fretz, and Shaw (2007, 2011) identify six facets of field notes that should be addressed in all ethnographies:

1. Contemporaneous.
2. Representational.
3. Selective.

4. Framing.
5. Descriptive.
6. Corpus-driven.

Field notes are written as events or phenomena happen (1), but are inherently representational because what is logged into a notebook reduces the classroom into a set of superficial accounts of teaching and learning (2). In this sense, field notes are selective (3), leaving out information that the researcher believes is unimportant, but at the same time framing the teaching and learning in new ways (4). Although field notes are later analyzed during the reporting stage, the contemporaneous nature of note-taking means that what is written down is largely descriptive; furthermore, field notes allow the researcher to describe in detail the context and setting, which is needed for a robust classroom ethnography (5). Field notes are made discretely, systematically, and chronologically, and thus collectively represent a corpus of data to be used later for research purposes (6).

The notes made while in the field are fundamental to classroom ethnographies, but an ethnographer must at some point incorporate field notes into a larger set of empirical observations. The notion of a thick description is one way of understanding how contextual information collected in the field must be transformed into detailed accounts of classroom discourse.

7.2.3 Thick descriptions

A thick description is a tool for uncovering the contextual nuances of classroom discourse. According to Geertz (1973), who popularized but did not coin the term (cf. Ryle, 2009), thick descriptions are needed because human behavior is far too complex to describe from one perspective and within the context of one event or situation. In this sense, ethnographic inquiry leads to thick descriptions in that ethnography requires classroom data to be collected over an extended period of time using different methods while adopting diverse perspectives. A thick description does not simply entail providing more detail or information to an observation. It is about weaving together all of the information gathered during an ethnography and presenting it to an audience as a coherent whole.

According to the definition provided above, research that adopts one methodological approach, such as CA, provides thin descriptions in that the focus of analysis in such work is, by and large, based on "factual" accounts of classroom discourse. Thin descriptions belie classroom discourse, as the linguistic, discursive, and communicative features that are the focus of "single-method" research do not fully capture the human experience.

Leeds-Hurwitz (2015, p. 2) provides an excellent, albeit long, description of what an ethnographer (or "analyst") should do when constructing a thick description:

> The analyst's task is to first document everything, and then to reduce hundreds of pages of notes, records, and recordings, concisely summarizing all – and

only – those essentials necessary for understanding the behavior under consideration … When the focus is human communication, the underlying processes, relationships, and identities are all potentially relevant. The goal is to ensure that readers/viewers come to understand the meanings and implications of the data presented as well as the participants, and the analysis of what has been learned through the collection and presentation of data is the final critical step. Obviously helping nonparticipants understand behavior as well as participants is an impossible goal, but it is the goal Geertz set.

The essence of a thick description, according to this quote, is the need to treat any piece of information collected during an ethnography as potentially relevant to the description, interpretation, and dissemination of data.

Additionally, Ponterotto (2006, p. 542) offers a more concrete list of characteristics that is based on the works of Denzin (1989) and others (e.g., Geertz, 1973); these thick description characteristics are paraphrased as follows:

1. Thick descriptions are accurate in description and interpretation.
2. Thick descriptions capture "the thoughts, emotions, and … social interaction" of the research participants.
3. Thick descriptions assign "motivations and intentions" to social action.
4. Thick descriptions bring readers into the classroom experience, as experienced by the research participants.
5. Thick descriptions lead to thick interpretations, which create thick meaning.

Thick descriptions do not merely describe; such descriptions include the interpretation of data (1 and 5), which leads to rich and meaningful accounts of classroom discourse (5). Thick descriptions attempt to account for all of the contextual variables that may shape classroom discourse (2), including the reasons why a behavior or phenomenon is organized in a particular way (3). Finally, thick descriptions are not only methodological tools for analyzing data, but they also (when done faithfully and earnestly) bring readers into the context in which the teaching and learning occurred (4). That is, thick descriptions are meant to be shared with an audience beyond the classroom setting.

The following examples provide a simple, though perhaps crude, way of juxtaposing thin and thick descriptions:

Thin description

Claudio spent an hour teaching a history lesson. The students were attentive and responded to questions when asked.

Thick description

Claudio entered the classroom looking cheerful. During an interview the previous day, it was discovered that he will be promoted to lead teacher of his school. The lesson began with Claudio describing the historical events leading up to the present discussion. The students are typically participatory, asking questions and demonstrating a passion for learning. Claudio asked many questions during the lesson, including some controversial topics related to the government's decision to require all students to pass a standardized examination. Some of the topics discussed challenged the students; however, they were motivated to learn. This motivation was demonstrated in their hand gestures, body positions, and eye gaze.

Although the second example is clearly better than the first, readers should use the five characteristics identified in the beginning of this section to evaluate what can be done to improve the thick description. For example, what additional perspectives can be added? Is there any information that could be included to bring the reader closer to the research setting and participants?

The next section builds on these discussion points by reviewing several ways that ethnographers can understand the context in which their investigations are based.

7.3 Understanding your context

The chapter has thus far established that ethnography has a special understanding of context and the role it plays in classroom discourse. Ethnography is committed to describing and interpreting classroom discourse as understood and experienced by teachers and students. While other approaches to classroom discourse are committed to participant-based accounts of teaching and learning, such as CA and narrative analysis, ethnography assumes that such methodologies must be coupled with other research tools in order to capture all of the important contextual variables involved in a communicative setting or event. To this end, the following discussion presents two types of ethnographic approaches that are particularly helpful in classroom discourse research: ethnography of communication and autoethnography. Like general ethnography, ethnography of communication and autoethnography can incorporate specific methodological tools, such as those offered in CA, DA, CDA, or narrative analysis, to study classroom discourse.

7.3.1 Ethnography of communication

Ethnography of communication (sometimes referred to as ethnography of speaking in earlier publications; see Hymes, 1962), is an approach to studying discourse established by Dell Hymes and John Gumperz; their work, which was published many decades ago (Gumperz & Hymes, 1964), continues to influence how scholars understand the role of context in language and communication. Ethnography of communication was, and continues to represent, an important contribution to ethnographic studies because it was one of the first approaches to celebrate the cultural elements of language (for a more detailed historical account, see Carbaugh, 2008).

Ethnography of communication, according to Saville-Troike (2003, pp. 1–2), possesses two empirical objectives:

> [Ethnography of communication] is directed at the description and understanding of communicative behavior in specific cultural settings, but it is also directed toward the formulation of concepts and theories upon which to build a global metatheory of human communication. Its basic approach does not involve a list of facts to be learned so much as questions to be asked, and means for finding out answers. In order to attain the goal of understanding both the particular and the general, a broad range of data from a large variety of communities is needed.

The conceptual overlaps between ethnography and ethnography of communication should be clear. Both approaches are interested in describing and interpreting "communicative behavior in specific cultural settings." Ethnography and ethnography of communication both put aside methodological debates and mandates in order to provide the most comprehensive understanding of classroom discourse possible. Put differently, both ethnographic approaches use whatever methodological tools are available to understand language and communication.

Two general questions drive much of the work done in ethnography of communication:

1. How is *communicative competence* demonstrated by the research participants?
2. What are the communicative norms and practices of the *speech community*?

Communicative competence is the ability to communicate (verbally or in writing) according to the norms and expectations of a speech community. A teacher and students collectively represent a speech community in that a classroom can, over time, establish specific ways of communicating (just like a larger community within a city or even a country). Communicative competence includes knowledge of linguistic structure (e.g., grammar and pronunciation), pragmatic norms (e.g., asking questions in a particular and appropriate way), and cultural practices (e.g., managing teacher–student roles and relationships).

Ethnography of communication is thus primarily concerned with how members of speech communities learn, demonstrate, and co-construct communicative competence. Although ethnography of communication has a long tradition of investigating communicative competence and speech communities, the approach can be used to provide thick descriptions of context.

The SPEAKING model, developed by Hymes (1964), is one such way of investigating communicative competence and speech community, as well as identifying the contextual nuances of a particular classroom setting or context. The SPEAKING model is a tool for collecting data in the field, and is thus a type of fieldwork. SPEAKING is a mnemonic title that represents eight components of context: setting, participants, ends, act sequences, key, instrumentalities, norms, and genres.

Setting is any spatial arrangement or factor that influences how teaching and learning unfolds. For instance, the physical dimensions and characteristics of a classroom, are spatial variables that may influence classroom discourse. Setting and context are often used interchangeably, but the two terms are different. Setting is only one of many contextual factors that may influence classroom discourse.

Participants are the people involved in teaching and learning; their age, language background, learning objectives, personalities, and communicative preferences, to name a few, are all contextual variables within this component that an ethnographer may wish to investigate.

Ends refer to the motivations and objectives of classroom discourse. The motivations for covering a particular lesson is one example of an end. Ends address why classroom discourse is organized in a particular way. For example, the desire to develop student understanding in a short period of time may lead to a teacher providing explicit corrections in the classroom.

Act sequences are the ways in which meaning is constructed in and through language and communication. Act sequences are the sequential and dialogic features of classroom discourse, such as how embodied movements and facial expressions are used to co-construct meaning within a communicative exchange.

Key is the tone and manner of classroom discourse. Examples of key are gestures, prosodic cues, voice amplitude, and laughter, to name a few.

Instrumentalities are the modes and forms of larger discourse structures and activities; they differ from act sequences in that instrumentalities are closer to the concept of register (i.e., the contextual reasons why communication unfolds in a particular way). The way a particular aspect of a classroom activity is organized, such as greeting students before the beginning of a lesson, is an example of an instrumentality.

Norms are the expectations of speech and written dialogue. The issue of whether it is acceptable for students to interrupt teachers to ask questions is an example of a classroom norm.

Genres are the specific types of speech or written dialogues that occur in classrooms. This component overlaps with a number of other components, such as instrumentality. Take, for example, email exchanges between students and teacher. This type of communication is a specific type of genre; the forms of communication that occur within these emails are instrumentalities, such as the terms of address used by students.

Although the eight components span a range of contextual variables, the SPEAKING model is a type of focused observation (refer back to Figure 7.1). That is, each component in the SPEAKING model establishes a top-down set of assumptions about what to observe in classrooms. As such, the SPEAKING model may overlook potentially important discursive features of a classroom that the eight components are not designed to observe. For example, historical or political issues and events may shape classroom discourse in subtle, but profound ways (cf. Chapter 5); the SPEAKING model is type equipped to address such contextual issues.

Despite its limitation, the SPEAKING model offers a relatively easy way of capturing some of the complexities of classroom discourse. The following questions offer some direction in this endeavor to understanding classrooms:

1. *Setting*: What are the situational factors?
2. *Participants*: Who are the classroom participants?
3. *Ends*: What are the goals of the classroom?
4. *Act sequences*: What is being discussed?
5. *Key*: How are things being discussed?
6. *Instrumentalities*: What is the medium of communication?
7. *Norms*: What are the rules and expectations?
8. *Genre*: What is the category of communication?

A more detailed account of the SPEAKING model is provided by Hymes (2005). Readers interested in conducting an ethnography of communication are encouraged to read the works Hymes (2005) and others (e.g., Carbaugh, 1989).

7.3.2 Autoethnography

Autoethnography is an approach that examines the experiences and feelings of the researcher (i.e., the self; or you, the reader). Autoethnographers, like general ethnographers, try to bring readers into the world or context being described and studied. However, in autoethnographies, it is the researcher's world that is being described and studied rather than the research participants. In autoethnographic classroom discourse studies, the self is often a teacher or student teacher (e.g., Canagarajah, 2012; Miller, 2009), though learner accounts of learning are not uncommon (e.g., Jenks, 2017b).

Autoethnography should not be confused with autobiography. In the latter approach, personal observations never move beyond an understanding of the self. This may entail simply writing about how one feels about a situation without critically examining the foundation of such a claim. In the former, observations of the self are understood from varied perspectives and using different theoretical frameworks.

Autoethnography utilizes autobiographic data, such as personal narratives. The approach subscribes to many of the principles discussed in general ethnography, including perhaps most importantly the value placed on providing deeper accounts of teaching and learning through field notes and thick descriptions.

Autoethnography is based on a number of theoretical positions that make the approach exceptionally unique (vis-à-vis other approaches to classroom discourse). These positions are as follows, and have been taken and modified from Adams, Jones, and Ellis (2015, pp. 9–10):

1. Autoethnography is skeptical of the possibility of establishing "universal truths, especially in regard to social relations."

2. Autoethnography is skeptical of the possibility "of making certain and stable knowledge claims about humans, experiences, relationships, and cultures."
3. Autoethnography celebrates "stories and storytelling as ways of knowing."
4. Autoethnography celebrates "affect and emotion."

Each position allows ethnographers to provide rich and detailed accounts of classroom discourse by freeing researchers from the belief that classroom observations must follow a narrow set of rules regarding what constitutes objective reality and rigorous empirical research. Accepting the complex and complicated nature of social relations and interaction allows researchers to explore classroom discourse using creative and interdisciplinary methods that value the true human experience. Such experiences are often best told in and through stories, as storytelling is not shackled to what an empirical observation must look like.

Like ethnography, autoethnography aims to provide detailed contextual descriptions of teaching and learning. Autoethnography views classrooms as exceptionally complex spaces that require taking into account multiple perspectives from the social to the institutional.

The value in doing autoethnography is captured succinctly by McIlveen (2008, p. 16):

> [Autoethnographies] inform the reader of an experience he or she may have never endured or would be unlikely to in the future, or of an experience he or she may have endured in the past or is likely to in the future, but has been unable to share the experience with his or her community of scholars and practitioners.

Autoethnographies are valuable in that they provide the space for researchers to balance "intellectual and methodological rigor [with] emotion, and creativity" (Adams et al., 2015, p. 2). That is, autoethnographic accounts celebrate the complex relationship between researchers and their research sites.

The ability to detail the complex relationship between the self and a research site requires attending to several methodological considerations. Anderson (2006, p. 378) distills these methodological considerations into five elements of autoethnography:

1. Complete member researcher status.
2. Analytic reflexivity.
3. Narrative visibility of the researcher's self.
4. Dialogue with informants.
5. Commitment to theoretical analysis.

Autoethnographers are completely immersed in the context of their study (1), such as a teacher that wishes to investigate her classroom and the ways in which her personal subjectivities and empirical goals shape, but are also shaped by, classroom discourse (2). Autoethnographic observations focus on the researcher, weaving the different field notes taken and data collected in the field into a text that highlights the experiences and feelings of the self (3). Although the self plays a central role in autoethnographic descriptions of classroom discourse, the approach requires ethnographers to attend to the researcher's interactions and relationships with other participants, such as students or colleagues (4). Finally, autoethnographies attempt, whenever possible, to make sense of the researcher's personal observations and subjectivities by incorporating theory and philosophy (5). For example, a three-month diary documenting a teacher's feelings about teaching in a new school provides the foundation for an excellent autoethnographic study. However, diary entries must go beyond simply describing what is happening, and include additional interpretive and explanatory work that draws from exogenous theory.

Autoethnographers have a number of research tools at their disposal to accomplish these goals, including field notes and other commonly used ethnographic methods. Autoethnography frequently use tools that are unique in their focus on the self, such as biographical statements, research diaries, and interactive interviews (for an explanation of these tools, see Chang, 2016).

The process of writing up autoethnographic accounts of classroom discourse also differs. Most autoethnographies possess all of the following writing characteristics:

1. The writing should be in the first person.
2. The writing should resemble a story.
3. The writing should privilege depth over breadth.
4. The writing should be personal.
5. The writing should be evocative.

Readers interested in conducting an autoethnography must be comfortable making themselves the object of study (1), using narrative approaches (2) to explain, in great detail (3), the intimate relationships (4) of the researcher and research participants, evoking feelings and thoughts about the story being told (5). Again, and in sum, a good autoethnography embraces the human experience by rejecting traditional scientific modes of knowing that flatten lives into categories that are conveniently constructed through the lens of the so-called objective researcher.

7.4 Key terms, constructs, and people

This final section of the chapter identifies ten key terms, constructs, and people associated with ethnography. The operative term here is "associated," as some of the terms and constructs identified are used in other approaches, including those discussed in this book. Each entry is followed with a brief description or explanation. The first three entries are key scholars in ethnography. The next seven entries are terms and constructs listed in alphabetical order.

The justification for including ten entries is simple. The concise list provides an accessible, albeit superficial, overview of the different terms, constructs, and people that have shaped ethnography. In other words, the list does not represent all of the key terms, constructs, and people in ethnography, but the entries nonetheless capture the core ideas of, and thinkers in, the approach. Furthermore, all of the entries have not been discussed in detail in this chapter, and thus offer a different perspective of ethnography than provided in the sections before.

A more comprehensive understanding of the key terms, constructs, and people of ethnography can be developed by reading the references included throughout this chapter.

1. *Paul Atkinson* has written extensively on the topic of ethnography. His book and journal publications on ethnography are used in many disciplines.
2. *Frederick Erickson* is an early contributor to the anthropology of education in general, and classroom ethnography in particular. His publications on the theoretical and methodological principles of ethnography have been especially impactful in classroom discourse studies.
3. *Dell Hymes* is one of the founders of the ethnographic study of language use. Although he is an influential figure in anthropology and ethnography, Dell Hymes is perhaps best known for his work on communicative competence.
4. *Artifact* refers to objects of study. Ethnographic studies of classrooms study how artifacts, such as a textbook, written sample, or computer screen, shape the discourse of teaching and learning.
5. *Bias* refers to the ways in which ethnographers shape the findings according to their subjectivities, personal feelings, and empirical objectives. It is a critical issue in ethnography because ethnographers are often intimately connected to the research site.
6. *Generalizability* is the extent to which the observations and findings of one study can be applied or extended to a different context. In ethnography, generalizability is often not an empirical goal, as detailed and nuanced descriptions are best achieved through a singular focus.
7. *"Going native"* is a term used in ethnography when researchers are unable to achieve objectivity because they are too involved in their research site.
8. *Membership* refers to whether an ethnographer is a member of the community under investigation. For some ethnographers, membership is obligatory in ethnography because it allows them to better understand their objects of investigation.
9. *Reflexivity* is when ethnographers reflect on how their positionality as researchers shape the research process. This involves being self-critical, revealing subjectivities, and being transparent in the research process, to name a few. Reflexivity is an important feature of ethnography.
10. *Triangulation* is the use of two or more research methods (e.g., field notes and interviews) to study the same classroom discourse phenomenon (e.g., teacher feedback). Triangulation is not simply about using several methods, but rather how the data gathered from such methods collectively provide a unique or particular observation.

8
REPORTING AND WRITING

Reporting on, and writing up, the observations made in a study is a key aspect of conducting classroom discourse research. This is because classroom discourse research is often shared to an audience, and therefore needs to be articulated in a way that allows readers to understand the merits of a particular study. In this sense, an empirical investigation is only as good as the writing that reports the study. That is to say, a good researcher is also a good writer.

Like riding a bicycle, writing is a skill that requires minimal theory and much practice. Although everyone approaches the writing process in slightly different ways, there are several principles that are shared by all good writers, such as careful planning and editing. Many of these principles are introduced in this chapter.

The aim of this chapter is to provide a practical overview of the reporting and writing up stage of classroom discourse research. As a practical overview of writing, much attention will be paid in this chapter to frameworks, lists, and examples, rather than providing elaborate descriptions of such ideas. This approach will allow readers to easily locate important principles, and practice adopting them in their own writing.

Before moving on to what these principles are, it is important to note that writing is a process. An extensive literature exists on this topic (e.g., Graham & Sandmel, 2011), and therefore much variation exists in what process writing entails. In this book, process writing consists of five stages:

1. Pre-writing.
2. Drafting.
3. Feedback.
4. Revision.
5. Editing.

Much of this book is based on conducting classroom discourse research, which typically occurs before the pre-writing (or planning) stage. That is, the pre-writing stage often begins after a researcher has collected and analyzed classroom discourse data. At this point, the researcher is ready to begin devising an outline, brainstorming ideas about how to structure a research paper, or synthesizing notes taken in the field, to name a few pre-writing methods.

All good research papers are a product of many drafts. Drafting entails adding to the writing done in the pre-writing stage; more importantly, drafting is the first attempt at piecing together notes into a coherent "whole." This coherent whole could be a complete draft or most of the necessary sections in a research report (see Section 8.4). Coherence is an important aspect of drafting, as the different sections in a research paper must flow seamlessly from one sentence and paragraph to another. Typically, each subsequent draft is based on extensive changes, such as reshuffling paragraphs, adjusting the writing style, adding important theory, or deleting unnecessary information. A helpful drafting strategy is to take a break from your project for at least one day, as returning to it may help you see your writing from a different perspective.

Feedback is a critical, yet often neglected, stage of writing. Instructors, fellow classmates, or even friends can be used to received feedback on drafts. However, finding people willing and able to provide such feedback may be difficult. In many other cases, writers simply think that their writing does not require feedback. It is important to resist this belief, as all good writing is a product of feedback. For example, a carefully constructed paragraph may be incomprehensible to readers, but writers may not know this until sharing their writing.

Revision can, but need not, follow the feedback stage. In an ideal environment, revisions are made after receiving feedback from a person knowledgeable of writing or an expert in the field. Not all feedback is useful, and again some writers may not have access to people willing to offer helpful suggestions. Nonetheless, revision is based on the idea that writing can always be improved, and some attention to detail must be made from one draft to another.

Editing is the fine-tuning stage of process writing. Editing is not the same as revising. The latter is often based on more substantive changes in a research paper, such as adding a new section on a theoretical framework. Editing is often based on small changes to sentence structure, punctuation, and writing style.

Again, writing need not follow these five stages, and much variation exists in how process writing is implemented. With that said, good writing, which can be defined as clearly articulated ideas that are tailored to a specific audience, is based on several universal principles. Many of these principles are discussed in the sections that follow.

8.1 Purpose and principles

A key reason to write is to share. Researchers share their research to bring about change in their schools or to contribute to a body of scholarship. Sharing is sometimes compulsory, such as when a student must submit a research paper to an instructor. In both situations, sharing is a necessary part of contributing to an academic community.

Who your readership is will influence what and how to write. For example, an instructor responsible for assessing your research paper will determine important writing guidelines, such as word count, citation requirements, and composition style. Furthermore, all writers must attend to their readership. For instance, it is important to omit unnecessary jargon if your readership possesses little technical knowledge. Similarly, a long, convoluted sentence may make sense to the author, but offer little meaning to readers. The decisions that are made during the writing process must reflect audience needs, expectations, and level of technical knowledge.

The process of sharing also leads to permanent records of classroom discourse research that can be later read and used for other empirical purposes. In this sense, research writing contributes to a much larger enterprise of knowledge production and dissemination. Although you may feel at times like an insignificant writer during the research process, your writing allows you to become a member of a network of scholars.

The scholars that inform the research that you conduct will likely possess their own set of expectations about how to report on and write about classroom discourse, such as the differences in writing style between conversation analysts and critical discourse analysts. Paying particular attention to how scholars describe their research will help you grow as a writer, as well as conform to important writing conventions.

Although analytic approaches, such as CA and CDA, have their own set of writing conventions (e.g., how much context to introduce, and what aspects of context to include in an analysis), there are several aspects of writing that all classroom discourse research must follow. Lester and Lester (2015, p. 22) argue that there are three such aspects of writing, which have been expanded here to reflect classroom discourse research:

1. *Analysis*: Your writing must establish (typically in the introduction, but also in the literature review) what the major classroom issues are of your study. Your analysis of classroom data can then, through systematic observations, establish how your study builds on existing research.
2. *Evidence*: Your observations of classroom data must be backed up, or supported by, other scholars working in the same area of your study. This cross-referencing exercise is often done in the data analysis section, but can occur in any section of your paper.
3. *Discussion*: Your writing must situate your study within a larger discussion of teaching and learning. For example, how should readers interpret your findings? What is the takeaway message of your research? How can your study be applied to different classroom contexts? Such writing often takes place in the discussion and conclusion sections.

Hopkins (2014, p. 172) also offers a similar account of what writers should attend to when reporting on their research. The four aspects of writing identified by Hopkins are modified and expanded here to reflect the needs of classroom discourse researchers:

1. *Replicability*: Your writing should clearly and accurately describe your investigation, and how it was conducted, so that readers can replicate it if they wish to do so. This writing typically takes place in the methodology section of your research paper.
2. *Thesis*: Your writing should clearly and succinctly establish the objectives of your study. This is often done at the end of the introduction section, and can be written as research questions or thesis statements. The objectives may also reappear in the methodology section.
3. *Uptake*: Your writing should establish how you want readers to interpret the significance of the study. You can do this throughout the essay by adding meta-commentaries, which are short pieces of writing that explicitly tell the reader what you, as the writer, are thinking about the study.
4. *Accessibility*: Your writing should be devoid of unnecessary jargon and elaborate explanations so that readers can easily interpret your observations and findings.

While the previous lists establish aspects of writing that are important and must be followed, there are a number of common reporting problems that should be avoided in a research paper. To this end, Woods (2005, pp. 185–188) identifies seven problems that are particularly relevant to classroom discourse research:

1. *Straw man*: A straw man argument is based on an idea that either does not exist or is incorrectly presented to readers.
2. *Overstating*: When an idea or finding is amplified or exaggerated in order to make a stronger argument.
3. *Understating*: When an idea or finding is not presented in its entirety in order to devalue an opposing belief.
4. *Utopianism*: When an author creates an ideal, but not completely accurate depiction of, a classroom, such as the notion that all of the students in a class are eager to learn.
5. *Sloppiness*: Inconsistent claims, use of terms, and application of theory leads are examples of sloppy writing.
6. *Zealousness*: When writers are too structured and deductive in their writing, which makes reading your research more challenging. Zealousness is the opposite of sloppiness.
7. *Exactness*: Presenting classroom discourse as a perfectly organized and easily interpreted phenomenon, which is problematic, as such depictions never reflect the realities of teaching and learning.

Drafting a research paper is a time-consuming task that requires attending to a number of writing principles. While good research writing is informed by writing principles, developing into a good writer takes much practice and effort. That is, the principles discussed in this section do not alone provide a sufficient base from which to develop into a good writer. It is again important that writing is built into the research process so that sufficient time is allocated to practice and revision.

Good research writing also requires sufficient planning. Before any substantial writing is done, it is important to reflect on what type of research paper will be written and who will read your work. To this end, the following list provides a set of questions that can be used to create an outline for the writing process:

1. *Overview*: What is the overview of your study? Who are the classroom participants? Who will benefit from your study? Why is your study important?
2. *Objective*: What would you like to argue? Do you plan on critiquing a particular issue? What is your research question? Are you trying to solve a teaching problem?
3. *Audience*: Who is your audience? Will your audience assess your research paper? Does your audience possess writing expectations? Is your audience skeptical or possess different views?
4. *Timing*: When does the research paper need to be submitted? How much time will be spent on writing each week? Is there enough time to create multiple drafts? How much time is needed to receive feedback?

These planning questions represent an important part of the pre-writing stage of process writing. The answers compiled for the four categories should be written down and then later used to create a first draft.

8.2 Describing your research

Research writing is a process of careful planning and execution. While the general writing principles identified in the previous section make up a large part of how a research paper is constructed and disseminated, researchers must also possess several composition skills that are specific to the task of reporting on a study of classroom discourse. These skills can be divided into two, interdependent aspects of writing: describing a study and analyzing data. This section addresses the former, and the latter skill is discussed subsequently.

A research paper must contain several description requirements: (1) a description of your objectives, (2) a description of the relevant literature, and (3) a description of your classroom setting and its contextual variables:

1. *Describing objectives* (i.e., thesis statements and research questions).
2. *Describing the literature* (i.e., review what has and has not been done).
3. *Describing a classroom* (i.e., providing important contextual facts).

8.2.1 Identifying your objectives

The first description requirement can be accomplished by either constructing a thesis statement or research questions. A key difference exists between these two research objectives. That is, a thesis statement is a declarative sentence that establishes what the research believes and will argue, for example:

1. Task-based learning does not work in South Korea.
2. Translingual approaches to writing are inclusive and effective.
3. Explicit feedback demotivates students.

A research question, conversely, is exploratory, and does not explicitly establish a specific position or argument. Take, for example, the following research questions:

1. What are the unique challenges of implementing task-based learning in South Korea?
2. How can translingual approaches successfully meet the diverse learning needs of multilingual classrooms?
3. How do students respond to explicit teacher feedback?

In both types of research objectives, the sentences are concise, clear, and focused. The decision to use a thesis statement or research question will depend on what an author is trying to accomplish. Position papers are likely to include thesis statements, as the evidence supporting a particular argument has already been gathered. Research questions are more common in classroom discourse research, as most studies of this type are exploratory and based on data that will be analyzed after such sentences are constructed.

Thesis statements and research questions are important aspects of writing because they provide direction for readers, establish a reference point for assessing the merits of an investigation, and help authors determine what should and should not be included in a report.

8.2.2 Reviewing the literature

A literature review is a critical description of what has and has not been done in your area of investigation. It is important to highlight both what has, and has not, been investigated, as a literature review allows you to establish how your research builds on existing work. However, a literature review is not a list of disparate studies that are relevant to your study. All good literature reviews provide essential background information and weaves together past work into a compelling story. A literature review is a crucial aspect of research writing, as it helps readers understand the larger empirical context from which your study is situated. The following list summarizes these observations:

1. A literature review is not an annotated bibliography.
2. A literature review often includes a discussion of what needs to be done.
3. A literature review synthesizes past work into a coherent story.
4. A literature review guides readers through the strengths of past work.
5. A literature review is a type of persuasive, and not descriptive, writing.

Some questions that can be asked when planning a literature review include:

1. What are the main issues in your area of investigation?
2. What are the main research gaps in your area of investigation?
3. How does your study add to existing work?
4. What are the seminal studies in your area of investigation?
5. Who is conducting cutting-edge research in your area of investigation?
6. What are the main research questions in your area of investigation?
7. What methodological approaches are commonly used (or neglected)?
8. Why is it necessary to continue investigating your area of investigation?
9. What are the conceptual inconsistencies of your area of investigation?
10. What are the different schools of thought in your area of investigation?

Although reviewing past work is a highly variable writing task that changes according to research objectives, it is helpful to explore an example of a less than ideal literature review in order to understand what to avoid. The following example is not a complete literature review, but the writing provides enough information to build on the five characteristics identified in the beginning of this section.

> Kemp (2008) investigates the collaborative practices of students in tertiary education in Hong Kong. Her investigation of 20 first year students demonstrates that collaborative practices are often carried out in online settings.
>
> Collaborative practices are examined by Park and Park (2019). The authors study how primary schools provide opportunities for students to share and debate ideas. Their findings demonstrate that although schools value collaborative learning, classrooms offer few spaces for students to learn from each other.
>
> Jones (2017) explores the ways in which students engage in task-based learning. Several tasks are investigated in this study, including information gap tasks, debating exercises, and collaborative writing. The author establishes important connections between task design characteristics and collaborative practices, such as the relationship between mode of communication and student questions.

This literature review is problematic because no connections are made between the three paragraphs. The writer reviews each study in isolation, leaving it to readers to makes sense of how the studies are relevant to each other. Each review also lacks criticality. For example, the writer is completely descriptive in reviewing the literature, providing no qualitative statements about the value of each study.

The following example of a literature review offers a better example of writing.

> In a seminal investigation of collaborative learning, Kemp (2008) examines how students in tertiary education in Hong Kong provide support for each other while completing group projects. Her investigation is cutting-edge in that it is the first to follow the collaborative practices of students over a three-month period. The findings show that collaborative practices evolve over time and are adopted for specific learning needs. Similarly, in the present study, I seek to understand how collaborative practices develop over a one-year period, thus building on the important work done by Kemp (2008).
>
> Although Park and Park (2019) do not examine university students, their study of collaborative practices in primary schools contributes to the literature by showing how classrooms establish the conditions for such learning to occur. For instance, the spatial arrangement of a classroom is a key factor in how students engage in collaborative learning. Classrooms with a fixed seating arrangement hinder opportunities for collaborative learning, forcing students to engage in individual work. The observations made by Park and Park (2019) are relevant to university learning, as there are little spatial differences between both primary and university classrooms.
>
> In a similar study of how contextual variables can influence classroom discourse, Jones (2017) establishes important connections between task design characteristics and collaborative practices, such as the relationship between mode of communication and student questions. The study fills a gap in the literature by uncovering how specific tasks, such as information-gap activities, debating exercises, and collaborative writing, provide or hinder opportunities to engage in collaborative learning.

This literature review adds to the previous one in a number of ways. First, the writer makes connections between each paragraph. This is done as transition statements, such as the beginning of the sentence "Although Park and Park (2019) do not examine university students." This statement allows the writer to attend to the difference between the previous study and the one being presently reviewed. Although such transition statements are not obligatory, they help readers better understand what has and has not been done in previous work. The writer also relates the literature review to her own research in the final sentence of the first paragraph. Although there is no obvious chronology or logical order, this second literature review begins with a "seminal" (and earlier) study, and then reviews later investigations that build on this work. The second literature review is also critical, moving beyond the descriptive by adding interpretive comments, such as "The study fills a gap in the literature by uncovering how specific tasks." Such statements also help readers establish a better understanding of past studies.

A more in-depth discussion of literature reviews is provided by Randolph (2009).

8.2.3 Explaining your study

Describing the parameters of your study, and the research setting and participants, is a critical aspect of research writing. Often found in a section titled "The study," such descriptions are useful because they help readers do the following:

1. Replicate your investigation.
2. Assess the merits of your study in general, and data analysis in particular.
3. Understand the unique contextual dimensions of your classroom.
4. Appreciate how your study builds on existing research.
5. Understand the procedural challenges of your empirical work.

Addressing this list requires writing about different aspects of your research: theory, methodology, method, classroom, and procedure. The extent to which theory, methodology, method, classroom, and procedure are included in descriptions of a study varies according to what a researcher is attempting to investigate. Furthermore, the order in which theory, methodology, method, classroom, and procedure are discussed is dependent on a researcher's objectives. Nonetheless, it is helpful to unpack what these different levels of writing entail.

1. *Theory*: This entails writing about the theoretical framework that informs how you conduct your study (e.g., post-structuralism) and implement your data analysis (e.g., approaches to identity).
2. *Methodology*: This entails writing about how you analyze your data, and the justifications for doing so in a particular way. For example, are you following traditional conventions or deviating from the norm? CA and DA are examples of methodologies.
3. *Method*: This entails writing about the tools used to conduct your study, such as recording devices, interviews, and field notes, to name a few. Method should not be confused with methodology, which entails how you administered these tools, and the ways in which data were analyzed.
4. *Classroom*: This entails describing the classroom and the research participants. Detailed ethnographic descriptions are typically not needed for most methodologies, but the writing should provide enough information for the reader to understand the unique characteristics of your research setting and participants.
5. *Procedure*: This entails describing how the study was conducted. Example topics that can be discussed include, but are not limited to, how many days were spent conducting your study, why a particular school was selected for investigation, and the challenges faced when collecting data.

162 Understanding and reporting

The following questions offer a way of ensuring that theory, methodology, method, classroom, and procedure are accounted for in your research paper. The questions function as a checklist for devising an outline, but it is always best practice to see what other established scholars do when describing their investigations.

1. What and who am I investigating?
2. What are the characteristics of the classroom?
3. How did I collect and analyze my data?
4. What are the logistical and procedural challenges of my study?
5. How did I plan and carry out my study?

It is important to reflect on audience needs and expectations when describing the parameters of your study, and the research setting and participants. Your research objectives will again determine what to describe and the level of detail provided. The goal of describing your study is to convey enough information to reveal what you are investigating and how you went about doing so (for more detailed information about describing your study, see Wallwork, 2011, p. 217).

8.3 Presenting your data excerpts

A critical part of writing a research paper on classroom discourse is presenting the data excerpts from which your observations and findings are based. A data excerpt is a segment of information taken from a larger recording or record of classroom discourse. For example, imagine that the following data excerpt was taken from a much longer two-hour recording of a lesson.

```
1      Teacher         what does foundational mean?
2                      (1.0)
3                      does anyone know?
4      Student A       does it mean beginning?
```

The observations that would typically follow this excerpt form the data analysis. This task was addressed in Chapters 3–6 using empirical topics commonly examined in CA, DA, CDA, and narrative analysis.

However, data excerpts also need to be presented. Data presentation entails two writing tasks: the information that precedes a data excerpt and the data itself. The information that precedes a data excerpt is needed because all observations of classroom discourse – both spoken and written – must be presented with some context. This is because data excerpts are already taken out of context and presented without all necessary information. Contextual information may include who the interactants are and what they are doing (for a more detailed discussion, see Chapter 7). Note how the contextual information provided in the example in Figure 8.1 frames the data excerpt in a way that allows readers to better understand the discourse and classroom participants.

> In the data excerpt below, the teacher and students have been discussing terminology commonly found in research papers. *The students are all advanced English-language learners and are enrolled in this class because they wish to pursue their university studies further. The classroom participants have established a culture where students feel comfortable nominating themselves as the next speaker, such as in the following example:*
>
> ```
> 1    Teacher        what does foundational mean?
> 2                   (1.0)
> 3    Teacher        does anyone know?
> 4    Student A      does it mean beginning?
> ```

FIGURE 8.1 Presenting context

Second, data presentation entails organizing data excerpts in a way that is legible to readers. For example, it is important to be mindful of how data are presented, as ostensible trivial decisions, such as adopting a particular spacing format or not thinking about this issue at all, will influence how readers process your excerpts. The transcript in Figure 8.2 is presented in two ways to illustrate this point.

The differences between the two examples are small. The top example uses variable-width font (i.e., letters and characters do not occupy the same amount of space) and does not include wide column spaces. The bottom example uses fixed-width font (i.e., letters and characters use the same space) and includes wide column spaces. Despite these small differences, the bottom example is more legible. It is easier to follow the flow of communication, and identify specific aspects of the discourse, when the text is not bunched together with little spacing. That is, the top example is harder to follow, as the line numbers, speaker column, and utterances blend into each other. The use of fixed-width font in the bottom example creates uniformity in the text and looks more professional. Although the two transcripts are based on spoken communication, these observations apply to written discourse.

Approaches to classroom discourse have unique ways of presenting data. For example, the contextual information provided by a critical discourse analyst before a data excerpt will likely be different than what a conversation analyst offers. Similarly, approaches to classroom discourse also have different understandings of how to organize data excerpts. For instance, conversation analysts often have very specific expectations regarding the type of font used in transcripts (i.e., fixed-width or monospaced font), as the micro details of talk and interaction are the focus of investigation and therefore need to be presented systematically and uniformly.

Although much variation exists in data presentation, there are several universal principles and guidelines that can be used to ensure that your data are presented in a convincing and legible way. The first set of principles and guidelines are related to presenting context:

164 Understanding and reporting

---

1 Teacher: what does foundational mean?
2 (1.0)
3 Teacher: does anyone know?
4 Student A: does it mean beginning?

```
1    Teacher      what does foundational mean?
2                 (1.0)
3    Teacher      does anyone know?
4    Student A    does it mean beginning?
```

FIGURE 8.2 Presenting data

1. Data must be presented with contextual information.
2. This contextual information must go before the data.
3. Contextual information should include information to help readers understand the data.
4. Contextual information can be used to divide longer stretches of discourse into smaller data excerpts.
5. Contextual information is sometimes just as important as the data being presented.

For presenting data, readers should be aware of the following principles and guidelines:

1. Data excerpts should be, whenever possible, concise.
2. Data excerpts must be easy to read.
3. Data excerpts are typically presented before an analysis is provided.
4. Data excerpts must be uniformly presented: follow a presentation format or transcription system.
5. Data excerpts should be presented logically or sequentially, using numbers or any other form of identification, including names (e.g., data excerpt 1, 2, and 3).

The type of classroom research discussed in this book is observational, naturalistic, and process-oriented (Lazaraton, 2002). In terms of data presentation, what this means for you is ostensibly simple. The contextual information that accompanies data excerpts must present classroom discourse as a life event and human experience that involves real people and social goals. Simply put, data excerpts must be presented with enough contextual information for readers to understand not just the discursive phenomenon under investigation, but also the classroom and classroom participants. Similarly, the data presented in the form of excerpts must represent classroom discourse, as much as possible, as it was experienced by the teachers and students. What this means in practice is based on the methodology used to analyze classroom discourse (cf. Chapters 3–6).

8.4 Key sections of a research report

The writing process can be broken into many stages of composition, and followed in a linear fashion from pre-writing to drafting. At times during the writing process, however, it is helpful to zoom out and reflect on what shape a research paper will take.

To this end, the following list identifies the key sections of a research report. This list can be used to create an outline of what will be included in your research paper. The list includes sections with traditional names, such as "Introduction" and "Literature review." However, scholars often use different names to be more precise about what is being reported in each section. Like all aspects of writing, what is ultimately included in a research paper should reflect the expectations of your readership. More importantly, the writing must reflect the purpose of each section:

1. *Title*: The purpose of the title is to capture the main theme or idea of your research paper. A good title is descriptive, concise, and includes keywords that signal to the reader the type of study conducted.
2. *Abstract*: The purpose of the abstract is to summarize the main aspects of your study. An abstract is a mini-overview of your research paper. This section often includes your research objective, methodology for data analysis, key findings, and the importance of such analytic observations.
3. *Keywords*: The purpose of keywords is to capture the main aspects of your research paper. Like your title, keywords help potential readers locate your study using search engines or research databases. Keywords should reflect what you studied and how you went about it. Using keywords that are commonly included in recent and popular studies will help readers locate your research paper.
4. *Introduction*: The purpose of this section is to draw readers into your paper by establishing the importance of your study, providing important background information, and identifying the research objectives (see Section 8.2.1).
5. *Literature review*: The purpose of this section is to account for what has and has not been done in your area of investigation (see Section 8.2.2).
6. *The study*: The purpose of this section is to explain how your study was conceptualized and conducted. This section often includes a discussion of the methodology and methods used to collect and analyze data, an account of the classroom and classroom participants, and any information that can be used to replicate or evaluate the merits of your study (see Section 8.2.3).
7. *Data analysis*: The purpose of this section is the report on your findings. This section includes your data excerpts and analytic observations. In qualitative classroom discourse research, the discussion of your findings are often included in this section.

8. *Conclusion*: The purpose of this section is to establish the significance of your study by summarizing your findings, applying such analytic observations to other classroom situations, and identifying opportunities for future research. A good conclusion does not merely repeat the main findings, but rather synthesizes them.
9. *References*: The purpose of this section is to list all of the studies cited in your research paper. Studies read, but not directly quoted or used, are not included (cf. bibliography). Your references should follow a specific style, such as APA or Chicago.
10. *Appendix*: The purpose of this section is to provide readers with materials that help them better understand your study. Such materials may include transcription conventions, interview questions used to collect data, journal entries, or classroom lessons, to name a few.

REFERENCES

Adams, T.E., Jones, S.H., & Ellis, C. (2015). *Autoethnography*. Oxford, UK: Oxford University Press.
Agar, M. (1980). Stories, background knowledge and themes: Problems in the analysis of life history narrative. *American Ethnologist, 7*, 223–239.
Akbari, R. (2007). Reflections on reflection: A critical appraisal of reflective practices in L2 teacher education. *System, 35*, 192–207.
Amin, N. (1997). Race and the identity of the nonnative ESL teacher. *TESOL Quarterly, 31*, 580–583.
Anderson, L. (2006). Analytic autoethnography. *Journal of Contemporary Ethnography, 35*, 373–395.
Andrews, S. (2001). The language awareness of the L2 teacher: Its impact upon pedagogical practice. *Language Awareness, 10*, 75–90.
Antaki, C. (2007). Mental-health practitioners' use of idiomatic expressions in summarising clients' accounts. *Journal of Pragmatics, 39*, 527–541.
Antón, M.M. (1996). Using ethnographic techniques in classroom observation. *Foreign Language Annals, 29*, 551–561.
Appleby, R. (2013). Desire in translation: White masculinity and TESOL. *TESOL Quarterly, 47*, 122–147.
Ashton, J.R. (2016). Keeping up with the class: A critical discourse analysis of teacher interactions in a co-teaching context. *Classroom Discourse, 7*, 1–17.
Atkinson, J.M., & Heritage, J. (1984). *Structures of social action*. Cambridge, UK: Cambridge University Press.
Atkinson, P., Coffey, A., Delamont, S., Lofland, J., & Lofland, L. (2007). *Handbook of ethnography*. London, UK: Sage.
Auerbach, E.R. (1993). Reexamining English only in the ESL classroom. *TESOL Quarterly, 27*, 9–32.
Aukrust, V.G. (2008). Boys' and girls' conversational participation across four grade levels in Norwegian classrooms: Taking the floor or being given the floor? *Gender and Education, 20*, 237–252.
Bailey, K.M. (1991). Diary studies of classroom language learning: The doubting game and the believing game. In E. Sadtono (Ed.), *Language acquisition and the second/foreign language classroom* (pp. 60–102). Singapore: SEAMEO Regional Language Centre.

Baker, P. (2012). Acceptable bias? Using corpus linguistics methods with critical discourse analysis. *Critical Discourse Studies, 9*, 247–256.
Ball, S.J. (2013). *Foucault, power, and education*. London, UK: Routledge.
Bamberg, M., & Georgakopoulou, A. (2008). Small stories as a new perspective in narrative and identity analysis. *Text & Talk, 28*, 377–396.
Barkhuizen, G. (2014). Revisiting narrative frames: An instrument for investigating language teaching and learning. *System, 47*, 12–27.
Barkhuizen, G. (2016). Narrative approaches to exploring language, identity and power in language teacher education. *RELC Journal, 47*, 25–42.
Barkhuizen, G., Benson, P., & Chik, A. (2014). *Narrative inquiry in language teaching and learning research*. London, UK: Routledge.
Barkhuizen, G., & Wette, R. (2008). Narrative frames for investigating the experiences of language teachers. *System, 36*, 372–387.
Barnard, R., & Burns, A. (2012). *Researching language teacher cognition and practice*. Bristol, UK: Multilingual Matters.
Barraja-Rohan, A.M. (2011). Using conversation analysis in the second language classroom to teach interactional competence. *Language Teaching Research, 15*, 479–507.
Bathmaker, A.M., & Harnett, P. (2010). *Exploring learning, identity and power through life history and narrative research*. London, UK: Routledge.
Benson, P. (2014). Narrative inquiry in applied linguistics research. *Annual Review of Applied Linguistics, 34*, 154–170.
Blake, R.J. (2011). Current trends in online language learning. *Annual Review of Applied Linguistics, 31*, 19–35.
Blommaert, J. (2001). Context is/as critique. *Critique of Anthropology, 21*, 13–32.
Blommaert, J. (2005). *Discourse: A critical introduction*. Cambridge, UK: Cambridge University Press.
Borg, S. (1998). Teachers' pedagogical systems and grammar teaching: A qualitative study. *TESOL Quarterly, 32*, 9–38.
Borg, S. (2003). Teacher cognition in language teaching: A review of research on what language teachers think, know, believe, and do. *Language Teaching, 36*, 81–109.
Borg, S. (2006). *Teacher cognition and language education: Research and practice*. London, UK: Continuum.
Boyd, M.P. (2015). Relations between teacher questioning and student talk in one elementary ELL classroom. *Journal of Literacy Research, 47*, 370–404.
Boyer, W. (2010). Empathy development in teacher candidates. *Early Childhood Education Journal, 38*, 313–321.
Brinton, L.J. (1996). *Pragmatic markers in English*. Berlin, Germany: Mouton de Gruyter.
Brinton, L.J. (2017). *The evolution of pragmatic markers in English: Pathways of change*. Cambridge, UK: Cambridge University Press.
Brock, C.A. (1986). The effects of referential questions on ESL classroom discourse. *TESOL Quarterly, 20*, 47–59.
Brooks, C.F. (2016). Role, power, ritual, and resistance: A critical discourse analysis of college classroom talk. *Western Journal of Communication, 80*, 348–369.
Brown, G., & Yule, G. (1983). *Discourse analysis*. Cambridge, UK: Cambridge University Press.
Bucholtz, M. (2000). The politics of transcription. *Journal of Pragmatics, 32*, 1439–1465.
Bucholtz, M. (2007). Variation in transcription. *Discourse Studies, 9*, 784–808.
Bucholtz, M., & Hall, K. (2005). Identity and interaction: A sociocultural linguistic approach. *Discourse Studies, 7*, 585–614.
Canagarajah, A.S. (2012). Teacher development in a global profession: An autoethnography. *TESOL Quarterly, 46*, 258–279.

References

Candela, A. (1999). Students' power in classroom discourse. *Linguistics and Education, 10*, 139–163.

Carbaugh, D. (1989). The critical voice in ethnography of communication research. *Research on Language and Social Interaction, 23*, 261–281.

Carbaugh, D. (2008). Ethnography of communication. In W. Donsbach (Ed.), *The international encyclopedia of communication* (pp. 1592–1598). Malden, MA: Wiley-Blackwell.

Carson, J.G., & Longhini, A. (2002). Focusing on learning styles and strategies: A diary study in an immersion setting. *Language Learning, 52*, 401–438.

Chang, B. (2013). Voice of the voiceless? Multiethnic student voices in critical approaches to race, pedagogy, literacy and agency. *Linguistics and Education, 24*, 348–360.

Chang, H. (2016). *Autoethnography as method*. London, UK: Routledge.

Chao, X., & Kuntz, A. (2013). Church-based ESL program as a figured world: Immigrant adults learners, language, identity, power. *Linguistics and Education, 24*, 466–478.

Charles, Q.D. (2017). *Black teachers in South Korea* (Doctoral dissertation). Philadelphia: University of Pennsylvania.

Chaudron, C., & Richards, J. (1986). The effect of discourse markers on the comprehension of lectures. *Applied Linguistics, 7*, 113–127.

Chomsky, N. (1999). *Profit over people: Neoliberalism and global order*. New York, NY: Seven Stories Press.

Chun, C.W. (2009). Contesting neoliberal discourses in EAP: Critical praxis in an IEP classroom. *Journal of English for Academic Purposes, 8*, 111–120.

Cook, G. (1990). Transcribing infinity: Problems of context presentation. *Journal of Pragmatics, 14*, 1–24.

Copley, K. (2018). Neoliberalism and ELT coursebook content. *Critical Inquiry in Language Studies, 15*, 43–62.

Coulthard, M. (2014). *An introduction to discourse analysis*. London, UK: Routledge.

Cremin, T., Flewitt, R., Mardell, B., & Swann, J. (2016). *Storytelling in early childhood: Enriching language, literacy and classroom culture*. London, UK: Routledge.

Crookes, G.V. (2015). Redrawing the boundaries on theory, research, and practice concerning language teachers' philosophies and language teacher cognition: Toward a critical perspective. *Modern Language Journal, 99*, 485–499.

De Costa, P.I. (2015). *Ethics in applied linguistics research*. London, UK: Routledge.

De Fina, A., & Georgakopoulou, A. (2008). Introduction: Narrative analysis in the shift from texts to practices. *Text & Talk, 28*, 275–281.

De Fina, A., & Georgakopoulou, A. (2019). *The handbook of narrative analysis*. Malden, MA: Wiley-Blackwell.

Denzin, N.K. (1989). *Interpretive interactionism*. London, UK: Sage.

Dewey, J. (1933). *How we think: A restatement of the relation of reflective thinking to the education process*. Lexington, MA: D.C. Heath & Company.

Duranti, A., & Goodwin, C. (1992). *Rethinking context: Language as an interactive phenomenon*. Cambridge, UK: Cambridge University Press.

Edelsky, C. (1981). Who's got the floor? *Language in Society, 10*, 383–421.

Edwards, D., & Mercer, N. (1989). Reconstructing context: The conventionalization of classroom knowledge. *Discourse Processes, 12*, 91–104.

Edwards, J.A., & Lampert, M.D. (2014). *Talking data: Transcription and coding in discourse research*. New York, NY: Psychology Press.

Ellis, D.G. (1999). Research on social interaction and the micro–macro issue. *Research on Language and Social Interaction, 32*, 31–40.

Ellis, R., Basturkmen, H., & Loewen, S. (2002). Doing focus-on-form. *System, 30*, 419–432.

Emerson, R.M., Fretz, R.I., & Shaw, L.L. (2007). Participant observation and fieldnotes. In P. Atkinson, A. Coffey, S. Delamont, J. Lofland, & L. Lofland (Eds.), *Handbook of ethnography* (pp. 352–368). London, UK: Sage.

Emerson, R.M., Fretz, R.I., & Shaw, L.L. (2011). *Writing ethnographic fieldnotes.* Chicago, IL: University of Chicago Press.

Engin, M. (2011). Research diary: A tool for scaffolding. *International Journal of Qualitative Methods, 10,* 296–306.

Erickson, F. (2010). Classroom ethnography. In P. Peterson, E. Baker, & B. McGaw (Eds.), *International encyclopedia of education* (pp. 320–325). Oxford, UK: Elsevier.

Eriksson, P., & Kovalainen, A. (2016). *Qualitative methods in business research.* London, UK: Sage.

Ernst-Slavit, G., & Pratt, K.L. (2017). Teacher questions: Learning the discourse of science in a linguistically diverse elementary classroom. *Linguistics and Education, 40,* 1–10.

Evans-Winters, V.E., & Twyman Hoff, P. (2011). The aesthetics of white racism in pre-service teacher education: A critical race theory perspective. *Race Ethnicity and Education, 14,* 461–479.

Fairclough, N. (2013). *Critical discourse analysis: The critical study of language.* London, UK: Routledge.

Farrell, T. (2003). Reflective practice: The principles and practices. *English Teaching Forum, 41,* 14–21. Retrieved from https://americanenglish.state.gov/resources/english-teaching-forum-2003-volume-41-number-4.

Farrell, T., & Mom, V. (2015). Exploring teacher questions through reflective practice. *Reflective Practice, 16,* 849–865.

Fife, W. (2005). *Doing fieldwork: Ethnographic methods for research in developing countries and beyond.* Basingstoke, UK: Palgrave Macmillan.

Fitch, F., & Morgan, S.E. (2003). "Not a lick of English": Constructing the ITA identity through student narratives. *Communication Education, 52,* 297–310.

Foster, P., & Ohta, A.S. (2005). Negotiation for meaning and peer assistance in second language classrooms. *Applied linguistics, 26,* 402–430.

Foucault, M. (1984). *The Foucault reader.* New York, NY: Pantheon.

Fung, L., & Carter, R. (2007). Discourse markers and spoken English: Native and learner use in pedagogic settings. *Applied Linguistics, 28,* 410–439.

Garton, S. (2012). Speaking out of turn? Taking the initiative in teacher-fronted classroom interaction. *Classroom Discourse, 3,* 29–45.

Gee, J.P. (2014). *How to do discourse analysis: A toolkit.* London, UK: Routledge.

Geertz, C. (1973). *The interpretation of cultures: Selected essays.* New York, NY: Basic Books.

Gilbert, R. (1992). Text and context in qualitative educational research: Discourse analysis and the problem of contextual explanation. *Linguistics and Education, 4,* 37–57.

Godley, A.J., & Loretto, A. (2013). Fostering counter-narratives of race, language, and identity in an urban English classroom. *Linguistics and Education, 24,* 316–327.

Graham, S., & Sandmel, K. (2011). The process writing approach: A meta-analysis. *Journal of Educational Research, 104,* 396–407.

Gray, J. (2010). *The construction of English: Culture, consumerism and promotion in the ELT global coursebook.* Basingstoke, UK: Palgrave Macmillan.

Gray, J. (2010). The branding of English and the culture of the new capitalism: Representations of the world of work in English language textbooks. *Applied Linguistics, 31,* 714–733.

Gumperz, J., & Hymes, D. (1964). The ethnography of communication. *American Anthropologist, 66,* part 2.

Hafner, C.A., & Candlin, C.N. (2007). Corpus tools as an affordance to learning in professional legal education. *Journal of English for Academic Purposes, 6,* 303–318.

Hall, J.K. (2007). Redressing the roles of correction and repair in research on second and foreign language learning. *Modern Language Journal, 91*, 511–526.
Hall, J.K. (2018). From L2 interactional competence to L2 interactional repertoires: Reconceptualising the objects of L2 learning. *Classroom Discourse, 9*, 25–39.
Hall, J.K., Hellermann, J., & Pekarek Doehler, S. (2011). *L2 interactional competence and development*. Bristol, UK: Multilingual Matters.
Halliday, M.A.K. (1961). Categories of the theory of grammar. In G.R. Kress (Ed.), *Halliday: System and function in language* (pp. 52–72). Oxford, UK: Oxford University Press.
Hammersley, M., & Traianou, A. (2012). *Ethics in qualitative research*. London, UK: Sage.
Haney López, I.F. (1994). The social construction of race: Some observations on illusion, fabrication, and choice. *Harvard Civil Rights–Civil Liberties Law Review, 29*, 1–62.
Hart, C. (2011). *Critical discourse studies in context and cognition*. Amsterdam, the Netherlands: John Benjamins.
Harvey, D. (2005). *The new imperialism*. Oxford, UK: Oxford University Press.
Heigham, J., & Croker, R.A. (2009). *Qualitative research in applied linguistics: A practical introduction*. Basingstoke, UK: Palgrave Macmillan.
Hellermann, J. (2003). The interactive work of prosody in the IRF exchange: Teacher repetition in feedback moves. *Language in Society, 32*, 79–104.
Hellermann, J., & Vergun, A. (2007). Language which is not taught: The discourse marker use of beginning adult learners of English. *Journal of Pragmatics, 39*, 157–179.
Helm, F. (2009). Language and culture in an online context: What can learner diaries tell us about intercultural competence? *Language and Intercultural Communication, 9*, 91–104.
Hepburn, A., & Bolden, G.B. (2013). The conversation analytic approach to transcription. In J. Sidnell & T. Stivers (Eds.), *The handbook of conversation analysis* (pp. 57–76). Malden, MA: Wiley-Blackwell.
Hilliard, L.J., & Liben, L.S. (2010). Differing levels of gender salience in preschool classrooms: Effects on children's gender attitudes and intergroup bias. *Child Development, 81*, 1787–1798.
Hirano, E. (2008). Learning difficulty and learner identity: A symbiotic relationship. *ELT Journal, 63*, 33–41.
Hobbs, V. (2007). Faking it or hating it: Can reflective practice be forced? *Reflective Practice, 8*, 405–417.
Holborow, M. (2007). Language, ideology and neoliberalism. *Journal of Language and Politics, 6*, 51–73.
Holstein, J.A., & Gubrium, J.F. (2012). *Varieties of narrative analysis*. London, UK: Sage.
Hopkins, D. (2014). *A teacher's guide to classroom research*. Berkshire, UK: McGraw-Hill.
Hu, G., & Duan, Y. (2019). Questioning and responding in the classroom: A cross-disciplinary study of the effects of instructional mediums in academic subjects at a Chinese university. *International Journal of Bilingual Education and Bilingualism, 22*, 303–321.
Hutchby, I., & Wooffitt, R. (2008). *Conversation analysis*. Cambridge, UK: Polity.
Hyland, K., & Paltridge, B. (2011). *Continuum companion to discourse analysis*. London, UK: Continuum.
Hymes, D. (1962). The ethnography of speaking. In T. Gladwin & W. Sturtevant (Eds.), *Anthropology and human behavior* (pp. 15–53). Washington, DC: Anthropological Society of Washington.
Hymes, D. (1964). *Language in culture and society: A reader in linguistics and anthropology*. New York, NY: Harper & Row.
Hymes, D. (2005). Models of interaction of language and social life: Toward a descriptive theory. In S.F. Kiesling & C.B. Paulston (Eds.), *Intercultural discourse and communication* (pp. 4–16). Malden, MA: Wiley-Blackwell.

Hyon, S., & Sulzby, E. (1994). African American kindergartners' spoken narratives: Topic associating and topic centered styles. *Linguistics and Education, 6,* 121–152.

Janks, H. (1997). Critical discourse analysis as a research tool. *Discourse: Studies in the Cultural Politics of Education, 18,* 329–342.

Jaworski, A., & Coupland, N. (2006). *The discourse reader.* London, UK: Routledge.

Jenks, C.J. (2007). Floor management in task-based interaction: The interactional role of participatory structures. *System, 35,* 609–622.

Jenks, C.J. (2011). *Transcribing talk and interaction.* Amsterdam, the Netherlands: John Benjamins.

Jenks, C.J. (2013a). Working with transcripts: An abridged review of issues in transcription. *Language and Linguistic Compass, 7,* 251–261.

Jenks, C.J. (2013b). "Your pronunciation and your accent is very excellent": Orientations of identity during compliment sequences in English as a lingua franca encounters. *Language and Intercultural Communication, 13,* 165–181.

Jenks, C.J. (2014). *Social interaction in second language chat rooms.* Edinburgh, UK: Edinburgh University Press.

Jenks, C.J. (2017a). *Race and ethnicity in English language teaching: Korea in focus.* Bristol, UK: Multilingual Matters.

Jenks, C.J. (2017b). The semiotics of learning Korean at home: An ecological autoethnographic perspective. *International Journal of Bilingual Education and Bilingualism, 20,* 688–703.

Jenks, C.J. (2018). English for sale: Using race to create value in the Korean ELT market. *Applied Linguistics Review, 10,* 517–538.

Jenks, C.J., & Lee, J.W. (2016). Heteroglossic ideologies in world Englishes: An examination of the Hong Kong context. *International Journal of Applied Linguistics, 26,* 384–402.

Johnson, K.E. (2015). Reclaiming the relevance of L2 teacher education. *Modern Language Journal, 99,* 515–528.

Johnson, K.E., & Golombek, P.R. (2002). *Teachers' narrative inquiry as professional development.* Cambridge, UK: Cambridge University Press.

Johnson, K.E., & Golombek, P.R. (2011). The transformative power of narrative in second language teacher education. *TESOL Quarterly, 45,* 486–509.

Jones, R.H. (2011). Data collection and transcription in discourse analysis. In K. Hyland & B. Paltridge (Eds.), *Continuum companion to discourse analysis* (pp. 9–21). London, UK: Continuum.

Jones, R.H. (2012). *Discourse analysis: A resource book for students.* London, UK: Routledge

Jones, R.H., & Thornborrow, J. (2004). Floors, talk and the organization of classroom activities. *Language in Society, 33,* 399–423.

Jung, D., & Himmelmann, N.P. (2011). Retelling data: Working on transcription. In G. Haig, N. Nau, S. Schnell, & C. Wegener (Eds.), *Documenting endangered languages: Achievements and perspectives* (pp. 201–220). Berlin, Germany: Mouton de Gruyter.

Käänta, L. (2010). *Teacher turn-allocation and repair practices in classroom interaction: A multisemiotic perspective.* Jyväskylä, Finland: Jyväskylä Studies in Humanities.

Kasper, G. (2009). Categories, context, and comparison in conversation analysis. In H. Nguyen & G. Kasper (Eds.), *Talk-in-interaction: Multilingual perspectives* (pp. 1–28). Honolulu, HI: National Foreign Language Resource Center.

Keddie, A. (2016). Children of the market: Performativity, neoliberal responsibilisation and the construction of student identities. *Oxford Review of Education, 42,* 108–122.

Kennison, M.M., & Misselwitz, S. (2002). Evaluating reflective writing for appropriateness, fairness, and consistency. *Nursing Education Perspectives, 23*(5), 238–242.

Koole, T. (2007). Parallel activities in the classroom. *Language and Education, 21,* 487–501.

Koshik, I. (2002). Designedly incomplete utterances: A pedagogical practice for eliciting knowledge displays in error correction sequences. *Research on Language and Social interaction, 35,* 277–309.

Koshik, I. (2005). Alternative questions used in conversational repair. *Discourse Studies, 7,* 193–211.

Kramsch, C. (1986). From language proficiency to interactional competence. *Modern Language Journal, 70,* 366–372.

Kroskrity, P.V. (2010). Language ideologies: Evolving perspectives. In J. Jaspers, J. Östman, & J. Verschueren (Eds.), *Society and Language Use* (pp. 192–211). Amsterdam, the Netherlands: John Benjamins.

Kroskrity, P.V. (2015). Language ideologies: Emergence, elaboration, and application. In N. Bonvillain (Ed.), *The Routledge handbook of linguistic anthropology* (pp. 95–108). London, UK: Routledge.

Kubanyiova, M., & Feryok, A. (2015). Language teacher cognition in applied linguistics research: Revisiting the territory, redrawing the boundaries, reclaiming the relevance. *Modern Language Journal, 99,* 435–449.

Kubota, R., & Lin, A. (2006). Race and TESOL: Introduction to concepts and theories. *TESOL Quarterly, 40,* 471–493.

Kumaravadivelu, B. (1999). Critical classroom discourse analysis. *TESOL Quarterly, 33,* 453–484.

Lamy, M.N. (2012). Click if you want to speak: Reframing CA for research into multi-modal conversations in online learning. *International Journal of Virtual and Personal Learning Environments, 3,* 1–18.

Lazaraton, A. (2002). Quantitative and qualitative approaches to discourse analysis. *Annual Review of Applied Linguistics, 22,* 32–51.

Lee, J.W., & Jenks, C.J. (2016). Doing translingual dispositions. *College Composition and Communication, 68,* 317–344.

Lee, J.W., & Jenks, C.J. (2018). Aestheticizing language: Metapragmatic distance and unequal Englishes in Hong Kong. *Asian Englishes, 21,* 128–141.

Lee, L. (2008). Focus-on-form through collaborative scaffolding in expert-to-novice online interaction. *Language Learning & Technology, 12,* 53–72.

Lee, Y. (2007). Third turn position in teacher talk: Contingency and the work of teaching. *Journal of Pragmatics, 39,* 180–206.

Lee, Y. (2008). Yes–no questions in the third-turn position: Pedagogical discourse processes. *Discourse Processes, 45,* 237–262.

Leeds-Hurwitz, W. (2015). Thick description. In K. Tracy (Ed.), *The international encyclopedia of language and social interaction* (pp. 1–5). Malden, MA: Wiley-Blackwell.

Lerner, G.H. (1995). Turn design and the organization of participation in instructional activities. *Discourse Processes, 19,* 111–131.

Lester, J.D., & Lester, J.D. (2015). *Writing research papers: A complete guide.* Essex, UK: Pearson.

Levy, M. (2015). The role of qualitative approaches to research in CALL contexts: Closing in on the learner's experience. *CALICO Journal, 32,* 554–568.

Lewontin, R.C. (1972). The apportionment of human diversity. *Evolutionary Biology,* 381–398.

Li, L., & Walsh, S. (2011). "Seeing is believing": Looking at EFL teachers – beliefs through classroom interaction. *Classroom Discourse, 2,* 39–57.

Liebscher, G., & Dailey-O'Cain, J. (2003). Conversational repair as a role-defining mechanism in classroom interaction. *Modern Language Journal, 87,* 375–390.

Liggett, T. (2014). The mapping of a framework: Critical race theory and TESOL. *Urban Review, 46,* 112–124.

Loughran, J.J. (2002). Effective reflective practice: In search of meaning in learning about teaching. *Journal of Teacher Education, 53,* 33–43.

Luke, A. (2002). Beyond ideology critique: Critical discourse analysis. *Annual Review of Applied Linguistics, 22,* 96–110.

Lyster, R., & Saito, K. (2010). Oral feedback in classroom SLA: A meta-analysis. *Studies in Second Language Acquisition, 32,* 265–302.

Macbeth, D. (2004). The relevance of repair for classroom correction. *Language in Society, 33,* 703–736.

Maitlis, S. (2012). Narrative analysis. In G. Symon & C. Cassell (Eds.), *Qualitative organizational research: Core methods and current challenges* (pp. 492–511). London, UK: Sage.

Makalela, L. (2014). Fluid identity construction in language contact zones: Metacognitive reflections on Kasi-taal languaging practices. *International Journal of Bilingual Education and Bilingualism, 17,* 668–682.

Mandelbaum, J. (1990). Beyond mundane reason: Conversation analysis and context. *Research on Language and Social Interaction, 24,* 333–350.

Manke, M.P. (1997). *Classroom power relations: Understanding student-teacher interaction.* Mahwah, NJ: Lawrence Erlbaum Associates.

Markee, N. (2000). *Conversation analysis.* New York, NY: Routledge.

Markee, N. (2008). Toward a learning behavior tracking methodology for CA-for-SLA. *Applied Linguistics, 29,* 404–427.

Markee, N. (2015). *The handbook of classroom discourse and interaction.* Malden, MA: Wiley-Blackwell.

Marti, L. (2012). Tangential floor in a classroom setting. *System, 40,* 398–406.

Martin-Jones, M., & Saxena, M. (1996). Turn-taking, power asymmetries, and the positioning of bilingual participants in classroom discourse. *Linguistics and Education, 8,* 105–123.

Martínez-Roldán, C.M. (2005). Examining bilingual children's gender ideologies through critical discourse analysis. *Critical Inquiry in Language Studies, 2,* 157–178.

Martínez-Roldán, C.M., & Malavé, G. (2004). Language ideologies mediating literacy and identity in bilingual contexts. *Journal of Early Childhood Literacy, 4,* 155–180.

Mayo, P. (2015). *Hegemony and education under neoliberalism: Insights from Gramsci.* London, UK: Routledge.

Mazak, C.M., & Herbas-Donoso, C. (2014). Translanguaging practices and language ideologies in Puerto Rican university science education. *Critical Inquiry in Language Studies, 11,* 27–49.

McAllister, G., & Irvine, J.J. (2002). The role of empathy in teaching culturally diverse students: A qualitative study of teachers' beliefs. *Journal of Teacher Education, 53,* 433–443.

McCarthy, M. (1991). *Discourse analysis for language teachers.* Cambridge, UK: Cambridge University Press.

McIlveen, P. (2008). Autoethnography as a method for reflexive research and practice in vocational psychology. *Australian Journal of Career Development, 17,* 13–20.

McHoul, A.W. (1990). The organization of repair in classroom talk. *Language in Society, 19,* 349–377.

McNamara, T. (2012). Poststructuralism and its challenges for applied linguistics. *Applied Linguistics, 33,* 473–482.

Mehan, H. (1979). *Learning lessons: Social organization in the classroom.* Cambridge, MA: Harvard University Press.

Menard-Warwick, J. (2008). "Because she made beds. Every day": Social positioning, classroom discourse, and language learning. *Applied Linguistics, 29,* 267–289.

Meyer, M. (2001). Between theory, method, and politics: Positioning of the approaches to CDA. In R. Wodak & M. Meyer (Eds.), *Methods of critical discourse analysis* (pp. 14–31). London, UK: Sage.

Meyerhoff, M. (2015). *Introducing sociolinguistics.* London, UK: Routledge.

References 175

Meyerhoff, M., Schleef, E., & MacKenzie, L. (2015). *Doing sociolinguistics: A practical guide to data collection and analysis.* London, UK: Routledge.

Miao, P., & Heining-Boynton, A.L. (2011). Initiation/response/follow-up, and response to intervention: Combining two models to improve teacher and student performance. *Foreign Language Annals, 44,* 65–79.

Miller, A. (2009). Pragmatic radicalism: An autoethnographic perspective on pre-service teaching. *Teaching and Teacher Education, 25,* 909–916.

Mondada, L. (2013). The conversation analytic approach to data collection. In J. Sidnell & T. Stivers (Eds.), *The handbook of conversation analysis* (pp. 32–56). Malden, MA: Wiley-Blackwell

Moodie, I., & Feryok, A. (2015). Beyond cognition to commitment: English language teaching in South Korean primary schools. *Modern Language Journal, 99,* 450–469.

Mori, J. (2002). Task design, plan, and development of talk-in-interaction: An analysis of a small group activity in a Japanese language classroom. *Applied Linguistics, 23,* 323–347.

Mortensen, K., & Hazel, S. (2011). Initiating round robins in the L2 classroom: Preliminary observations. *Novitas-Royal (Research on Youth and Language), 5,* 55–70.

Müller, S. (2005). *Discourse markers in native and non-native English discourse.* Amsterdam, the Netherlands: John Benjamins.

Nakayama, T.K., & Krizek, R.L. (1995). Whiteness: A strategic rhetoric. *Quarterly Journal of Speech, 81,* 291–309

Nassaji, H., & Wells, G. (2000). What's the use of "triadic dialogue"?: An investigation of teacher-student interaction. *Applied Linguistics, 2,* 376–406.

Nofsinger, R.E. (1975). The demand ticket: A conversational device forgetting the floor. *Communications Monographs, 42,* 1–9.

Norrick, N.R. (2000). *Conversational narrative: Storytelling in everyday talk.* Amsterdam, the Netherlands: John Benjamins.

Norton, B., & Early, M. (2011). Research identity, narrative inquiry, and language teaching research. *TESOL Quarterly, 45,* 415–439.

Nunn, R. (1999). The purposes of language teachers' questions. *International Review of Applied Linguistics in Language Teaching, 37,* 23–42.

O'Halloran, K.L. (2004). *Multimodal discourse analysis: Systemic-functional perspectives.* London, UK: Continuum.

Orelus, P.W. (2016). *Language, race, and power in schools: A critical discourse analysis.* London, UK: Routledge.

Pavlenko, A. (2007). Autobiographic narratives as data in applied linguistics. *Applied Linguistics, 28,* 163–188.

Pekarek Doehler, S., & Berger, E. (2016). L2 interactional competence as increased ability for context-sensitive conduct: A longitudinal study of story-openings. *Applied Linguistics, 39,* 555–578.

Phillipson, R. (2009). *Linguistic imperialism continued.* London, UK: Routledge.

Pike, K. (1967). *Language in relation to a unified theory of the structure of human behavior.* The Hague, the Netherlands: Mouton de Gruyter.

Polat, B. (2011). Investigating acquisition of discourse markers through a developmental learner corpus. *Journal of Pragmatics, 43,* 3745–3756.

Pole, C., & Hillyard, S. (2016). *Doing fieldwork.* London, UK: Sage.

Pomerantz, A., & Bell, N.D. (2011). Humor as safe house in the foreign language classroom. *Modern Language Journal, 95,* 148–161.

Ponterotto, J.G. (2006). Brief note on the origins, evolution, and meaning of the qualitative research concept thick description. *Qualitative Report, 11,* 538–549.

Pryde, M. (2014). Conversational patterns of homestay hosts and study abroad students. *Foreign Language Annals, 47*, 487–506.

Psathas, G. (1995). *Conversation analysis*. Thousand Oaks, CA: Sage.

Pun, J., & Macaro, E. (2019). The effect of first and second language use on question types in English medium instruction science classrooms in Hong Kong. *International Journal of Bilingual Education and Bilingualism, 22*, 64–77.

Rampton, B., Roberts, C., Leung, C., & Harris, R. (2002). Methodology in the analysis of classroom discourse. *Applied Linguistics, 23*, 373–392.

Randolph, J. (2009). A guide to writing the dissertation literature review. *Practical Assessment, Research, and Evaluation, 14*(1), 13.

Rapley, T. (2008). *Doing conversation, discourse and document analysis*. London, UK: Sage.

Raschka, C., Sercombe, P., & Chi-Ling, H. (2009). Conflicts and tensions in codeswitching in a Taiwanese EFL classroom. *International Journal of Bilingual Education and Bilingualism, 12*, 157–171.

Rau, A., Elliker, F., & Coetzee, J. (2018). Collecting data for analyzing discourses. In U. Flick (Ed.), *The Sage handbook of qualitative data collection* (pp. 300–313). London, UK: Sage.

Richards, K. (2006). "Being the teacher": Identity and classroom conversation. *Applied Linguistics, 27*, 51–77.

Rojas-Sosa, D. (2016). The denial of racism in Latina/o students' narratives about discrimination in the classroom. *Discourse & Society, 27*, 69–94.

Ryle, G. (2009). Collected essays 1929–1968 (Vol. 2). London: Routledge.

Rymes, B. (2015). *Classroom discourse analysis: A tool for critical reflection*. London, UK: Routledge.

Sacks, H., Schegloff, E.A., & Jefferson, G. (1974). A simplest systematics for the organization of turn-taking for conversation. *Language, 50*, 696–735.

Sagor, R. (1992). *How to conduct collaborative action research*. Alexandria, VA: Association for Supervision and Curriculum Development.

Saville-Troike, M. (2003). *The ethnography of communication: An introduction*. Malden, MA: Wiley-Blackwell.

Sayer, P., Martínez-Prieto, D., & Carvajal de la Cruz, B. (2019). Discourses of white nationalism and xenophobia in the United States and their effect on TESOL Professionals in Mexico. *TESOL Quarterly, 53*, 835–844.

Schegloff, E.A. (2007). *Sequence organization in interaction*. Cambridge, UK: Cambridge University Press.

Schegloff, E.A., Jefferson, G., & Sacks, H. (1977). The preference for self-correction in the organization of repair in conversation. *Language, 53*, 361–382.

Schiffrin, D. (1987). *Discourse markers*. Cambridge, UK: Cambridge University Press.

Schmidt, R., & Frota, S. (1986). Developing basic conversational ability in a second language: A case study of an adult learner of Portuguese. In R.R. Day (Ed.), *Talking to learn* (pp. 237–326). Rowley, MA: Newbury House.

Schumann, F.E., & Schumann, J.H. (1977). Diary of a language learner: An introspective study of second language learning. In H.D. Brown, R.H. Crymes, & C.A. Yorio (Eds.), *On TESOL '77: Teaching and learning English as a second language: Trends in research and practice* (pp. 241–249). Washington, DC: TESOL.

Seedhouse, P. (1996). Classroom interaction: possibilities and impossibilities. *ELT Journal, 50*, 16–24.

Seedhouse, P. (1999). Task-based interaction. *ELT Journal, 53*, 149–156.

Seedhouse, P. (2004). *The interactional architecture of the language classroom: A conversation analysis perspective*. Malden, MA: Wiley-Blackwell.

Seedhouse, P. (2007). On ethnomethodological CA and "linguistic CA": A reply to Hall. *Modern Language Journal, 91*, 527–533.

References

Sert, O. (2015). *Social interaction and L2 classroom discourse*. Edinburgh, UK: Edinburgh University Press.
Shelley, M., Murphy, L., & White, C. (2013). Language teacher development in a narrative frame: The transition from classroom to distance and blended settings. *System, 41,* 560–574.
Shepherd, M.A. (2014). The discursive construction of knowledge and equity in classroom interactions. *Linguistics and Education, 28,* 79–91.
Shin, H. (2015). Everyday racism in Canadian schools: Ideologies of language and culture among Korean transnational students in Toronto. *Journal of Multilingual and Multicultural Development, 36,* 67–79.
Sidnell, J., & Stivers, T. (2013). *The handbook of conversation analysis*. Malden, MA: Wiley-Blackwell.
Silverstein, M., & Urban, G. (1996). *Natural histories of discourse*. Chicago, IL: University of Chicago Press.
Simpson, J. (2005). Conversational floors in synchronous text-based CMC discourse. *Discourse Studies, 7,* 337–361.
Sinclair, J., & Coulthard, M. (1975). *Towards an analysis of discourse*. Oxford, UK: Oxford University Press.
Smith, B. (2008). Methodological hurdles in capturing CMC data: The case of the missing self-repair. *Language Learning & Technology, 12,* 85–103.
Smith, B. (2012). Eye tracking as a measure of noticing: A study of explicit recasts in SCMC. *Language Learning & Technology, 16,* 53–81.
Spencer, S. (2006). *Race and ethnicity: Culture, identity and representation*. London, UK: Routledge.
Stoddart, M.C.J. (2007). Ideology, hegemony, discourse: A critical review of theories of knowledge and power. *Social Thought & Research, 28,* 191–225.
Stryker, S., & Serpe, R.T. (1994). Identity salience and psychological centrality: Equivalent, overlapping, or complementary concepts? *Social Psychology Quarterly, 57,* 16–35.
Subtirelu, N.C. (2015). "She does have an accent but …": Race and language ideology in students' evaluations of mathematics instructors on RateMyProfessors.com. *Language in Society, 44,* 35–62.
Talib, N., & Fitzgerald, R. (2016). Micro–meso–macro movements: A multi-level critical discourse analysis framework to examine metaphors and the value of truth in policy texts. *Critical Discourse Studies, 13,* 531–547.
Tannen, D., Hamilton, H.E., & Schiffrin, D. (2015). *The handbook of discourse analysis*. Malden, MA: John Wiley & Sons.
Taylor, L. (2006). Wrestling with race: The implications of integrative antiracism education for immigrant ESL youth. *TESOL Quarterly, 40,* 519–544.
Taylor, S. (2010). *Narratives of identity and place*. London, UK: Routledge.
Theodórsdóttir, G. (2018). L2 teaching in the wild: A closer look at correction and explanation practices in everyday L2 interaction. *Modern Language Journal, 102,* 30–45.
Toohey, K. (2008). Ethnography and language education. In K.A. King & H. Hornberger (Eds.), *Encyclopedia of language and education* (pp. 177–187). New York, NY: Springer.
Tsui, A.B.M. (2007). Complexities of identity formation: A narrative inquiry of an EFL teacher. *TESOL Quarterly, 41,* 657–680.
Üstünel, E., & Seedhouse, P. (2005). Why that, in that language, right now? Code-switching and pedagogical focus. *International Journal of Applied Linguistics, 15,* 302–325.
van Dijk, T.A. (1993). Principles of critical discourse analysis. *Discourse & Society, 4,* 249–283.

Varonis, E.M., & Gass, S. (1985). Non-native/non-native conversations: A model for negotiation of meaning. *Applied linguistics*, *6*, 71–90.
Vasquez, V.M. (2014). *Negotiating critical literacies with young children*. London, UK: Routledge.
Wallwork, A. (2011). *English for writing research papers*. New York, NY: Springer.
Walsh, S. (2006a). *Investigating classroom discourse*. London, UK: Routledge.
Walsh, S. (2006b). Talking the talk of the TESOL classroom. *ELT Journal*, *60*, 133–141.
Walsh, S. (2011). *Exploring classroom discourse: Language in action*. London, UK: Routledge.
Walsh, S. (2012). Conceptualising classroom interactional competence. *Novitas-ROYAL (Research on Youth and Language)*, *6*, 1–14.
Walsh, S., & Mann, S. (2015). Doing reflective practice: A data-led way forward. *ELT Journal*, *69*, 351–362.
Wannagat, U. (2007). Learning through L2: Content and language integrated learning (CLIL) and English as medium of instruction (EMI). *International Journal of Bilingual Education and Bilingualism*, *10*, 663–682.
Waring, H.Z. (2009). Moving out of IRF (initiation–response–feedback): A single case analysis. *Language Learning*, *59*, 796–824.
Waring, H.Z. (2011). Learner initiative and learning opportunities in the language classrooms. *Classroom Discourse*, *2*, 201–218.
Warren, J.T. (2001). Doing whiteness: On the performative dimensions of race in the classroom. *Communication Education*, *50*, 91–108.
Warriner, D.S. (2016). "Here, without English, you are dead": Ideologies of language and discourses of neoliberalism in adult English language learning. *Journal of Multilingual and Multicultural Development*, *37*, 495–508.
Watson, C. (2006). Narratives of practice and the construction of identity in teaching. *Teachers and Teaching: Theory and Practice*, *12*, 509–526.
Watson-Gegeo, K.A. (1988). Ethnography in ESL: Defining the essentials. *TESOL Quarterly*, *22*, 575–592.
Watson-Gegeo K.A. (1997). Classroom ethnography. In N.H. Hornberger & D. Corson (Eds.), *Encyclopedia of language and education* (pp. 135–144). New York, NY: Springer.
Wei, L. (2011). Moment analysis and translanguaging space: Discourse construction of identities by multilingual Chinese youth in Britain. *Journal of Pragmatics*, *43*, 1222–1235.
Wells, G. (1993). Reevaluating the IRF sequence: A proposal for the articulation of theories of activity and discourse for the analysis of teaching and learning in the classroom. *Linguistics and Education*, *5*, 1–37.
Wetherell, M., Taylor, S., & Yates, S.J. (2001). *Discourse as data: A guide for analysis*. London, UK: Sage.
Wiggins, S. (2016). *Discursive psychology: Theory, method and applications*. London, UK: Sage.
Wiley, T.G., & Lukes, M. (1996). English-only and standard English ideologies in the US. *TESOL Quarterly*, *30*, 511–535.
Wilkins, A. (2012). Push and pull in the classroom: Competition, gender and the neoliberal subject. *Gender and Education*, *24*, 765–781.
Wodak, R., & Meyer, M. (2015). *Methods of critical discourse studies*. London, UK: Sage.
Wong, J., & Waring, H.Z. (2010). *Conversation analysis and second language pedagogy: A guide for ESL/EFL teachers*. New York, NY: Routledge.
Woods, P. (2005). *Inside schools: Ethnography in educational research*. London, UK: Routledge.
Wooffitt, R. (2005). *Conversation analysis and discourse analysis*. London, UK: Sage.
Young, R.F. (2008). *Language and interaction: An advanced resource book*. New York, NY: Routledge.

Zembylas, M. (2005). Beyond teacher cognition and teacher beliefs: The value of the ethnography of emotions in teaching. *International Journal of Qualitative Studies in Education*, *18*, 465–487.

Zemel, A., & Koschmann, T. (2011). Pursuing a question: Reinitiating IRE sequences as a method of instruction. *Journal of Pragmatics*, *43*, 475–488.

Ziegler, G., Sert, O., & Durus, N. (2012). Student-initiated use of multilingual resources in English-language classroom interaction: Next-turn management. *Classroom Discourse*, *3*, 187–204.

INDEX

Page numbers in *italics* refer to illustrations and those in **bold** refer to tables.

access (of researcher) 21–22
access (to information and knowledge), and power 91
action research 17
activism, in critical discourse analysis 108
Adams, T.E. 149
Akbari, R. 123, **124**
Amin, N. 103
Anderson, L. 150
anonymization 37–38, 39
anthropology 137
Antón, M.M. **136**
archiving 33
artifacts, in ethnography 152
Ashton, J.R. **94**
Atkinson, J.M. 41
Atkinson, P. **136**, 152
Auerbach, E.R. **12**
Aukrust, V.G. 73
autoethnography 115, 149–151; *see also* diaries and journals

backing-up data 33
Bailey, K.M. 125
Bamberg, M. 113, **129**, 131
Barkhuizen, G. **111**, 112, 115, **129**, 130
Barnard, R. **120**
Barraja-Rohan, A.M. **60**
Bathmaker, A.M. **116**
Benson, P. **111**, 112
bias, in ethnography 152

bilingual classrooms **11**, **12**, **80**, **94**, **98**
bookmarking data 33
Borg, S. 115, 117, **120**
Boyd, M.P. 77, **80**
Brinton, L.J. 81
Brooks, C.F. **94**
Brown, G. **66**, 67
Bucholtz, M. 34, 38

Candela, A. **94**
Carbaugh, D. 146
Carson, J.G. **128**
Cazden, C. 86
Chang, B. **105**
Chang, H. 151
Chao, X. **8**
Chaudron, C. **84**
Chun, C.W. **7**, 99, **102**
classroom discourse analysis *see* discourse analysis (DA)/classroom discourse analysis
classroom materials, as data 32
classroom (setting): access 21–22; defining, and research planning 5–9, *6*; *see also* nontraditional classroom settings; traditional classroom settings
competence: communicative competence 147, 152; interactional competence 57–59, **60**
consent 25
context: in conversation analysis **61**, 64, 139; in critical discourse analysis 106,

107, 139; in data presentation 162, 163–164, *163*; in discourse analysis 85, 86, 139; in ethnography 138–140, 146; methodological issues (overview) **15**, 16; in narrative analysis **129**, 139; recording contextual information 32, 142–144, *143*, 151

conversation analysis (CA) 45–64; context **61**, 64, 139; data analysis **61**; data collection 60–62, **61**; data presentation **61**; vs. discourse analysis 65, 68; and discourse structure analysis 13; interactional competence 57–59, **60**; introduction to 45–46, **46**; key scholars 63; key terms and constructs 64; methodological issues 59–63, **61**; pauses 48–49, 53; repairs 55–57, **57**, 58; research questions 48–49; transition relevance places (TRPs) 53–54; turn constructional units (TCUs) 52–54; turn shape and placement 52–54, **54**; turn-taking *see* turn-taking

Cook, G. 40, 139
Copley, K. 99, **102**
corrections vs. repairs 55, 56–57, **57**
Coulthard, M. 9, 86

critical discourse analysis (CDA) 88–109; context 106, **107**, 139; data analysis 106, **107**, 139; data collection 96, 100, 103, **107**; data presentation 106, **107**; defined 89–90; introduction to 88–89, **89**; key scholars 108; keywords 101, 104; language ideologies **12**, 94–97, **98**; methodological issues 105–108, **107**; neoliberalism **12**, 88, 97–101, **98**, **109**; power **12**, 88, 90–93, **94**, 104; racism 88, **89**, 93, **98**, 101–104, **105**; reflective questions 91, 93, 95–96, 100; theoretical assumptions 106–108; *see also* discourse analysis (DA)/classroom discourse analysis

critical pedagogy 109
critical race theory 104, **105**; *see also* race and racism
cultural stereotypes 93

data analysis: in conversation analysis **61**; in critical discourse analysis 96–97, 106, **107**; in discourse analysis 77, **85**; methodological issues (overview) **15**, 16; in narrative analysis 113–114, 118–119, 122, **129**, 130; preliminary analysis 33–34; transcription *see* transcription and transcripts

data collection 26–27; access to classroom/data 21–22; classroom/supporting materials 32; consent 25; in conversation analysis 60–62, **61**; in critical discourse analysis 96, 100, 103, **107**; data volume 30–31; in discourse analysis **85**; equipment and software *see* recording equipment and software; in ethnography 32, 140–144, *143*, 151; field notes 32, 142–144, *143*, 151; methodological issues (overview) 14, **15**; in narrative analysis 115, 116–118, 119–123, 125–127, **129**, 130; nonverbal data 8–29; online learning spaces 29; planning learning activities for 30; written discourse analysis 31–32; *see also* fieldwork

data-driven research, and transcripts 35
data management and archiving 33
data presentation: context in 162, 163–164, *163*; in conversation analysis **61**; in critical discourse analysis 106, **107**; in discourse analysis **85**; in ethnography 144–146; methodological issues (overview) **15**, 16; in narrative analysis **129**; transcript readability 36, **37**

Day, R.R. **128**
De Fina, A. 111, **111**, 112, 131
Denzin, N.K. 145
diaries and journals 115, 116–117, 119–121, 120; learner diaries, 123–127, **128**; *see also* autoethnography; reflective practices
discourse actions 9–11, **10**, **11**; *see also* first language (L1) use; floor management; repair strategies; triadic dialogues and IRF/IRE sequences; turn-taking

discourse analysis (DA)/classroom discourse analysis 64, 65–87; analysis of teacher questions 75–79, **80**; context **85**, 86, 139; vs. conversation analysis 65, 68; data analysis 77, **85**; data collection **85**; data presentation **85**; defined 3–5, 13–14, 65; discourse markers 79–83, **84**; floor management **11**, 71–75, **74**, 95; introduction to 65–66, **66**; key scholars 86–87; key terms and constructs 87; keywords 76; methodological issues 13–16, **15**, 83–86, **85**; reflective questions 75, 76; research questions 67, 69, 71, 73–74, 82–83, 86; triadic dialogues and IRF/IRE sequences 67–71, **70**, 91–92, **94**; and type of learning 6; value of 17–19; written discourse analysis 31–32; *see also* conversation analysis (CA); critical

discourse analysis (CDA); narrative analysis
discourse, defined 9
discourse markers 79–83, **84**
discourse structures (orientation to) 9–13, **10**, **12**; *see also* gender; language ideologies; linguicism; neoliberalism; power
discrimination 88, 93, 101–102; *see also* race and racism
display questions 77–79
dissemination of research *see* reporting and writing up
Duranti, A. **15**

echoic vs. epistemic teacher questions 76–77
economic issues *see* neoliberalism
Edelsky, C. 71–72, **74**
Edwards, D. 139–140
Edwards, J.A. **85**
Ellis, D.G. **15**
embodied actions/nonverbal data: in conversation analysis 47, 48, 51, 54, **54**; data collection 28–29; gaze 36, 47, 48, 51, 54; and transcripts 35, 37
Emerson, R.M. 143–144
emic perspective 59–60, 63
Engin, M. **128**
entextualization 34
epistemic vs. echoic teacher questions 76–77
equipment and software: data collection *see* recording equipment and software; data transcription 23–24, 33
Erickson, F. **136**, 137, 138, 152
Eriksson, P. 141–142
Ernst-Slavit, G. **80**
ethics *see* research ethics
ethnography/classroom ethnography 135–152; autoethnography 115, 149–151; characteristics of 138; context 138–140, 146; ethnography of communication 146–149; field notes 32, 142–144, *143*, 151; fieldwork 140–142; introduction to 135–138, **136**; key scholars 152; key terms and constructs 152; participant-based ethnography 143; thick descriptions 144–146
ethnography of communication 146–149
ethnomethodology 64

Fairclough, N. 88, **89**, 108
Farrell, T. 76, **80**, 122–123

feedback (in IRF sequences) *see* triadic dialogues and IRF/IRE sequences
field notes 32, 142–144, *143*, 151
fieldwork 140–142
first language (L1) use **11**, **80**; *see also* bilingual classrooms
Fitch, F. **116**
Flick, U. **107**
floor management **11**, 71–75, **74**, 95
footing 87
frame 87
Fung, L. 79, 82, **84**

Garton, S. **11**, **54**
gatekeepers 22
gaze 36, 47, 48, 51, 54
Gee, J.P. **15**, **66**
Geertz, C. 144
gender **12**
generalizability 31, 131, 152
genre 87
Gilbert, R. **85**
Godley, A.J. **105**
"going native," in ethnography 152
granularity of transcription 36–37
Gray, J. **12**
Gumperz, J. 146

Hafner, C.A. **8**
Haig, G. **129**
Hall, J.K. **57**, **60**
Halliday, M.A.K. 67
Hammersley, M. 25
Hart, C. **107**
Harvey, D. 99
hegemony 91, 93, 99, 109
Hellermann, J. **7**, 82, **84**
Helm, F. **128**
Hepburn, A. **61**, 62
Hilliard, L.J. **12**
Hirano, E. **128**
Hobbs, V. **124**
Holstein, J.A. **129**
Hopkins, D. 156
Hu, G. **80**
Hutchby, I. **46**, **61**
Hyland, K. **85**
Hymes, D. 146, 147–149, 152

identities, in narrative analysis 112–115, **116**
imperialism 93
impressionistic observations 143; *see also* field notes
indexing, in narrative analysis 132

interactional competence 57–59, **60**
interpretive reading of data, in narrative analysis 118–119
intersubjectivity 64, 140
intertextuality 109
intonation, transcription 36, **40**
IRF/IRE sequences **11**, 67–71, **70**, 91–92, **94**

Janks, H. **107**
Jaworski, A. 4, 13
Jefferson, G. 63
Jenks, C.J. **8**, **11**, **15**, 36, 38, 39, **40**, 73, 99, 101
Johnson, K.E. **120**
Jones, R. **74**
Jones, R.H. **66**, **85**
journals *see* diaries and journals
Jung, D. **129**

Käänta, L. **54**
Keddie, A. **102**
keywords: for literature searching 6, **7**, 8–9, **8**, 76, 101, 104, 115; of published research paper 165
King, K.A. **136**
Koole, T. **74**
Koskrity, P.V. 95
Kramsch, C. 58, **60**
Kubota, R. 101
Kumaravadivelu, B. 88, 89, **89**

Lamy, M.N. 29
language ideologies **12**, 94–97, **98**
Lazaraton, A. 65
learner diaries, in narrative analysis 123–127, **128**; *see also* diaries and journals
learning, types of, and classroom discourse organization 6
learning vs. competence 58–59
Lee, J.W. **12**, **98**
Lee, L. 30
Lee, Y. 71
Leeds-Hurwitz, W. 144–145
Lerner, G.H. **54**
Lester, J.D. 155
Levy, M. 29
Li, L. **7**
Liebscher, G. **57**
life history 115, **116**
Liggett, T. **105**
linguicism **12**
literature reviews: databases 6; keywords 6, **7**, 8–9, **8**, 76, 101, 104, 115; planning 159;
writing up 158–161; *see also* secondary research
lived experienced, in narrative analysis 132
Loughran, J.J. 123, **124**

Macbeth, D. **57**
Maitlis, S. **129**
Mandelbaum, J. **61**
Manke, M.P. **94**
marginalization **94**, 100–101, 105; *see also* discrimination; race and racism
Markee, N. 9, **46**, 59
Marti, L. **74**
Martin-Jones, M. **12**, **94**
Martinez-Roldan, C.M. **98**
Mazak, C.M. **98**
McCarthy, M. 13
McHoul, A.W. **11**, **57**
McIlveen, P. 150
McNamara, T. 106
Mehan, H. **136**
membership, in ethnography 152
Menard-Warwick, J. 67
metacognition 125
Meyer, M. **107**
Meyerhoff, M. **15**, 27
Miao, P. **70**
microphones 28
mobile phones, use for data recording 27
Mondada, L. 62
Moodie, I. **120**
Mortensen, K. **54**
motivated looking *see* unmotivated looking
Müller, S. **84**

narrative analysis: context **129**, 139; data analysis 113–114, 118–119, 122, **129**, 130; data collection 115, 116–118, 119–123, 125–127, **129**, 130; data presentation **129**; identities 112–115, **116**; introduction to 110–112, **111**; key scholars 131; key terms and constructs 132; learner diaries 123–127, **128**; methodological issues **111**, 127–131, **129**; reflection data 14, 110, 112, 121, 123; reflective practices 119–123, **124**; reflective questions 114, 121; research questions 112, 117; teacher cognition 115–119, **120**; value of 110–111, **111**
narrative frame 132
narrative inquiry 115
narrative space 132
Nassaji, H. **11**
neoliberalism **12**, 88, 97–101, **98**, **109**

next-turn proof procedure 64
nontraditional classroom settings: example studies **8**; online learning spaces 29; and research planning 7–9
nonverbal data *see* embodied actions/ nonverbal data
Norton, B. **116**

online learning spaces 29
Orelus, P.W. 90
Other, in narrative analysis 132

participation data 14, 110
pauses: in conversation analysis 48–49, 53; transcription 35, **40**
Pavlenko, A. **111**, 112
Pekarek Doehler, S. **60**
Peterson, E. **136**
planning *see* research planning
Polat, B. **84**
Pole, C. 141
Ponterotto, J.G. 145
positioning, in narrative analysis 132
post-structuralism 109
postcolonialism 109
postmodernism 109
power **12**, 88, 90–93, **94**, 104
practices and actions in turn-taking 51
procedural consequentiality 64
Pryde, M. **70**
Psathas, G. **46**, **61**
pseudonyms *see* anonymization
Pun, J. **80**

race and racism: in critical discourse analysis 88, **89**, 93, **98**, 101–104, **105**; defined 101–102; White normativity 103–104
Rampton, B. **66**
Rapley, T. **61**, 62
Raschka, C. **11**
Rau, A. **107**
recasts and reformulations 77
recipient design 64
recontextualization 87
recording equipment and software 24; microphones 28; mobile phones 27; online data recording 29; testing 29–30; video recording devices 28–29
referential questions 77–79
reflection data 14, 110, 112, 121, 123; *see also* narrative analysis
reflective practices 119–123, **124**; *see also* diaries and journals
reflexivity 16, 150, 152

reformulations and recasts 77
register 87
relevance 64
repair strategies **11**
repairs 55–57, **57**, 58
reported speech 87
reporting and writing up 153–166; accessibility 155, 156; common problems 156; explaining the study 161–162; key report sections 165–166; literature review 158–161; planning questions 157; purpose and principles 154–157; reflexivity 16, 150, 152; stages of writing 153–154; statement of objectives 158; wider literature in 155; *see also* data presentation
research, defined 16–17
research ethics 24–25; anonymization 37–38, 39; in narrative analysis **116**; and transcription 37–38
research methodologies *see specific methodologies*
research planning: access 21–22; and classroom setting 5–9, *6*; empirical issues (overview) 26; ethical advice and approval 24–25; learning activities for data collection 30; literature reviews *see* literature reviews; logistical considerations (overview) 20–21, *21*; methodological issues (overview) 13–16, **15**; planning tool **18**, *19*; technological considerations 23–24; time constraints 23
research questions (in general) 158
researcher: identities **116**; motivation 18–19; reflexivity 16, 150, 152
Riessman, C. 131
rigor 130
Ryle, G. 144
Rymes, B. 16, 89, **89**

Sacks, H. 53, 63
sample size 31
Saville-Troike, M. 147
Schegloff, E.A. **46**, 55, 63
Schiffrin, D. 79, 81
Schmidt, R. **128**
Scollon, R. 87
secondary research 17, 22; *see also* literature reviews
Seedhouse, P. 6, **50**, **57**
Self, in narrative analysis 132
sequence and organization in turn-taking 49–50, 51, 58; *see also* triadic dialogues and IRF/IRE sequences

Sert, O. **50**
Shepherd, M.A. **74**
Shin, H. **105**
Sidnell, J. 47, **61**
Silverstein, M. 36
Simpson, J. **8**
Sinclair, J. 7, 67
Smith, B. 29
socially distributed cognition 64
SPEAKING model 147–149
speed of speech, transcription **40**
Spencer, S. 101
Stoddart, M.C.J. 90
Subtirelu, N.C. **98**

Talib, N. **107**
Tannen, D. **66**
Taylor, L. **105**
teacher questions, analysis of 75–79, **80**
teachers: cognition 115–119, **120**; identities 115, **116**; marginalization **94**, 100–101; reflective practices 121–123, **124**; White normativity 103–104
teaching materials: and neoliberalism 99, **102**; and power 93
textbook discourse 88
textuality 87
thematic reading of data, in narrative analysis 118
Theodórsdóttir, G. **8**
thesis statements (in general) 158
thick descriptions 144–146
time constraints 23
Toohey, K. **136**
traditional classroom settings: example studies **7**; and research planning 6, 8–9
transcription and transcripts: conventions 36, 40–41, **40**; in conversation analysis 62–63; defined 34; and embodied/non-verbal data 35, 37; entextualization 34; ethical considerations 37–38; as incomplete representations 40; intonation 36, **40**; open vs. closed transcripts 34–35, *35*; practical approach 39; representational issues 36–39, **37**; services 23; standardization vs. vernacularization 38; time taken 30–31, **31**; tools 23–24, *33*; *see also* data presentation

transition relevance places (TRPs) 53–54
triadic dialogues and IRF/IRE sequences 11, 67–71, **70**, 91–92, **94**
triangulation 152
trustworthiness 130–131
Tsui, A.B.M. **116**
turn-allocation 53, **54**
turn constructional units (TCUs) 52–54
turn shape and placement 52–54, **54**
turn-taking 11, **11**, 47–52, **50**, 58, **60**, **94**; *see also* triadic dialogues and IRF/IRE sequences

unmotivated looking: in conversation analysis 62–63; in discourse analysis 86
Üstünel, E. **7**

van Dijk, T.A. 88, **89**, 108
Varonis, E.M. 76
vernacularization vs. standardization (transcripts) 38
video recording devices 28–29

Walsh, S. 45, **124**
Wannagat, U. **7**
Waring, H, Z. **7**, **50**, **70**
Warriner, D.S. **102**
Watson, C. **116**
Watson-Gegeo, K.A. 32, 138
Wei, L. **8**
Wells, G. **70**
Wetherell, M. **85**
White normativity 103–104
Wiggins, 2016 27
Wilkins, A. **102**
Wodak, R. 88, **89**, **107**, 108
Wong, J. **50**, 58, 62
Woods, P. 140, 156
Wooffitt, R. **46**
writing up *see* reporting and writing up
written discourse analysis 31–32

Young, R.F. 58

Zembylas, M. **120**
Zemel, A. 68, **70**
Ziegler, G. **54**

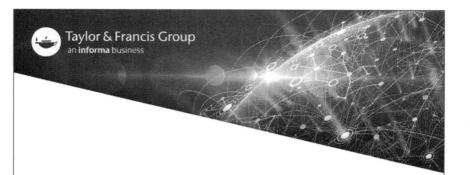